Now with a new epilogue:
How Abraham Lincoln and Sam Houston
tried to keep Texas in the Union

"Like our country itself, *Sam Houston & the Alamo Avengers* staggers,
inspires, and reminds us of the power of real leaders."
— BRAD MELTZER, author of *The First Conspiracy*

"We Texans know how special our history is. Now, thanks to Brian
Kilmeade's new book, the rest of the country can also celebrate the way
defeat gave way to glory."
— MARK CUBAN, owner of the Dallas Mavericks

"Kilmeade tells a tale of early Texas history that echoes vibrantly today
in the courage, honor, and commitment of the U.S. military serving
around the world. A masterpiece!"
— ADMIRAL JAMES STAVRIDIS, 16th Supreme Allied
Commander of NATO and author of *Sailing True North*

"A fast-paced romp through the Texas Revolution that feels more like a
novel than nonfiction. Kilmeade presents the leaders of the Lone Star
State as the flawed and fearless heroes they truly were, and their David
and Goliath story that changed American history is riveting reading."
— STEPHEN L. MOORE

SAM
HOUSTON
and the
ALAMO
AVENGERS

ALSO BY BRIAN KILMEADE

George Washington's Secret Six
Thomas Jefferson and the Tripoli Pirates
Andrew Jackson and the Miracle of New Orleans

SAM HOUSTON

and the

ALAMO AVENGERS

THE TEXAS VICTORY THAT
CHANGED AMERICAN HISTORY

BRIAN KILMEADE

★ SENTINEL ★

SENTINEL
An imprint of Penguin Random House LLC
penguinrandomhouse.com

First published in hardcover in the United States by Sentinel,
an imprint of Penguin Random House LLC, in 2019.

This paperback edition with a new afterword and updated epilogue published in 2020.

Most Sentinel books are available at a discount when purchased in quantity for sales
promotions or corporate use. Special editions, which include personalized covers, excerpts,
and corporate imprints, can be created when purchased in large quantities. For more
information, please call (212) 572-2232 or e-mail specialmarkets@penguinrandomhouse.com.
Your local bookstore can also assist with discounted bulk purchases using the Penguin
Random House corporate Business-to-Business program. For assistance in locating
a participating retailer, e-mail B2B@penguinrandomhouse.com.

Page 268 constitutes an extention to this copyright page.

ISBN 9780525540540 (trade paperback)

Library of Congress Cataloging-in-Publication Data

Names: Kilmeade, Brian, author.
Title: Sam Houston and the Alamo Avengers : The Texas Victory
That Changed American History / Brian Kilmeade.
Other titles: Texas victory that changed American history
Description: [New York] : Sentinel, [2019] | Includes
bibliographical references and index. |
Identifiers: LCCN 2019022817 (print) | LCCN 2019022818 (ebook) |
ISBN 9780525540533 (hardcover) | ISBN 9780525540564 (epub)
Subjects: LCSH: Houston, Sam, 1793–1863. | Texas—History—Revolution,
1835–1836. | Alamo (San Antonio, Tex.)—Siege, 1836. |
Governors—Texas—Biography. | Legislators—United States—Biography. |
Texas—History—To 1846.
Classification: LCC F390.H84 K55 2019 (print) | LCC F390.H84 (ebook) |
DDC 976.4/04092 [B]—dc23
LC record available at https://lccn.loc.gov/2019022817
LC ebook record available at https://lccn.loc.gov/2019022818

Printed in the United States of America

7th Printing

BOOK DESIGN BY MEIGHAN CAVANAUGH

MAPS BY DANIEL LAGIN

To my mother, my greatest supporter, defender, and inspiration.
May her legacy of toughness, kindness, and loyalty live on
in all those who were lucky enough to know her.

My son, take this musket and never disgrace it; for remember, I had rather all my sons should fill one honorable grave, than that one of them should turn his back to save his life. Go, and remember, too, that while the door of my cottage is open to brave men, it is eternally shut against cowards.

—Elizabeth Houston

CONTENTS

The Lessons of Battle

Experience is the teacher of all things.

—JULIUS CAESAR

No small target at six-foot-two, young Sam Houston wasn't thinking about getting hit. He was thinking about getting even. Running through a hail of musket balls, spears, and arrows, he and his fellow soldiers sprinted toward an eight-foot-tall barricade. Behind it was an army of Red Stick Creek American Indians who had massacred three hundred men, women, and children at a Mississippi Territory stockade town called Fort Mims seven months earlier. For months Houston and his fellow soldiers serving under General Andrew Jackson had been attempting to retaliate, only to have the Red Sticks escape them time and time again. But now Jackson and his men had discovered their main camp, here at Horseshoe Bend, and they were not leaving without revenge.

The first man over the barricade took a bullet to the skull and fell back lifeless. Just behind him, Sam Houston never wavered.

On enlisting a year earlier as a private, Houston had immediately attracted notice. Tall and strong, his eyes a piercing blue, he looked every inch a leader. Promoted to drill sergeant, Houston's deep voice rang with authority; in a matter of months, he was promoted twice more. His superiors saw him as "soldierly [and] ready to do, or to suffer, whatever the obligation of . . . military duty imposed."[1] Now that resolution would be tested.

As the second man to top the wall, Houston did not hesitate. Waving his sword, he called for his men to follow. He immediately drew enemy fire, and he leapt to the ground inside the Red Stick fort, an arrow plunged deep into his upper thigh.

Houston refused to be turned aside. Despite the pain, he remained standing, fighting on with the shaft of the arrow protruding from his leg. His platoon, joined by reinforcements, soon drove the Red Sticks back. Only then did Houston look to his wound.

At Sam Houston's order, another lieutenant tried—but failed—to pull the arrow from his thigh. At Houston's insistence, the officer yanked a second time, but still the arrow refused to budge. Houston, sword in hand, demanded a third attempt, saying, "Try again and, if you fail this time, I will smite you to the earth."[2] This time the barbed arrowhead tore free, releasing a gush of blood and opening a deep gash.

Most men would have been done for the day and, after a surgeon field dressed his gaping wound, Houston rested. When General Jackson came to check the wounded, he recognized the young man who had helped lead the charge and honored him for his bravery—but he also ordered Houston out of the fight. Houston objected, but Jackson was firm.

Houston admired Jackson as the sort of father he'd always wanted, but he wasn't about to be kept out of the battle by anyone or anything. A short time later, when Jackson called for volunteers to storm a last Red Stick stronghold built into a ravine, Houston got to his feet and grabbed a musket. Limping and bloodied, he charged. When he stopped to level his gun, musket balls smashed into his right shoulder and upper arm, and his shattered limb fell to his side. Houston barely managed to make his way out of the range of fire before collapsing to the earth.

In the hours that followed, the Red Sticks were finally routed; hundreds of fighters lay dead. Fort Mims had been avenged, and the British deprived of a key ally in their attempt to destroy the young United States.

But Houston had paid a high price for his part in this victory, and he was about to learn that perhaps his drive to be in the action at any cost was not the best way to serve his country.

After Houston was carried from the field, a surgeon removed one of the musket balls but halted the procedure before digging deeper to extract the second lead projectile. In the cold triage of the battlefield, he saw no reason to inflict more suffering. In his judgment, this man would not survive the night. Houston would spend "the darkest night of [my] life" on the damp ground, alone and "racked with the keen torture of . . . many wounds."[3] But he lived to see the dawn.

Houston would carry to his grave the musket ball fragments in his shoulder, and the wound on his thigh never entirely healed. And just a few months later, the wounds tortured him in a different way when, upon arriving in Washington, D.C., he experienced a moment of horror. The British had burned the Capitol and the president's house shortly before. As he looked upon the ruins, he later remembered, "My blood boiled and I experienced one of the keenest pangs of my life in the thought that my right arm should be disabled at such a moment, and while the foe was still prowling through the country."[4]

The wounded and wiser Sam Houston came face-to-face with the limits of bravery. Eager to be a hero at any cost, he had instead become a casualty in a bloody battle, with wounds that left him unable to defend his young country from an even bigger threat. He had recognized how fragile both his own life and the American project were. And he learned a key lesson about war: Courage must be calculated, because courage without calculation could get you killed.

ONE

General Jackson's Protégé

Poor Houston rose like a rocket and fell like a stick.

—GOVERNOR WILLIAM CARROLL

S am Houston's wounds healed slowly. He underwent several surgeries to repair his arm and thigh. But the young soldier's subsequent rise to power and prominence was surprisingly swift.

By the time Houston returned to active duty in the infantry, General Jackson and his army had won a stunning victory at the Battle of New Orleans, in January 1815, ending once and for all American battles with the British. But even as the war came to a close, Houston's relationship with Jackson continued to grow. Houston became Jackson's protégé—and more, almost a son to Old Hickory—after the twenty-two-year-old, at Andrew Jackson's personal request, was assigned to the general's staff in Nashville, Tennessee.

And Houston needed a father. His own had died when he was thirteen, and he had spent his early teens in frontier Tennessee, with a rocky relationship with his mother. Finally at age sixteen, unhappy with life on his mother's farm, he ran away, finding a home with Chief Oo-Loo-Te-Ka of the Cherokee nation. Houston embraced life with the

Cherokee, since he liked "the wild liberty of the Red Men better than the tyranny of his own brothers."[1]

The Cherokee had trained the restless young man, equipping him for a life of war. Now Houston wanted to be equipped for a life of politics, and he needed someone from his own culture to take him under his wing. Jackson, perhaps perceiving Houston's need and remembering his own fatherless youth, became that man.

When Houston resigned his commission, in 1818, to start a legal career, Jackson continued to support him. Thanks to his mentoring, Houston gained an insider's view of the intricacies of Tennessee politics and was appointed general of the Tennessee militia, a post Jackson once held. And he became a regular visitor to Jackson's beloved plantation home, the Hermitage, where not only Andrew Jackson, but his wife, Rachel, continued to embrace him as if he were a son.

Supported by Jackson, Houston flourished, eventually running, with Jackson's encouragement, to represent Tennessee in Congress. Jackson became a U.S. senator in the same election cycle, and the two men together headed for Washington. Houston's rise didn't stop there. Five years later, he was back in Tennessee as governor and seemed destined for a long and prosperous political career. America was young and growing, and there was much a young man with courage and ambition could do. It seemed that a fatherless child raised in poverty and then by Cherokee was going to make it to the top.

Seeming to cap his success was his luck in love. On January 22, 1829, the thirty-five-year-old Houston and lovely Eliza Allen exchanged marriage vows, by candlelight, in her father's sprawling plantation house. The best of Nashville society toasted to the couple's happiness and to the groom's rise to ever-greater political success.

But the marriage was the turning point in Houston's luck. Just three months later, Eliza abruptly left her husband to return to her father's house. Houston had questioned her faithfulness, and whispers and rumors blossomed into a full-blown scandal. Few details surfaced, but it seems Eliza was vindicated, suggesting Houston to be in the wrong. He disclaimed any accusation, but their relationship was ruined and so was his political career. By allegedly insulting her honor, Houston had violated the social code of the day, leaving him no choice but to resign as governor. As his predecessor, Governor Billy Carroll, observed, "Poor Houston rose like a rocket and fell like a stick."[2]

Houston left Tennessee. He found refuge with the Cherokee once again. Nearly twenty years after he had first asked them for help, the chief welcomed Houston's return.

The man who only weeks before had seemed destined to be president of the United States disappeared entirely from American political life. Tortured, he did all he could to forget his former world. He abandoned his city clothes, the English language, and his birth name, once again becoming known in Cherokee as *Co-lon-neh* ("the Raven"). For months, he attempted to numb his pain with alcohol, admitting later that he "buried his sorrows in the flowing bowl."[3] His huge liquor consumption soon earned him a second name, *Oo-tse-tee Ar-dee-tah-skee*—Cherokee for "the Big Drunk."[4]

TEXAS LOST

Sam Houston's fall from grace was far from President Jackson's only concern. While his protégé was off drowning his sorrows with the Cherokee, Jackson worked hard to undo what he saw as one of the biggest mistakes of the previous occupant of the White House, John Quincy Adams.

To put it bluntly, Jackson hated Adams. First of all, he hated him for having beaten him in the presidential election of 1824. Although Jackson won the popular vote by a solid margin, he got less than the required majority of electoral votes. The House of Representatives had decided in Adams's favor, thanks to the support of Henry Clay. Adams rewarded Clay by naming him secretary of state,* and Jackson accused Adams of making a "corrupt bargain" in accepting "thirty pieces of silver" from Clay, whom Jackson called the "Judas of the West." Despite the outcry from Jackson and others, Adams took possession of the president's house.

But Jackson's dislike of Adams went back further and deeper than the presidential defeat. He thought that the New Englander fundamentally misunderstood the needs of the frontier—and that he had given away land necessary to America's future. Years before, in May 1818, General Jackson and his army, as part of a campaign to protect his fellow citizens from the Seminole Indians, captured the port city of Pensacola in Spanish Florida. The next year Spain agreed to cede Florida to the United States in a treaty negotiated by none other than John Quincy Adams, then serving as James Monroe's secretary of state. This would have been good news for Jackson, had it not been for what Adams gave up in return for Florida.

President Thomas Jefferson had believed Texas to be part of the 1803 Louisiana Purchase. It was a link to the expanse of territory extending to the Pacific, as well as a buffer with Spain's colony, Mexico, to the south. Jefferson had also understood the region's potential value: "The province of Techas will be the richest state of our Union," he told James Monroe.[5] But in negotiating with Spain, Adams agreed to make the Sabine River—rather than the Rio Grande—the new border between American territory and Spanish, effectively handing over all of Texas to Spain.

In Andrew Jackson's mind, that left him with two Adams wrongs to

---

* In the early nineteenth century, becoming secretary of state was regarded as a stepping-stone to the presidency, the path taken by Jackson's four immediate predecessors, Jefferson, Madison, Monroe, and John Quincy Adams.

right: The first he corrected, in 1828, when he became president, defeating the incumbent Adams in a landslide. The second—the giveaway of Texas—would take longer to fix.

For one thing, the players had changed. Mexico had gained its independence from Spain in 1821. Then, three years later, the new nation south of the border adopted a federal constitution that echoed on the U.S. Constitution. Instead of freeing Texas from a European colonial power, Jackson would now have to coax it away from a democratic republic that had also recently won its freedom. And that was exactly what he hoped to do, sending an emissary to Mexico just a few months after his election.

Jackson wasn't the only U.S. citizen with an interest in Texas: By the thousands, American settlers were flooding over the Louisiana line to homestead in the rich farmland of Texas, which Mexico was making available cheaply to any who wanted it.

Earlier in the century, Americans looking to settle the frontier had been able to buy land on credit. But in 1820, Congress passed a new land act, which made it much, much harder for the average settler to afford it. Now settlers were required to buy a minimum of eighty acres, to be paid for in gold or silver, for $1.25 per acre. That hundred-dollar entrance fee closed the door to lots of people—when, just over the border, a settler could buy land for 12½¢ per acre. For those lacking the cash, the government in Mexico City extended credit, thinking they would have a firmer hold on Texas if they had more people residing in its largely empty expanse. As a result, Americans who wanted a fresh start poured over the border with the blessing of Mexico.

To Jackson, restoring Texas—where his countrymen had rapidly become a majority—to American ownership only made sense, but he knew the bargaining for it would be tough. On Jackson's orders, Colonel Anthony Butler made the Mexicans an offer. The United States would pay $5 million in return for the territory framed by the Sabine

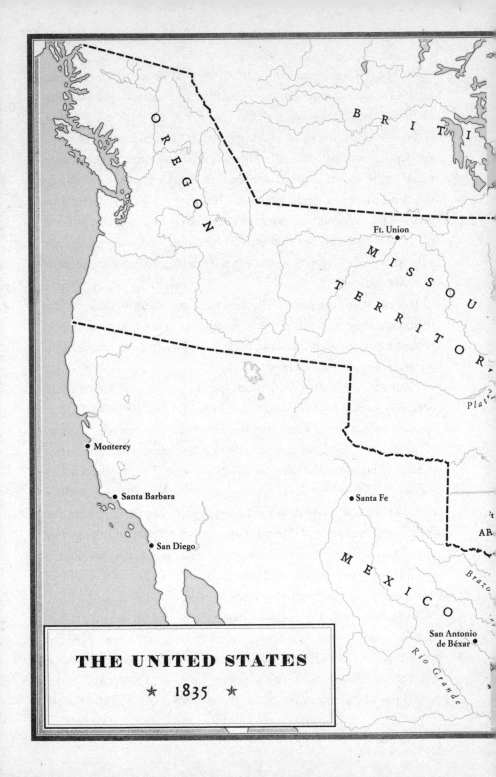

OREGON

BRITI

Ft. Union

MISSOU

TERRITOR

Plat

Monterey

Santa Barbara

San Diego

Santa Fe

't

AR

MEXICO

San Antonio
de Béxar

Brazo

Rio Grande

THE UNITED STATES

★ 1835 ★

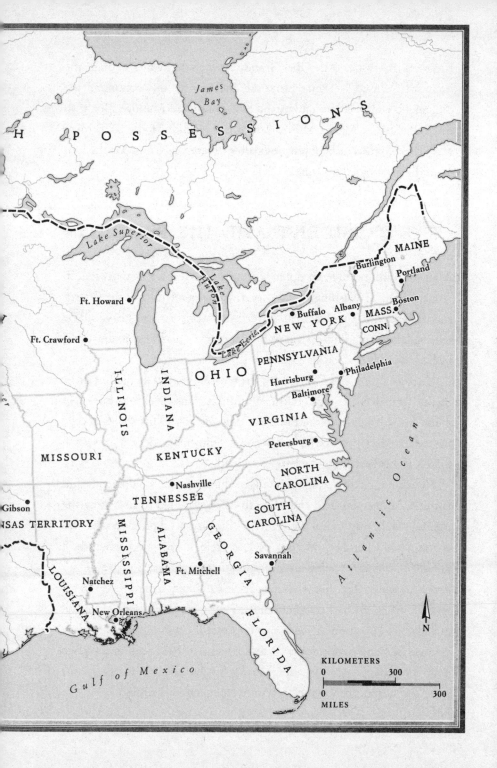

River on the east and the Rio Grande to the southwest. Though the Mexicans refused Jackson's proposal, the two nations continued the diplomatic conversation, and Americans continued to move. But with the leadership of Mexico shifting from one election to the next, there was little progress to be made. Jackson's dream was foiled for the moment. Jackson bided his time.

THE PRESIDENT AND HIS PRODIGY

After his withdrawal from polite society, Sam Houston reappeared, in January 1830, in Washington, D.C., arriving as a member of the Cherokee delegation to the American government. Unsure how he would be received, he wanted his arrival to be a surprise. "Don't say to any one," he had instructed a cousin, "that I will be in tomorrow."[6]

He took a room at an old haunt, Brown's Hotel. But he did not dress in the formal tailcoat of stylish Washingtonians. Wearing buckskin pants and a brightly colored blanket draped around his shoulders, he looked like the Cherokee he had become. Shiny metal decorations sewn loosely to his coat jangled when he walked.

Houston quickly became the talk of the town. Both old friends and entrenched enemies held their breath as they waited to hear how the general would respond to the return of his disgraced protégé, who was representing Cherokee interests, no less. Jackson's reaction, whatever it might be, would be public at a diplomatic reception at the president's house, to which the Cherokee delegation had been invited.

Even when dressed conventionally, Houston's height made him unmistakable. He stood at least six feet, two inches tall, though some claimed he stood six-four or even six-foot-six. At the reception, a turban wrapped around his head added to his height, making it easy for the president to spot his former lieutenant from across the room.

When the president called out to him, the crowd parted. Jackson approached. To the relief of many, the aging, rail-thin president pulled Houston to him, wrapping the younger and taller man in a bear hug. The message was clear: Whatever he had done, and wherever he had been, the general's affection for Sam Houston was undiminished.

For much of the next two years, Houston would remain with his adopted Native American family. In his sober moments, he served as a council leader. He married again, in 1830, this time taking for his wife a Cherokee woman, Tianh, known in English as Dianah Rogers. (Although they were not formally divorced until 1833, Houston and Eliza had already ceased to be man and wife under Cherokee law because they had "split the blanket.")[7] Houston traveled deep into the Arkansas Territory, acting as a Cherokee ambassador, a peacemaker negotiating with the Osage, Creek, and Choctaw. He and Tianh operated a trading store, selling kettles, blankets, soap, and rope to their Native American brethren. Houston represented the Cherokee on trips to Washington, too, arguing that government agents had consistently cheated his adopted people. His former standing in the nation's capital helped him win some small victories. Then, early in 1832, his Cherokee association entangled Houston in a legal case that almost ended Houston's career once again.

During a debate on the Jackson administration's Indian policy, on March 31, 1832, Ohio congressman William Stanbery suggested Houston had been part of a scheme to defraud the government. When Houston read about Stanbery's speech, he was furious. He tried to confront the man who had slandered both him and General Jackson, but for two weeks Stanbery managed to avoid the seething Houston. Then, by chance, Houston spied him as he strolled along Pennsylvania Avenue after dark.

Stanbery was armed with pistols, but Houston was undaunted. After politely inquiring, "Are you Mr. Stanbery?" Houston lit into him with a cane that he had carved from a hickory tree growing at the Hermitage.[8] As Stanbery told the story, "Mr. Houston . . . struck me with the bludgeon he held in his hand . . . repeatedly with great violence."[9]

Stanbery tried to run, but Houston, despite a nearly useless right arm from his Horseshoe Bend wounds, leapt on Stanbery's back and dragged him to the ground, still battering him with his cane. Stanbery tried to fend off his attacker with a pistol, but it misfired. Houston tore the firearm from Stanbery's grip, then delivered a few more licks with his cane. According to one witness, the last blow, aimed below Stanbery's belt, "struck him elsewhere."[10]

At Stanbery's insistence, Houston was arrested and, a month later, tried in Congress on charges of battery and contempt of Congress. Frank Key, a Washington attorney (and the man later remembered by his full name, Francis Scott Key, and as the author of "The Star Spangled Banner"), helped Houston argue his case on the House floor. General Jackson paid for the fashionable suit Houston wore and welcomed Houston to the president's house for updates on the proceedings during the month-long trial. When the case finally drew to a close, Houston, suffering from a brutal hangover after a long night of drinking, gave his own summation. The long speech won the gallery over; it was met with tumultuous applause and calls of *Bravo!* and *Huzzah!* Yet, despite the defendant's persuasive words, the House, after deliberating four days, found him guilty.

The punishment decreed was more symbolic than real—a reprimand from the Speaker of the House—but at Stanbery's insistence, a court case soon followed. Houston was fined the tall sum of $500, along with court costs. But the bizarre events had made him the talk of the town and even the nation, thanks to the newspapers, and he found the attention energizing and redemptive after his long years of obscurity.

"I was dying out," he remembered much later, "and had they taken me before a justice of the peace and fined me ten dollars it would have killed me." Instead, though his reputation was again tarnished, the very public congressional proceeding gave Houston new standing and gained him new confidence. "They gave me a national tribunal for a theatre," he remembered later, "and that set me up again."[11] He was a public paradox, a ruined man *and* a proud hero more famous and admired than ever.

Though reinvigorated, Houston did not try to revive his political career. For one thing, there was little chance of him going beyond his earlier achievements. For another, he needed to come up with the $500 he owed the government. He had been granted a year to pay his fine—to a typical laborer it amounted to roughly a year's wages—and he had an idea of where he might find the money. *Texas* was a place where a man could make his fortune. But it was a place for adventurers, for men like Houston, who might also be called second-chance men.

Some of those who headed for Texas looked to leave past misdemeanors—or worse—behind. Others wanted success and to accumulate wealth. Some were running away; some were seekers, just looking for a chance to prove themselves. Texas had become a place for new beginnings, for men on the make and for families—and for Sam Houston. In Texas, everyone lived in the present and nobody cared about your past.

THE TEXAS ENTERPRISE

"I will ride to the Hermitage this evening, and see the old Chief," Houston wrote to an acquaintance in August 1832.[12] General Jackson was taking refuge from the pressures of Washington politics for a few months back home in Tennessee when Houston arrived on his doorstep. Sadly, "Aunt Rachel" would not be there to join them. Jackson's beloved wife had passed away almost four years before.

On this visit, Houston hoped to secure Jackson's support for his trip. He knew that his mentor's interest in Texas was still strong, that he believed owning it was essential if America was to expand. During Houston's visit to the Hermitage, their conversation inevitably turned to Texas.

This wasn't the first time Houston had proposed to go to Texas. At the time of his first exile three years before, he had boasted of his ambitions for "breaking [Texas] off from Mexico, and annexing it to the United States."[13] This brag had been foolhardy, coming while Jackson and his ambassador to Mexico were in the middle of negotiations. On hearing that Houston, in a drunken state, had claimed "he would conquer Mexico or Texas, and be worth two millions in two years,"[14] Jackson rebuked him. Writing to Houston, the general expressed wonder that Houston would even contemplate "so wild a scheme" and demanded then that Houston pledge "never [to] engage in any [such] enterprise."[15]

In the years since, the two men had corresponded—sometimes on the record, at times off in private letters—and periodically they had met in Washington and Nashville. During that time, diplomacy had produced little progress regarding the acquisition of Texas. Ambassador Butler had suggested to Jackson that they again offer to buy Texas, raising the price from $5 million to $7 million. Jackson had refused, thinking the price too high at a time when he worried about the national debt. When Butler later proposed another tack—a half million dollars or more in bribes—Jackson ran out of patience. He rejected the notion of bribery, writing sharply back to Butler that he must make a deal if he was capable of it. If not, he confided to Colonel Butler, the time might come when circumstances "compel us in self defense to seize that country by force and establish a regular government there over it."[16]

Only a few months later, Houston arrived on the scene. A bankrupt man looking to remake his fortunes, his confidence renewed and his military and diplomatic skills still strong, he was eager to head to Texas. Perhaps he could help win it for America, he thought. In any case, he planned to act upon a deal he had negotiated with New York financiers to acquire lands in the Mexican territory. He believed a Texas venture might prove profitable, confiding in a cousin, "My business in Texas is of some importance to my pecuniary interest, and as such, I must attend to it."[17] But his journey would put him in a place where he could do much more than advance his own finances.

Did Jackson explicitly ask Houston to be his eyes and ears on the ground? Did the two men agree that Houston should seek ways to do what both had dreamed of for years—bringing the territory back into American hands? No record of such orders remains, but the assistance Jackson offered Houston was striking. At Jackson's instructions, the secretary of state issued Houston a new passport, intended to ease his passage through Indian territory, where, officially, Houston would represent Jackson's government in negotiating with the Native Americans. Jackson also loaned him the substantial sum of $500, with which Houston could go much further and perhaps accomplish much, both for himself, for independence-minded settlers in Texas, and in seeking to fulfill Jackson's vision for the United States.

TWO

Gone to Texas

G.T.T.

—A COMMON NINETEENTH-CENTURY TERM, CHALKED
ON HOUSE DOORS AND NOTED IN TOWN RECORDS,
SHORT FOR "GONE TO TEXAS."

On December 10, 1832, Sam Houston, after crossing the Sabine, planted his boot on Texas turf for the first time. He had stopped en route to bid farewell to his Cherokee wife, Tianh, giving her the trading post, farm, and wigwam they shared. He would not return to her.

Now, entering the territory he'd dreamed of winning for America, he headed for Nacogdoches, just west of the river, where he hoped to make his new home. Perhaps the oldest town in Texas—a Native American settlement for centuries, it had become a Spanish mission town in 1716—Nacogdoches (*Nak-uh-doh-chiz*) seemed to Houston the perfect place to establish a law practice. He needed to find a way to support himself once Jackson's money ran out. He also needed to set about the business of learning Spanish and becoming Catholic, since, according to Mexican law, only Catholics could own land and practice law.

Not that everyone in Texas was a Spanish-speaking Catholic—

although the state of Texas belonged to Mexico, most of those Houston encountered were settlers from the United States. As recently as a dozen years before, the territory had been home to few beyond the fierce, nomadic Comanche, other Native Americans, and wild animals. But now Texas was full of adventurous and ambitious American settlers, thanks to one Stephen F. Austin. And he was a man Houston knew he needed to meet.

Just weeks after arriving, Houston set out from Nacogdoches to the village of San Felipe de Austin on a mission to meet the man who was organizing Texas. Finding him was worth the 180-mile journey, a journey along the old Spanish camino real, a route that Stephen Austin's father had traveled years earlier.

Born in Connecticut before the American Revolution, the young Moses Austin was an entrepreneur at heart. After working as a merchant, he moved to Missouri to invest in mining. Then, after losing his fortune there, he looked west again. In 1821, the fifty-nine-year-old Moses Austin obtained permission from the Mexican governor of Texas, who was eager to populate the sparsely occupied state, for three hundred American settlers to establish a colony there.

Tragically, Moses would not live to settle the land he had negotiated. Just weeks after settling the deal, he died of pneumonia. Not willing to give up his dream, on his deathbed, he pleaded for his son to take up his cause. "Tell dear Stephen," Moses Austin told his wife, "that it is his dieing fathers last request to prosecute the enterprise he had Commenced."[1]

When he took up his father's role as an empresario of Texas, Stephen Fuller Austin, a slender man of twenty-seven, hardly looked like the adventurer type; gentle and genteel, he seemed better suited to the drawing room than an unsettled wilderness. But he spent months in Mexico City, gaining the required seals and signatures to grant him full authority to establish a colony, and then found a suitable site along the

Brazos River, where buffalo and other wild game were abundant, the soil rich, and timber plentiful.

Austin had set about surveying, plotting out land grants, establishing a headquarters, and fulfilling his father's expansive vision. He wanted a port of entry, where goods from outside Texas could be imported and traded. Accordingly, he founded San Felipe de Austin, which served as a capital for his little colony.

By the time Houston arrived in Texas a decade later, Austin's venture had inspired a wave of immigration. Word of his project spread quickly; several hundred immigrants arrived by 1824, and by 1825, the count was over twelve hundred. The promise of more elbow room, a new land of opportunity, a place to flourish, lured some ten thousand more Americans in the late 1820s, people hungry for land. They called themselves "Texians," and in return for taking an oath to the Mexican government, settlers were given large grants of land: 640 acres for each able-bodied man, 320 for his wife, and 160 more for each child. By the beginning of the 1830s, the roughly fifteen thousand Texians outnumbered the Spanish-speaking Tejanos five to one.*

Though an 1830 bill passed by the Mexican congress closed the border, effectively prohibiting further American immigration, a lack of enforcement meant that the ban did less to discourage new arrivals than it did to encourage a sense of solidarity among the Anglo settlers. Immigrants—like Sam Houston—still poured into Texas.

Now, as Houston traveled along the weedy track of the camino, he was eager to learn Austin's plans. Did he hope for independence? Would

---

* The label "Texan" didn't come into general use until after Texas, having been annexed by the United States, gained statehood in 1845. In earlier days, "Texian" distinguished recent arrivals from the United States from the Tejanos, residents of Spanish descent. According to some sources, "Texians" was pronounced *Tex-yans* in the 1830s. J. H. Kuykendall Papers, cited in Huston, *Deaf Smith, Incredible Texas Spy* (1973), p. 5.

he cooperate with Houston's hopes? He was a conservative man, perhaps likely to favor the current state of affairs, but Houston needed to find out.

Houston turned south at the Brazos River, then reached San Felipe, which thirty families called home. He found Austin's homestead without difficulty, but, to his surprise, the hand he shook on the veranda wasn't Stephen Austin's. Austin was traveling elsewhere in the colony. Instead, Houston stood face-to-face with another Texas adventurer, one James Bowie.

WELCOME TO TEXAS

Jim Bowie and Sam Houston even looked like natural allies. A physically imposing six-footer, Bowie was, according to his brother, "about as well made as any man I ever saw." Bowie was as fond of drink as Houston and had also joined Jackson's army during the War of 1812. Born in Kentucky but raised on a hardscrabble Georgia farm, the handsome Bowie—"young, proud, and ambitious"—had, like Houston, left his humble origins behind in order to seek his fortune in Texas.[2]

His light-colored hair tinged with red, Bowie was likable, with an engaging smile and an easy and open manner. His reputation, however, wasn't all sweetness and light; when someone or something set off his hair-trigger temper, it "frequently terminated in some tragical scene."[3] One such moment, in 1827, had left Bowie nearly dead.

In a brawl fought on a sandbar of the Mississippi, Bowie had taken a bullet to his hip and a bloody knife gash to his chest. Neither prevented him from grabbing one attacker by the shirt and pulling him down on the blade of Bowie's long knife, "twisting it to cut his heart strings."[4] The man died quickly, but Bowie fought on, sustaining two more bullet wounds and another from a knife. He survived and always after wore at his side that long and instantly legendary knife as a badge of honor.

In Texas, he mastered Spanish, joined the Catholic Church, and accumulated vast tracts of land. He married Maria Ursula de Veramendi, the striking daughter of the vice governor of the province, and settled into a quieter life.

Upon meeting Houston at Austin's, Bowie volunteered to escort him to San Antonio, the next stop on Houston's Texas tour.[5] Houston eagerly accepted. Always the politician, he wanted to get to know his new place and meet its important people. They traveled in a small group and, at Bowie's insistence, posted a guard each night to watch for Indians.

Bowie was just one of a rapidly growing circle of Houston's connections in Texas. In San Antonio, Bowie introduced Houston to his in-laws, the Veramendis, and other influential Texians, who showed Houston around the adobe homes of the picturesque town. By coincidence, a group of Comanche happened to be in San Antonio at the same time, and Houston fulfilled an obligation to Jackson when he got them to agree to meet with Indian commissioners in U.S. territory.

Heading back east, he stopped in San Felipe, this time finding Austin at home. Houston saw a man of moderate height and sober habits, unmarried but dedicated to Texas (Austin was known to say, "Texas is my mistress"). As for Austin, he recognized in this tall stranger a man worthy of a major land grant in one of his colonies.

By Christmas Eve, Houston became a Texas landowner. For $375 and an American horse, he took ownership of a league of land along the Gulf Coast, a plat of some 4,428 acres. Houston's status as a full-fledged Texian was further affirmed when, on his return to Nacogdoches, he learned that the townspeople had chosen him as a delegate to a convention of Texians. Houston's fame had preceded him, and the Texians had decided they needed his political expertise for the challenge facing them.

The purpose of the convention was to petition that the Mexican government grant Texas statehood status in the Mexican federation, separating it from another Mexican state, Coahuila. Houston and a committee of other settlers would soon draft a constitution for such a new Mexican state, one based on the 1780 charter of Massachusetts. Texians were unhappy at Mexico's restrictions on immigration; even if they had little impact, they felt like an infringement. The linkage to Coahuila felt alien; while Texas was strongly Anglo, the province to the south and west was predominantly Tejano. But the biggest source of concern was actually a single man, a dangerous man, with what appeared to be an insatiable lust for power and wealth.

EL PRESIDENTE SANTA ANNA

Mexico's president seemed to believe that cruelty was usually the best strategy.

General Antonio López de Santa Anna's life story was, in some ways, not so different from Sam Houston's. At about the same time that twenty-one-year-old Houston was defending American independence by fighting the Red Sticks, Santa Anna, one year younger, had also been at war. Unlike Sam Houston, though, he was fighting against his country's independence. In 1813, the young warrior was serving under General Arredondo, a general in the Royal Spanish Army, seeking to put down a rebellion against Spain's control of Mexico.

Like Houston, Santa Anna had risen rapidly in the ranks. Born into a well-to-do family, he had joined the military at age sixteen as a "gentleman cadet." Also like Houston, he sustained an arrow wound early, during a skirmish with the Indians in the Sierra Madre. And, like Houston, his early war experience had formed him.

Where Houston had learned that bravery must be tempered with prudence, Santa Anna had recognized an appreciation of the power of pure brutality. Serving under Arredondo at the Battle of Medina, he was part of the Royal Army that had executed 112 rebels after they surrendered. They pursued more men who fled toward eastern Texas and the United States, putting to death any that they captured. In the end, they killed over a thousand men; only ninety-three managed to escape.

The brutality effectively ended resistance to the oppressive royalist government, but the Mexican desire for freedom from Spain was too strong to stay down forever. Just a few years later, Mexico saw another fight for independence, this time with Santa Anna, a man who could read which way the wind was blowing, on the side of the rebels.

In 1821, sensing a power shift, Lieutenant Colonel Santa Anna switched sides, leaving service to the Spanish king to join the insurgents seeking freedom from Spain. After Mexico gained her independence, Santa Anna's successes helped make him one of the new nation's most powerful military men. In the turbulent years that followed, his power grew. He helped fight off a Spanish invasion in 1829, an attempt by the mother country to recapture its former colony. In the decisive Battle of Tampico, Santa Anna defeated the invaders just as Andrew Jackson had beaten the British at New Orleans, and he was celebrated as the nation's savior and even many in Texas supported him. However, in early 1833, he became more than a general: He was elected president of Mexico. He possessed not only military prowess but the shrewd instinct of a political gamesman and a gift for self-promotion. He did not demure when his admirers described him as the "Napoleon of the West."

Once in control of Mexico, the ambitious Santa Anna consolidated his hold on power. He eliminated all constitutional restraints on his dictatorial authority, explaining that it was foolish to allow the Mexican people to be free. "A hundred years to come my people will not be fit for liberty," he told the U.S. ambassador to Mexico. "They do not know . . . unenlightened as they are [that] despotism is the proper government for them."[6] He thought of his people as children; he believed they needed him to be the adult, to make decisions for them. To Santa Anna, the Texians were ungrateful foreign immigrants.

This was the man who was making decisions about Texas now. His words didn't sit well with all Mexicans—and they certainly didn't sit well with the English-speaking Texians who had come to Texas seeking liberty. Among the newest of those, Sam Houston brought both long experience in reading shifting political tides and a continuing obligation to Andrew Jackson.

Houston soon sent a letter to Washington. He reported on his meeting with the Comanche, but he knew his official duties in regard to tribal affairs would interest his old commander less than an assessment of what he had seen and heard in the heart of Anglo Texas.

"I have travelled near five hundred miles across Texas," he wrote. "It is the finest country to its extent upon the globe," he assured General Jackson, ". . . richer and more healthy, in my opinion, than west Tennessee." He imagined a bright future. "There can be no doubt, but the country East of [the Rio Grande] would sustain a population of ten millions of souls."

The gregarious Houston, in visiting Nacogdoches, San Felipe, San Antonio, and parts in between, in getting acquainted with Bowie and Austin and others, had taken their temperature on independence. "I am in possession of some information," he confided in Jackson, "[that] may be calculated to forward your views, if you should entertain any, touching the acquisition of Texas, by the government of the United States."

That news, too, was excellent. "That such a measure is desirable by nineteen twentieths of the population of the Province," Houston assured Jackson, "I can not doubt."[7]

THREE

"Come and Take It"

We must rely on ourselves, and prepare for the worst.

—STEPHEN AUSTIN, AUGUST 31, 1835

Stephen Austin did everything he could to prevent an uprising. He had gone to Mexico City in the spring of 1833, but, despite his measured manner—and more than a decade of cooperation with the Mexican government—his mission had gone very wrong.

He carried a petition seeking for Texas the status of a state separate from Coahuila, but his firm but reasonable words produced only months of delays and no progress. Austin had despaired. "Nothing is going to be done," he wrote home, his patience exhausted, on October 2, 1833. Unfortunately for Austin, his pen didn't stop there.

Weary and frustrated, he urged the town council of San Antonio to act together with other towns. They should, he wrote, "unite in organizing a local government . . . even though the general government refuses its consent."[1] The runaround he'd faced in Mexico had done nothing to alleviate his worries concerning the future infringement of Texian rights; he knew that his fellow Texians, most of whom had been raised on the principles their fathers and grandfathers had fought for in the American Revolution, were with him.

When Santa Anna's Mexican government got wind of the letter, they arrested Austin. They accused him of sedition and threw him into the Inquisition prison. For a year he would remain in a cell, then he spent more months under house arrest, forbidden to leave Mexico City. He felt lucky when, in late July 1835, he was finally permitted to head home to Texas.

During those same months, Sam Houston kept a low profile, traveling around Texas and, in April 1834, visited Washington—and, undoubtedly, President Jackson. Neither man wanted Texas any less, but they chose to wait and to react as events unfolded—which they soon did.

Once more a free man, Austin made his way north, in the summer of 1835, stopping in New Orleans, where he confided in his cousin Mary Austin Holley, "It is very evident that Texas should be effectually, and fully, *Americanized*." One way or another, a philosophical Austin told Mary, independence would come, just "as a gentle breeze shakes off a ripe peach."[2]

Yet the peaceable Austin still hoped that Santa Anna might listen to reason. Austin feared the odds: After his many months in Mexico City, he fully grasped the size of the enemy; he and his thirty thousand Texian settlers faced a fight with a nation of some *eight million*.

He wanted to believe Santa Anna might be an ally. After all, thought Austin, the man had helped secure his release. His cautious optimism was also fed by a promise Santa Anna had made—"General Santa Anna told me he should visit Texas next March—as a friend." On the other hand, Austin knew that such hopes flew in the face of other actions of El Presidente.[3]

Santa Anna had decreed the Mexican congress powerless and undone earlier liberal reforms. He intimidated his people. When the state of Zacatecas resisted the president's orders to give up their weapons, Santa Anna led the army into the region. In May of that very year, the rebels surrendered, but, according to rumors around the capital, the president permitted his soldiers to run wild, setting fires and pillaging. In fact, more than two thousand civilians in the town had been slaughtered, among them hundreds of women and children. Santa Anna's message was clear: He would be merciless in putting down any who opposed him.

Few doubted that that included Texians and even the United States. In the presence of French and British diplomats, he issued an unmistakable warning. As reported by Jackson's man in Mexico City, he promised he "would in due Season *Chastise*" the United States. He went further, warning that, as the British had done in 1814, "I will march to the Capital, I will lay Washington City in ashes."[4]

Despite Santa Anna's threats, Stephen Austin still wanted to believe he might agree to a solution to pacify the unruly Texians. A strikingly handsome man with deep brown eyes, Santa Anna's quiet willingness to listen had impressed Austin, leading him to hope that, somehow, he could secure the future of his colony without a violent uprising and a bloody fight with Santa Anna. But on returning to America, he wrote from New Orleans to his cousin, admitting that he now could see Santa Anna had no respect for the Texians, that he wanted to make them Mexicans. He wanted to make them bow to Mexicans, to Mexico, and above all to him. What made that suddenly and undeniably clear to Austin was news that Santa Anna had ordered five hundred Mexican troops, commanded by General Martín Perfecto de Cos, onto Texas soil. Santa Anna had decided it was time to teach the Texian rebels a lesson.

Cos and his men, coming from Coahuila, would land at the Texian port of Copano on the Gulf of Mexico. They had been sent to preempt Texian resistance. They would disarm the Texians, peaceably or by force—that didn't matter to Santa Anna. But both sides could see that, with committees of safety springing up in every town—volunteer militias, ready to fight—armed conflict was growing more likely by the day.

The shock of all this, added to his two years in Mexico, altered Stephen Austin's views of Texas's future. Never large or hearty, he looked thin and wan, but the change was deeper. The man who'd departed with an honest allegiance to Mexico had been forced to rethink; now, in a matter of a few September days, Austin would finally abandon his long-held faith in Mexico and in Santa Anna, the man he wanted to believe was an ally to Texas. Like many of the so-called Three Hundred, the first families of Texas, he was reluctant to rebel; he would have been content if Texas were to become an independent state under Mexican authority. But he also wanted the rights restored that Santa Anna's strongman rule had taken away. Now, however, along with the flood of new arrivals who had little patience for the Mexican regime,

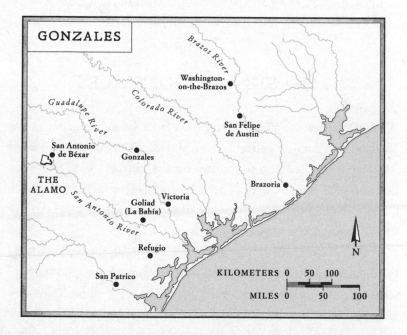

Austin recognized that war was inevitable. If Texas was to achieve its destiny, the Texians must be united in their resolve.

Returning after so many months to his colony at San Felipe de Austin, Austin accepted the chairmanship of the town's Committee of Safety, a volunteer company of rebels mustered in this moment of need, just as the Minutemen in Massachusetts had done in the revolutionary era. On almost the same day, the Committee of Public Safety in Nacogdoches put Sam Houston in charge of its militia. But it was Austin, in San Felipe, who issued a proclamation.

"There must now be no half way measures," Austin decreed as he worried about Cos's march north along the San Antonio River toward San Antonio. It must be, Austin added, "war in full. The sword is drawn and the scabbard must be put on one side until the [Mexican] military are all driven out of Texas."[5]

Little did he know that the war would soon begin a mere seventy-five miles away in the little town of Gonzales.

THE GUN AT GONZALES

When Gonzales had needed protection from Comanche attacks, the Mexican commandant at the nearby and larger San Antonio had loaned the town a small cannon to frighten off the Indians. Now, four years later, in 1835, with rumors of rebellion spreading fast, the Mexican military was eager to disarm any and all disgruntled Texians. As part of Cos's campaign, it was time to take the gun back.

The sleepy settlement of roughly two dozen families settled along the Guadalupe River posed no real threat to anyone. Nor did the half-forgotten little cannon, dismounted from its carriage with no ammunition available. But the Mexicans were determined to squash any opportunities for rebellion before they started, and as the sun-drenched days of September drew to a close, five Mexican soldiers marched into Gonzales to demand the return of the weapon.

The people of the isolated little town had been hearing whispers of Mexican efforts to disarm Texians. A rumor had recently gone around that soon only one man in ten would be permitted to carry a firearm. General Cos and five hundred Mexican troops were said to be coming to Texas to put down any unrest. And President Santa Anna loomed, far away but all-powerful and intimidating, an autocrat who ruled with an iron fist and whose goal of centralizing power and limiting democratic freedom was now clear to all. But whether any of the trouble would reach Gonzales had seemed less sure until the appearance of soldiers ready to confiscate Gonzales's only defensive weapon. Now the larger worries of Texas seemed very local.

Quickly convening a meeting to discuss the demands, the townspeople agreed that the order to hand over the gun made no sense if the Mexicans were looking out for Texian interests. San Antonio possessed at least eighteen better guns to protect it, and now Gonzales would have none. Never mind that they hadn't needed it to drive away Comanche in quite some time—the people of Gonzales correctly discerned that this was a move designed to weaken Texian defenses and destroy Texian morale. They decided to refuse to hand over the cannon. Mayor Andrew Ponton ordered the Mexican soldiers escorted out of town, the oxcart they had brought to carry the cannon left empty.

Their return cargo consisted of only a handwritten note, a message for the Mexican commandant at San Antonio. "The dangers which existed at the time we received this cannon still exist," Ponton wrote. "It is still needed here."[6] His words were half-true. Certainly, a threat remained—only now the biggest danger was not the Comanche, but men in Mexican army uniforms.

Though Ponton had politely offered a seemingly innocent excuse for defiance, it was defiance nonetheless. Everyone understood this would be a temporary standoff. No soldier in Santa Anna's army could let such evident insolence go unpunished. It was only a matter of time before a larger contingent of Mexican soldiers arrived to take the cannon by force.

Ponton looked around him: With just eighteen armed men ready to fight, Gonzales needed reinforcements—and fast. San Antonio was two days' ride away. If the Mexicans responded quickly, their avenging force could arrive in as little as four days, and eighteen Gonzales men would not be enough to fight them off. Desperate for help, one messenger galloped off for nearby Mina, another toward the Colorado River, passing the word to other Texian towns that Gonzales faced grave danger.

THE "OLD EIGHTEEN"

While the messengers were off rallying their fellow Texians, the men of Gonzales prepared to fight.* First, they evacuated the women and children. Some hid in the nearby forest, and others made their way to settlements along the Colorado River.

It was hard for twenty-five-year-old Almeron Dickinson to send away his wife, Susanna. The two of them, though they had been born in Tennessee, had adopted Texas as their native land four years before, settling in Gonzales in 1831. Dickinson tended their farm along the San Marcos River, and just a year earlier he and Susanna had welcomed their first child, a girl they named Angelina Elizabeth. But evacuation was the only sensible option for women and children, and, with Su-

---

* In later days, the survivors among these men took pride in identifying themselves as members of the "Old Eighteen," defenders of Gonzales. Miles, "Battle of Gonzales" (1899), p. 314.

sanna and Angelina safely gone, Dickinson turned his energy toward defending the home he'd come to love.

The first order of business was repairing the cannon—the truth was that the weapon the Texians were refusing to give up was not in good shape. Fortunately, as a U.S. Army veteran trained as an artilleryman, Dickinson knew a good deal about such guns. As a blacksmith, he knew how to repair them, too.

Dickinson fashioned a new carriage, making rough wheels of tree trunk rounds and inserting wooden axles through holes in their centers. He swabbed and cleaned the gun, and soon it was mounted and capable of being fired. But it really wasn't much of a weapon, Dickinson had to admit, since the cannon had been spiked to disable it years before by a retreating Mexican force. When the nail driven into its touchhole had been drilled out, the operation left an opening the size of a man's thumb. Dickinson did what he could to narrow the hole, but nothing would get this gun into top condition.

With no cannonballs to fire, ammunition had to be prepared. Dickinson and a second blacksmith set about hammering slugs of iron bar into crude balls that, together with pieces of chain and cut-up horseshoes, could be used as grapeshot.

Captain Albert Martin, Dickinson's neighbor, took charge of other preparations. He drilled his little band of men and talked strategy. Their best defense was the Guadalupe River, temporarily swollen by recent rain, which could function like a castle moat between them and enemies approaching from San Antonio in the west. Martin had the newly battle-ready cannon installed in a temporary fortification overlooking the river, and he ordered the ferryboat used for crossing the Guadalupe be moored well out of sight in a backwater hidden by trees upstream. The few remaining boats, too, were tied up on the east bank of the river, out of the reach of any Mexican soldiers.

The men collected the few guns they had—rifles, shotguns, and fowling pieces. Someone suggested a flag was needed, and soon volunteers went to work to make one. Using paint and a sheet of coarse cotton fabric as their canvas, they drew a simple likeness of the barrel of the disputed cannon. Above this symbol, they painted a five-point star to signify the state of Texas. Beneath, they wrote four words in black paint across the length of the six-foot flag. Large enough to be read from enemy lines, they posed a challenge: COME AND TAKE IT.[7]

Now Martin, Dickinson, and the other men waited, hoping that reinforcements would arrive before the enemy.

ONE HUNDRED DRAGOONS

The Mexicans appeared first. On Tuesday, September 29, a column of one hundred soldiers rode into sight. From across the Guadalupe they gazed on little Gonzales.

To these professional soldiers, this was just a routine mission, and their commanding officer, Lieutenant Francisco de Castañeda, had clear orders. He was to demand the cannon be handed over and, one way or another, bring to an end this insolence on the part of the upstart Texians.

Despite the long, two-day ride from San Antonio, the cavalrymen made an impressive appearance astride their horses and dressed in red uniform jackets. They carried nine-foot lances. Sabers and pistols hung from their belts and muskets jutted from their saddlebags.

The eighteen Texians were grateful that the rain-swollen river made crossing dangerous. They were not experienced fighters, but they did not need advanced knowledge of military tactics to understand that if the numbers didn't change—Martin and company were outnumbered more than five to one—this was not a winnable fight.

The Mexicans shouted across the Guadalupe that Lieutenant Castañeda, on behalf of the commander at San Antonio, wished to deliver a dispatch for the mayor of Gonzales. Captain Martin replied that a courier might swim over, and one of Castañeda's men crossed carrying his lieutenant's written demand.

Martin opened and read the dispatch. Its contents were no surprise, consisting of one demand: *The Texians must hand over the cannon.*

With reinforcements not yet there, Martin knew refusal would end badly. But there might be a way to buy time. Thinking quickly, he composed a meek response, saying that, with Mayor Ponton out of town, he lacked the authority to comply. Castañeda and his men would have to remain on the river's west bank overnight. The Mexicans, with an old-world respect for proper procedure, agreed.

As the Mexicans slept on the opposite bank, the men of Gonzales waited and prayed—and their petitions were answered. That evening reinforcements began to drift into Gonzales. Thirty men arrived from Mina; soon another fifty appeared, mustered from homesteads along the Colorado. The rumored arrival of Cos and his army had galvanized many in Texas, and these men came to fight not only for Gonzales but for freedom.

The following morning, the Texians managed to delay matters again; the mayor was still absent, Martin told Castañeda, but having been sent for, certainly he would return soon. Martin proposed scheduling the meeting for four o'clock that afternoon. With any luck, they'd be able by then to organize themselves enough to resist successfully.

At the appointed time, Lieutenant Castañeda returned to the river-bank, expecting to see Ponton crossing over. Instead, he saw a rebellious contingent of Texians gathered on the opposite bank. A Texian read a statement aloud, shouting it across the water. They would not "deliver up the cannon," the voice echoed. "The cannon is in the town and only through force will we yield. We are weak and few in number, nevertheless we are contending for what we believe just principles."[8]

Castañeda must have been shocked. Why would a tiny group of eighteen men think it could hold off one hundred trained Mexicans? Their resistance was irritating but could easily be put down. The day was coming to a close, but the next day he would march his men north to find an easier crossing, then travel south to Gonzales to teach the upstarts a lesson.

THE SKIRMISH

The Mexicans slowly marched north, eventually making camp that evening seven miles north of Gonzales. They occupied the fields of farmer Ezekiel Williams and helped themselves to his crop of watermelons. Secure in what they believed to be their vastly superior numbers, Lieutenant Castañeda and his troopers rested peacefully, blanketed by a deep fog that spread across the Guadalupe River Valley.

The Texians, with their homes and lives on the line, did not rest. As the Mexicans had retreated north, they had been busy accepting further reinforcements and organizing themselves under leaders. Now numbering more than one hundred sixty men, the volunteers elected John Moore as their commander, and Moore decided it was time to act. Martin's delaying tactic had bought enough time for volunteers to arrive from as far away as the Brazos River, and now the Texians outnumbered the enemy. No one knew whether more Mexicans were on the way, and it seemed prudent to act while the numbers were still in the Texian's favor. It seemed even more prudent to make that attack under cover of darkness.

That evening every available boat ferried men and horses across the Guadalupe. Once all the Texians were across, a Methodist preacher named W. P. Smith delivered a "patriotic address," exhorting the brave men to do their duty for God and Texas.[9] Then, on Colonel Moore's order, as one soldier remembered, the Texians moved north "with the greatest order and silence."[10]

The fog slowed progress, but at 4:00 A.M., warned by advance scouts that the Mexican encampment was a short distance ahead, the little army halted. The officers arranged the men into battle formation, with the fifty-man cavalry leading the way. Platoons of infantrymen marched on the right and left, flanking the artillery unit, with the brass cannon on its makeshift carriage and Almeron Dickinson heading its crew. A small guard brought up the rear. Still undetected, Moore's men resumed their advance on the Mexicans in a hushed silence.

A dog's bark broke the silence.

A moment later, a gunshot rang out, a Mexican picket firing into the predawn fog.

With visibility near zero, the Texians took cover in a nearby stand of trees. They waited: Had they been discovered? Or was the Mexican sentinel just jumpy? Either way, the fog was so thick that it would be foolhardy to attack now. They would wait and attack in the morning.

Even after sunrise, visibility remained poor as the fog gradually burned off. The sun slowly revealed that their presence had been discovered. Mexican dragoons stood in a triangular battle formation on a nearby rise, "their bright arms glittering in the sun."[11]

With the element of surprise entirely lost, Colonel Moore agreed to a parley. Meeting on middle ground, Castañeda once again demanded the cannon. The Texians refused. The cannon, they said, was rightfully theirs. Castañeda said his orders required him to remain in the vicinity and await further orders if the Texians refused to hand over the cannon.

Colonel Moore assured his opponent that he spoke for the people of Texas when he promised to "fight for our rights . . . until the last gasp."[12] He invited Castañeda to surrender.

The Mexican replied he must obey orders, and the negotiators returned to their respective lines.

With Mexican reinforcements undoubtedly coming from San Antonio, the Texians were not prepared to wait. Instead, they raised their banner—COME AND TAKE IT—over the cannon that was at the heart of the dispute. When a light was applied to its touchhole, Almeron Dickinson's weapon fired its load of iron shrapnel toward the Mexican line, and the band of farmers and settlers charged across the three hundred yards that separated the combatants.

To the Texians' great surprise, the Mexicans, at Castañeda's order, wheeled their horses and bolted.

"The Mexicans fled," remembered one of the Texians, "and continued to fly until entirely out of sight, on the road to San Antonio." The enemy was out of range before Dickinson's crew could fire off a second blast of iron scraps from the brass cannon.

Why had they fled? The Texians were not sure, but that was no reason not to celebrate the volunteers' victory over the trained forces. One or two Mexicans had been downed by the cannon's improvised ammunition, but the worst injury on the Texian side was a bloody nose suffered by a gunsmith whose horse had thrown him at the sound of the cannon.[13]

Strictly speaking, the Battle of Gonzales was scarcely a battle, and some of its participants would later call it just "the fight at Williams's place."[14] Nonetheless, the tale of the courageous men who'd held Gonzales, who'd defied the Mexicans, spread quickly. The threat of Mexican military action seemed suddenly very real, but in fact Casteñada had orders *not* to bring on a battle to the Texians, but at Gonzales the Texians believed they had defeated an invading army. They had taunted the powerful enemy with their challenge, *Come and take it*.

Gonzales was, quite simply, a moment to savor, a victory, a first victory, over the Mexicans. A wave of confidence spread. More than one account proudly termed the skirmish Texas's "Lexington and Concord moment," but the danger was far from past.

JOINING UP

Where there had been no Texian army, there would soon be one. And some of those who would fight for Texas came together in unexpected ways.

In the darkness at midnight, on October 9, a man on the run through the Texian wilderness listened carefully: Were the men on horseback, their voices barely distinguishable, friend or foe? Fearing they might be Mexican soldiers, he stood frozen, hoping to remain undetected.

He had come hundreds of miles across a desert plain from Monterrey. Despite long years in Texas and a sworn allegiance to Mexico, he had been jailed after Santa Anna became dictator. More than three months elapsed before he managed to slip away during a bathing session in a creek. Riding a fleet horse left him by a sympathetic friend, he raced for the Texas line. Now he could do nothing but wait, half-hidden in the mesquite thicket alongside the San Antonio River.

When one of the silhouetted riders raised a rifle in his direction, his freedom, even his life, might have ended with the report of the gun. But the first sound he heard wasn't the click of a trigger but a harsh demand.

"Who goes there?"

To the stranger's great relief, the rider spoke English.

"A friend," he responded; when he showed himself, some in the company recognized him. The stranger was Ben Milam, an early Texas settler and a man with nearly the status of Stephen Austin. His unexpected appearance was "like finding the dead to be alive."[15]

At forty-seven, Benjamin Rush Milam didn't look much like the soldier boy he once had been. Born in Lexington, he had gone to war with the Eighth Regiment of the Kentucky Infantry and defended his country during the War of 1812. In his late twenties, the restless young man had found a new home in Texas and, along with his friend Austin, encouraged other settlers to move westward, establishing what came to be known as Milam's Colony, located between the Guadalupe and Colorado rivers. He had led a venturesome life, accumulating large landholdings, as well as silver and other mining interests (which twice took him to England), and even investing in a project that led to the opening of the Red River to steamboats.

He had gone to the seat of government to stand up for those "who have built houses, mills and cotton gins, and introduced horses and cattle and hogs and sheep into the wilderness."[16] He had been rebuffed. Now, lined by the years and weathered by his journey, he still wore his tattered prison clothes. A sturdy man who stood six feet tall, Milam felt deeply betrayed by the Mexicans and was willing to fight for the rights of Texians.

When, after his discovery in the mesquite, he heard for the first time that the Texian rebellion had begun, "his heart was full. He could not speak for joy."[17] These men were volunteers, forming one of many bands around Texas who were looking to work together to fight off the Mexicans. Milam immediately volunteered to join the mission he had accidentally interrupted.

MILAM AND HIS NEW ASSOCIATES had a plan: They were looking to meet up with Captain George M. Collinsworth and join the ranks of his volunteer militia.

Hearing the call to arms just days before, Collinsworth, along with fewer than two dozen men, had departed the town of Matagorda near the mouth of the Colorado River. But on the march toward the newly contested heart of Texas, word of mouth brought more men to the cause from the surrounding coastal prairie. Tejanos concerned for their liberty also joined the ranks, bringing Collinsworth's count to more than a hundred men.

His objective was the nearby town of Goliad and its fortified mission building, La Bahía. Population seven hundred, Goliad occupied a hill-top overlooking the San Antonio River. A good, dry road and the navigable river extended south some forty miles to the port at Copano on the Gulf Coast; San Antonio was roughly the same distance north. This was the route General Cos and his troops had just taken, and it made Goliad, with its presidio, a natural base of operations in the region.

If Collinsworth and his volunteers could capture Goliad, the Texians would possess the perfect picket post from which to prevent the Mexicans from using the main supply route into the heart of Mexican Texas. Or, should the Texians persuade the nation of Andrew Jackson to lend assistance to their cause, the allies could land munitions and supplies from the United States.

In scouting the previous day, Collinsworth had gained valuable facts from several local Tejanos. These Spanish-speaking citizens told him the Mexican force holding the fort was small, a garrison of fewer than fifty enlisted men and a few officers. Collinsworth had sent a messenger asking them to surrender, but the mayor had refused.

Seeing no alternative, Collinsworth and his men prepared to attack on October 9. Led by Tejano scouts, three squads, with Milam at the head of one, moved quietly through the streets before midnight that Friday; a fourth band of soldiers remained with the horses outside the town. The mission and the attached imposing stone fortress looked impregnable, but acting on inside knowledge, Collinsworth's men went straight for the north wall.

Using axes, they chopped through a wooden door to reach an interior courtyard. One platoon headed for the quarters of the commandant. A sentinel fired on the attackers, but return fire silenced him. They quickly confronted the surprised Mexican commander, who threw up his hands in surrender. The Mexican defenders shot into the shadows; the Americans took careful aim at the enemy's muzzle flashes.

When a lull in the firing permitted one of Collinsworth's men to call upon the Mexicans to surrender, a Spanish voice agreed.

The short fight left one Mexican dead and three wounded, with a single Texian injured, his wound minor. The victors took two dozen prisoners, the rest of the Mexicans having escaped into the town.

A search of the presidio uncovered valuable weapons, including two brass cannons, six hundred spears, many bayonets, and ammunition. Less valuable were the stands of "Muskets and Carbins . . . the greater part . . . broken and entirely useless."[18] But there were large stores of supplies, including food and blankets and clothing. Ben Milam got a new set of clothes, although they were too small for the large man. Six inches or more of his ankles and arms stuck out like a scarecrow's.

Whatever the spoils, the result was clear: In Collinsworth's words, "I am now in possession of Goliad."[19] As at Gonzales, the Texians had demonstrated to the world—and to themselves—they could come together in common cause and fight effectively. After the news reached the distant East Coast later that year, the *New York Star* had admiring words for the Texians, calling them "mostly muscular, powerful men, and great marksmen; and whether at a distance with a rifle, or in close combat, they will be terrible."[20]

Another clear message had been sent, too: *Santa Anna, beware!*

GENERAL AUSTIN

By 8:00 A.M. on October 10, dispatches from Captain Collinsworth spread the word of Goliad's capture. In a matter of hours, the news reached Gonzales, where the armed force continued to grow by the day, even by the hour. From far-flung settlements, in the interior and on the coast, Texians came to join the fight.

"Recruits were constantly arriving, singly and in squads," remembered one soldier, ". . . [but] we soon had more officers than men."[21] Captain Moore no longer had clear charge of this motley band, the majority of whom hadn't yet arrived when he was chosen. A mix of lieutenants, colonels, and other captains would be required to command these men—but most of all the Texian rebels needed a general. A vote was scheduled for October 11; in keeping with militia tradition, the commander would be chosen by the men.

When Stephen Austin rode into camp early that Sunday afternoon, he didn't look well; "he was so feeble that his servant Simon [had] had to assist him to mount his horse."[22] But that didn't diminish the esteem his fellow Texians held for him and, one by one, the other candidates for the generalship bowed out. When the appointed hour of 4:00 P.M. rolled around, the rank and file unanimously chose Austin commander of the Volunteer Army of the People. He could claim no military experience beyond a few fights with marauding Indians and brief service in the Missouri militia during the War of 1812; still, he was the unimpeachable choice, founder and empresario, a man who'd gone to prison for his belief in Texas. His countrymen knew this citizen soldier would rise to any call to serve Texas.

Austin embraced his new role. Earlier that week he wrote to a friend in San Jacinto, "*I hope to see Texas forever free from Mexican domination of any kind.*" He said it in a private letter—"it is yet too soon to say this politically," he admitted—but he could read Texas's future.[23] The radical idea of *independence*, once held only by Houston and a handful of others, was rapidly becoming the will of the people.

Austin and his staff identified their next target: San Antonio. General Cos held that town; he had been sent to quell the uprising and, together with the five hundred men who had accompanied him from Mexico, the town's defenders were thought to number perhaps 650 men. Cos, a veteran soldier who had risen to the rank of brigadier general, headed a band of disciplined soldiers, fully armed professionals wearing matching blue uniforms with white sashes and tall hats. As Santa Anna had ordered, he was to put down the "revolutionists of Texas."[24]

Austin's officers included Colonel John Moore, commander of the main regiment, which now numbered about three hundred men. The scouts would report to Sam Milam, who had just arrived in Gonzales escorting three prisoners, the Mexican officers captured at Goliad. Responsibility for the artillery fell to Almeron Dickinson. And on October 13, Austin's band began the seventy-mile march, their heading due west.

The Texian "army" that marched out of Gonzales wore no official uniforms. The men, most in their twenties and thirties, wore the clothes of frontier settlers. For a typical volunteer that meant buckskin breeches gathered at the knee with Indian garters. Many wore shoes or moccasins and no socks. Almost none wore boots. Homemade buckskin hunting coats were common, worn atop rough linsey-woolsey shirts. A mix of sombreros and coonskin caps covered their heads.

The weapons included large hunting knives. Not everyone had a gun, but some did, many of them shotguns. The luckiest of them carried deadly accurate Kentucky long rifles. For those with firearms, priming horns and leather bullet pouches hung from their belts.

As his little army marched, Austin worried about the experienced and well-armed Mexican cavalry; most of the men were on foot, but his small mounted force consisted of men carrying homemade lances riding a mix of American horses, Spanish ponies, and mules. Another Austin worry was the hot-blooded nature of his men. Despite having no formal training and poor equipment, many were so keen to fight, so anxious to get into battle, that Austin wondered at his ability to restrain them until their odds improved. In his first official general orders, he warned them: "Patriotism and firmness will avail but little, without discipline and strict obedience to orders."[25]

The enemy outnumbered them, but the Texians were rising to this desperate occasion. Austin dispatched orders by courier for the soldiers from Goliad to join him en route. Two or three dozen new recruits were said to be arriving each day in San Felipe, and the general sent word that they, too, should join him on the march to San Antonio.

Austin also hoped to hear from Sam Houston, who was using his fame to help raise an army in East Texas. As reports of the action in central Texas arrived in Nacogdoches, Houston had, in early October, issued a call for volunteers from beyond the Sabine River, in the United States, appealing to men looking for adventure and a new start. Promising "liberal bounties of land," he implored readers in Arkansas, Tennessee, and Kentucky newspapers: "Let each man come with a good rifle, and one hundred rounds of ammunition, and to come soon." He closed with fighting words: "Our war cry is 'Liberty or death.'"[26] All that high talk was encouraging, but so far Austin had seen nothing of either Houston or his volunteers.

General Cos, a professional soldier with an experienced army, lay in wait, confident he could crush the upstart Texians whenever he wished. His opponent, the wary Austin, marched slowly toward San Antonio, consolidating his growing force. He would order his men into battle with the formidable Cos only when the time was right. Until then, he knew, everything was at risk.

FOUR

Concepción

The morning of glory is dawning upon us.
The work of liberty has begun.

—SAM HOUSTON, *Department Orders*, OCTOBER 8, 1835[1]

A ustin's Army of Texas covered only ten miles a day in its seventy-five-mile march to San Antonio, a slow pace that allowed fresh volunteers to catch up with the force. There was an air of optimism among the men, who were ready to fight for something they believed in—and, judging by the first fights, they were more than up to the task.

Among the new arrivals, together with a handful of his Louisiana friends, was Houston's friend Colonel Jim Bowie. Austin welcomed any and all fresh recruits, but this man's appearance in particular cheered the ragtag army. "Bowie's prowess as a fighter," remembered one who saw him that day, "made him doubly welcome."[2]

Before meeting Houston, Bowie had lived a rambling life. Childhood had taken him from his birthplace in Kentucky to Missouri and Louisiana; his gambling adulthood was spent in Louisiana, Arkansas, Mississippi, and finally Texas. He found a home only upon his marriage to Ursula, in 1831, and with the birth the next year of a daughter, Maria

Elva, and then a son, James Jr. When Houston first met him in Texas, the wanderer had found happiness with his growing family at home in San Antonio—but the next year, in a September 1833 cholera epidemic, Ursula and the two little ones had died. Overnight, Bowie became a childless widower.*

As Sam Houston had done after the implosion of his marriage, Bowie had tried to numb his heartbreak with alcohol. He resumed his iterant ways, traveling to New Orleans and Mexico, pursuing his passion for land. But in late September 1835, on his return to Texas from Natchez, Mississippi, he had heard the call to arms. He and his little company came at a gallop.

Bowie's willingness to fight for his friends was beyond question. After a recent brawl in San Antonio, he scolded a companion who hadn't joined the fight. "Why, Jim," his friend replied, "you were in the wrong." To Bowie, that was no excuse. "Don't you suppose I know that as well as you do? That's just why I needed a friend. If I had been in the right, I would have had plenty of them."[3]

This time Bowie's cause was in the right, though whether he had enough friends to win in the fight against Mexico remained to be seen. When he caught up with Austin's forces, he and his men joined them in the march toward San Antonio, where they would find out.

On reaching Salado Creek, on October 20, Austin ordered a halt to establish temporary headquarters. They were a mere half day's ride from San Antonio, but Austin wasn't ready for the Texians to fight.

Before leaving Gonzales, Austin had issued urgent pleas for supplies. "Send on, without delay, wagons, with what ammunition you can procure," he wrote to his friends back in San Felipe de Austin, "[and] cannon and small-arms—powder, lead, &c.; and also provisions, meal,

---

* Bowie's life story varies from source to source, and some historians now question whether Bowie fathered any of Ursula's children.

beans, sugar and coffee."⁴ But delivery was slow and now, after a week's march, the situation at the encampment looked more dire. "The men here are beginning to suffer greatly for the want of bread &c &c."⁵

Another challenge to Austin was the impending battle itself. He and his officers needed a strategy, a plan of attack. He could no longer count on the element of surprise—General Cos already knew the Texians were nearby since, a few days earlier, Ben Milam's scouts had engaged in a brief skirmish with a band of Mexican lancers that ended with the enemy force dashing back to San Antonio, carrying the news of the approaching Texians.

As inexperienced as he was in war, Austin understood he needed to know as much about his enemy as possible. *Did they have the rumored eight hundred or more men?* He knew too little about the town's defenses. *Where had they deployed their dozen or more cannons?* He had a hundred questions and few answers as his men entrenched along the little watercourse.

Austin needed somebody to venture closer to San Antonio, to look for information, as well as find corn, beans, and foodstuffs. He turned to his newest staff officer, Jim Bowie.

Austin recognized the way other men looked up to this fearless man. Having lived for years in San Antonio, Bowie also knew the town and its people very well. Austin assigned a slightly younger man, James Fannin, to be Bowie's co-commander. As the only one in the camp with any real military training (he'd spent two years at West Point), Fannin might be able to think tactically about the assault. Then, too, he might just offset the impulsive instincts of the scrappy Jim Bowie.

Bowie began by smuggling a letter into San Antonio. He learned from friends in the town that General Cos and his men (best estimate: six hundred Mexican troops) had fortified San Antonio with "adobe brick, with Port holes for their infantry." The enemy had mounted at least eight small cannons, some on rooftops. On the other hand, the

Mexicans had limited foodstuffs; "in *five days*," Bowie was told, "they can be *starved* out."[6] Bowie, Fannin, and company had also gone on small scouting missions and twice been "attacked by the enimy." But those skirmishes consisted of little more than brief exchanges of gunfire. Bowie asked Austin for fifty more men to assist him—*and* recommended that the Army of Texas move on San Antonio. He was confident of success.[7]

But Stephen Austin wasn't ready. He ordered the reconnoiterers back to camp. He wanted this fight to be on his terms, at a time he thought right. He also had to confront an immediate problem of Texian politics.

THE CONSULTATION

From a distance, the rider looked like just another volunteer. But as the stranger neared the temporary Texian camp, some thought they knew the identity of the man astride the little Spanish stallion. Soon the happy news began to ripple through the Army of Texas. The tall man on the little yellow horse, his feet almost touching the ground, was General Sam Houston.

The famous man arrived alone but instantly drew a crowd. Spontaneously, he delivered a speech to the excited men, "urging the necessity of concerted action among the colonists," as Noah Smithwick remembered it, and, "arguing that it should be for independence."[8] His audience needed no convincing and were thrilled to rally to the charismatic Houston. They cheered, heartened to have the great man on their side.

Oddly, though, Houston hadn't come to fight. His purpose was different: The new Texas needed a government. With Santa Anna having dissolved the legislature for the state of Coahuila y Tejas more than a year earlier, no form of representative government existed; in short,

Texas was "without a head."[9] And the rebellious Texians needed not only to stick together but to do it in an organized way.

The timing of Houston's appearance was no accident. In a matter of days, the Council of Texas, a body consisting of men from far-flung districts, planned to gather to sketch out a plan for governance. Delegates were already gathering in San Felipe de Austin, which had been chosen to take advantage of the just-arrived printing press and the newspaper it produced; the *Telegraph and Texas Register* could spread the word. But before beginning a formal session, the council needed a quorum. The purpose of Houston's visit was to corral the men already in the Army of Texas who had been chosen by their friends and neighbors to be delegates to the San Felipe Consultation.

That put Houston and Stephen Austin in direct conflict. Austin grasped the importance of the council's work, but he also knew, as general of this little army, he could hardly afford to lose a man. And he worried that the departure of some might lead to the departure of many. Instead of arriving to help in the fight, Houston would rob the army of fighters. Austin wasn't happy, but, always fair-minded, he looked for a solution.

On Sunday morning, October 25, he convened a meeting at the encampment. A number of other men spoke their minds, but Austin and Houston anchored the discussion. The central issue: *Stay and fight* vs. *Depart and debate.*

Houston made his case for the Consultation, arguing that they needed to organize a government for Texas and must do it swiftly. Then he spoke his mind about the ragtag band he saw before him. They needed more training, he told the troops. They were ill-equipped and, as Houston saw it, a lack of artillery doomed any assault on the well-barricaded town of San Antonio and its cannons. Rather than battling the well-armed and well-drilled regulars in the Mexican army, Houston told the assembled men, they would serve the cause of Texas better if they withdrew to Gonzales for winter camp, where they could make themselves into a real army.

These didn't sound like fighting words, but they were spoken by a fighter who, from harsh experience, knew the importance of prudence—and the costs of foolhardy courage.

When General Austin in his turn spoke to the crowd, he looked like the sick man he was; as one observer reported, he was "just able to sit on his horse." But despite the dysentery that caused him intense intestinal distress, he found the energy to deliver a deeply felt plea on behalf of his adopted land.

While he favored the purpose of the Consultation—*yes, certainly Texas needed a functioning government*—he passionately disagreed with Houston's plan to retreat back over hard-won ground; that would simply squander their first successes. The general promised his soldiers that he "would remain as long as 10 men would stick to [me], because the salvation of Texas depends on the army being sustained and at the same time the meeting of the convention."[10]

Houston and Austin, at odds with each other, had made their cases. The jury would be the fighting men, and a vote was taken. The vast majority of the men were angry and eager. They rejected retreat—but also recognized the need for the Consultation. The thorough airing of the matter permitted both a renewed commitment to the fight and an endorsement of a meeting of the council.

Despite their differences, Houston and Austin put their heads together; honoring the vote, they came to a compromise. Houston would go to San Felipe accompanied by the essential delegates, a total of fewer than twenty men. And he would carry a memorandum from Austin, who, understanding how critical the deliberations would be to the future of the region, wanted his opinions heard.

The debate in San Felipe would pit the radical faction, which some called the War Party, against the Peace Party, with the key tension between them whether they were fighting, on the one hand, for Texas's complete independence from Mexico or, on the other, for Mexican statehood and assurances of its citizens' rights under the Mexican Constitution of 1824, which Santa Anna had violated. In his letter, Austin made the case for remaining a Mexican state. But that would have to be resolved at the Consultation.

The next morning, Houston rode out the way he'd come, leaving Austin and the army to pursue a fight he thought misguided. As the big man departed, Austin was buoyed by the arrival of more than a hundred Tejano reinforcements, including a contingent of thirty-eight men led by Juan Seguín, the son of Austin's oldest Mexican friend. The army was growing more diverse, and it no longer looked like an entirely Anglo-versus-Mexican fight, but an uprising by all sorts of settlers resisting Santa Anna's iron rule.

With Houston gone, Austin issued the order for his troops, consisting of roughly four hundred effectives, to march west at last, moving closer to San Antonio. He had had enough waiting. As he'd promised the Council of Texas in the letter Houston carried, he would "press the operations as fast as my force will permit."[11]

"THE MOST ELIGIBLE SITUATION"

Barely a day after Houston left, Jim Bowie headed out toward San Antonio.[12] "You will select the best and most secure position that can be had on the river," General Austin ordered. The army needed a campsite close to San Antonio, one with pasturage for horses that was safe "from night attacks of the enemy."[13] And the general wanted it in time for the Army of Texas to make camp by nightfall.

Bowie and his division of ninety-two mounted men headed north from their base of operations at Mission San Francisco de la Espada.

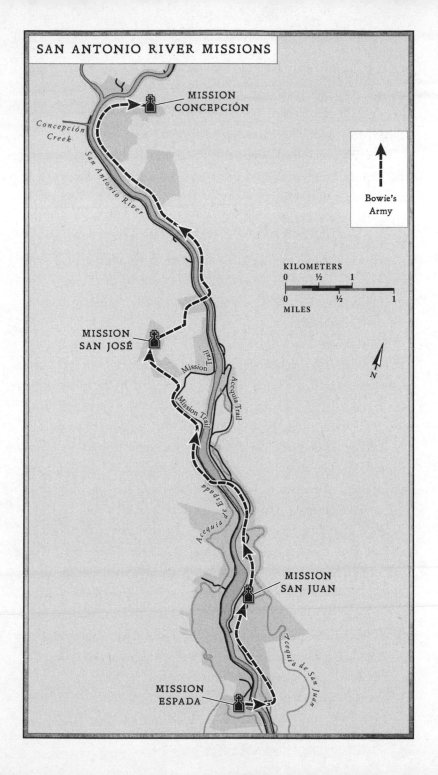

SAN ANTONIO RIVER MISSIONS

MISSION
CONCEPCIÓN

Concepción
Creek

San Antonio River

KILOMETERS
0   ½   1
0   ½   1
MILES

Bowie's
Army

MISSION
SAN JOSÉ

Mission Trail

Mission Trail

Acequia Trail

N

Acequia de Espada

MISSION
SAN JUAN

Acequia de San Juan

MISSION
ESPADA

They picked their way along the tree-lined bank of the San Antonio River and, two miles upstream, inspected Mission San Juan Capistrano. Although the abandoned church overlooked the river, the situation lacked the strategic advantages Austin wanted.

Three miles on, Bowie, together with Captain Fannin, inspected another site, but soon dismissed this one, a church called Mission San José, as indefensible. With the hours passing rapidly and Austin's words ringing in his ear ("with as little delay as possible"), Bowie urged the men further upstream.[14]

They encountered an enemy cavalry patrol, but after a brief skirmish, the outnumbered enemy withdrew. None of the Texians sustained injury, but General Cos would soon hear of their arrival in his immediate neighborhood.

Finally Bowie found just what he was looking for. Located just a quarter mile from another one-time Spanish mission, Concepción, he happened upon high ground at a U-shaped bend in the meandering river. It was a flat area, surrounded by stands of timber and scrub brush around the water's edge, behind which the men could take cover. The Mexicans could only advance through a narrow neck, and the nearly enclosed meadow would also provide a perfect field of fire for the Texians' long rifles. Best of all, the site lay within striking distance of their ultimate objective, just three miles from San Antonio.

They'd found the right place to camp, but one look at the sky indicated the short October day was drawing to a close.[15] There was no way Austin and the main force could reach Mission Concepción by dark, and that left Bowie a hard choice. The safest course would be to hightail it back to the main encampment. The alternative was to camp here to hold this strategic site, but that would be both risky—Bowie and his men would be outnumbered by Cos's troops, who were closer than the Army of Texas—and counter to Austin's orders.

Colonel Bowie, a man possessed of an independent streak wider than the Mississippi, never made decisions out of fear of friend or foe. Back in Louisiana, he'd won a reputation not merely for his knife fighting but as a tamer of wild horses and even for riding alligators. ("The trick was to get on [the alligator's] back, at the same time grasping his upper jaw firmly while gouging thumbs into his eyes. He couldn't see to do much and the leverage on his jaw would keep him from ducking under the water with the rider.")[16] He decided to ignore Austin's command.

Bowie's division would stay the night right where they stood, but, recognizing the possibility of attack, Bowie and Fannin established defensive positions. Forty-one soldiers under Bowie's command made camp on the north side of the roughly semicircular field, while Captain Fannin's company occupied the south side. Pickets were assigned to keep watch, including a detachment of seven men who occupied the cupola of the nearby mission with its broad view of the surrounding countryside.

Although the Mexicans lobbed a few cannonballs in the darkness from their camp on the other side of the river in the early evening, the Texians passed a quiet night, and the sentries raised no alarm. Bowie drank his share of a bottle of mescal before lying down to rest. This veteran of many fights had no great fear of what was to come. As one companion reported, "I never saw a man sleep more soundly than he did."

Back at the main camp, an anxious Austin waited. When a courier from Bowie finally arrived after dark, the general, already deeply worried about the fate of Bowie and his men, was frustrated. His army divided, he could do nothing until morning. Even then reinforcements would need two hours to reach Mission Concepción. After ordering his officers to prepare for a dawn march, Austin, unlike Bowie, spent a sleepless night, anxiously awaiting morning. He worried that he was about to lose what amounted to a quarter of his army.[17]

ACTION!

Shortly before dawn, Henry Karnes, one of Bowie's sentinels, heard hoofbeats. Tennessee born, the short, stocky Karnes rarely swore—but at that moment he must have been tempted. In the predawn light, speaking softly in his high-pitched voice, he urged the rifleman at his side to keep silent.

While Bowie slept, Austin's worst fear had been realized. General Cos, told by his spies that he outnumbered the ninety or so Americans camping in the horseshoe bend, had ordered one hundred troopers to slip across the river in darkness. Downstream from the Texian camp,

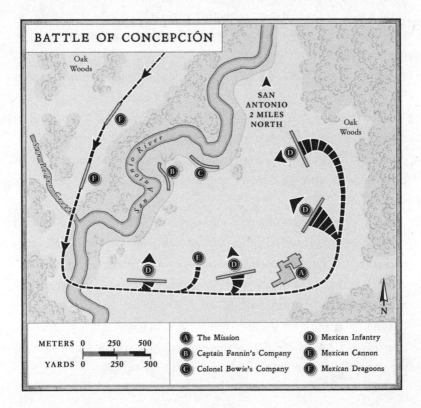

BATTLE OF CONCEPCIÓN

Oak Woods

San Pedro Creek

San Antonio River

SAN ANTONIO 2 MILES NORTH

Oak Woods

N

| METERS | 0 | 250 | 500 |
| YARDS | 0 | 250 | 500 |

Ⓐ The Mission
Ⓑ Captain Fannin's Company
Ⓒ Colonel Bowie's Company
Ⓓ Mexican Infantry
Ⓔ Mexican Cannon
Ⓕ Mexican Dragoons

the Mexican dragoons had waded ashore undetected, together with several companies of infantrymen and artillery detachments, totaling another two hundred, hauling a pair of field cannons.

The two Texian sentinels squinted into the mists, looking to see what they had heard. Then, just as Karnes glimpsed the legs of a horse in the middle distance, the report of a musket ripped the watchful silence.

The Texian rifleman quickly returned fire, and Karnes charged into the gloom, firing his pistol at the dim silhouette. But the Mexican horseman disappeared into the bank of fog, and again they heard the sound of hoofbeats, this time in rapid retreat. With that, the two lookouts fell back to their camp, where the other volunteers, their sleep shattered by the gunfire, leapt into action.

As the Texians scrambled for their guns, more unseen Mexicans opened fire. For a time, Jim Bowie later reported, they "kept up a constant firing, *at a distance*, [but] with no other effect than a waste of ammunition of their part."[18] Waiting for the morning fog to clear, the enemy didn't show themselves, and the firing soon ceased.

Meanwhile, the Texians prepared for an imminent attack. Some herded the horses to the riverbed below and tethered them to trees. At the edge of the clearing men hacked at bushes and vines with their hunting knives. Along the surrounding banks that descended to the river, they cut footholds, enabling them to step up and shoot before falling back and below the protective embankment, then reload and rise to fire again. Their defensive position, with the left flank angling away from the right, would put Mexicans who charged into the open ground in between and at the mercy of deadly raking fire.

"Keep under cover, boys," Bowie ordered, ". . . we haven't a man to spare."[19]

As the fog burned off, a battle line of Mexicans slowly became visible, two hundred yards away but ready to attack. The uniformed men filled the breadth of the hundred-yard-wide neck that provided the only land access to the horseshoe-shaped field of battle. At the center stood one hundred infantrymen, flanked on both sides by cavalry. Cannoneers brought up the rear. For any Texian considering retreat, a look over his shoulder revealed another two companies of Cos's dragoons on the opposite shore of the San Antonio River. Though it was a shock to the Texians to realize they were effectively surrounded, a gunsmith and Gonzales veteran named Noah Smithwick no doubt spoke for Bowie and Fannin and the rest when he said, "Retreat formed no part of our programme."[20]

At eight o'clock, a rifle shot signaled the Mexican attack.

The Mexican infantry marched forward as the field became a blaze of gunfire and billowing smoke. As they had been trained to do, the Mexicans fired their muskets in volleys while the Texians operated as individuals. Bowie's men fired less often—"but with good aim and deadly effect."[21] The ranks of the oncoming infantry thinned as the Texian marksmen dropped Mexicans, some dead, others wounded, to the ground.

Ten minutes into the fight, a Mexican cannon boomed. The four-pounder fired canister and grapeshot, which crashed harmlessly into the trees overhead. The only effect upon the crouching Texians was a shower of ripe pecans that rained down from above.

As the Mexican artillerymen worked to adjust the cannon's angle of fire, the Texians began shifting their position behind the bluff. After taking his shot each man would, as usual, step back and below the protective embankment to reload. But now, before rising to fire again, he would shift a few steps around the curve of the embankment, working closer to the position of the cannon.

One by one, the Texian fire brought down the exposed Mexican artillerymen. Although fresh gunners took their places, those, too, became the most-favored target of Bowie's men. When the second crew fell, a third took their place.

Slowed by their enemy's persistent and deadly marksmanship, the Mexican infantry regrouped, preparing to charge again. But Bowie issued his order first. Clambering out from behind their riverbank barricade for the first time, his men surged toward the brass cannon; in a matter of seconds, it was theirs. Finding the gun loaded and ready to fire, Bowie's men pivoted the weapon and emptied its load of iron at the Mexican infantrymen.

To their surprise, the cannon fire produced an immediate result. As the Texians observed in delight, the enemy was suddenly in full retreat. Stunned at the losses the Texians had inflicted, the Mexicans turned and fled back to San Antonio. In that moment, the battle was decided.

The Battle of Concepción ended in another decisive win for the Texians; as they had at Gonzales, the upstart settlers had taken on an impressive uniformed force, and again won a significant fight. Bowie's division sustained only two casualties, with two men wounded in the fighting. But as the guns went quiet, the screams of a soldier named Richard Andrews echoed across the battlefield.

Despite Bowie's orders, Andrews had ventured out from behind the bluff in the heat of the battle. An easy target, he had been quickly cut down when a shot tore into his left side; the iron ball exited his abdomen on the other. One of the first men to reach him had been Noah Smithwick.

"Dick, are you hurt?"

Andrews managed to reply to his friend, "Yes, Smith, I'm killed." Prone, in unbearable pain with his bowels protruding from his wound, Andrews would die hours later.[22]

The violent and public passing of their fellow soldier would be a reminder of what was at stake. Every man's life was on the line in the fight—but in just two hours, the Texians gained a clear victory in their first full-scale battle with Santa Anna's army.

"THE BRILLIANCY OF
THE VICTORY"

Thirty minutes after the Mexicans fled, General Austin arrived. On hearing distant gunshots, his army had quick-marched; when the firing had stopped, Austin, still at a distance, feared the worst. But on reaching Concepción, he saw the Mexican rear guard just visible in the distance, bound for San Antonio.

After being told of the rout of the Mexicans, Austin's first instinct was to order a pursuit of the fleeing and disorganized enemy: "The army must follow them right into town!"[23] Wouldn't San Antonio itself, with its defenders shocked and in disarray, be vulnerable?

His officers counseled caution. The town was fortified. According to Bowie's sources inside San Antonio, at least six cannons had been mounted on the walls of the church, a solid masonry building known as the Alamo. The artillery included an eighteen-pounder, and a handful more defended squares within the town. As for the Texians, their artillery trailed well behind. Attempting a frontal assault would expose Austin's army to deadly artillery fire and a spray of bullets from riflemen well protected by the adobe walls of the town. To storm San Antonio would put the entire army at risk.

Reluctantly, Austin contented himself with Bowie's morning success. Some three hundred Mexicans had surrounded a mere ninety-four Texians, but Bowie and Fannin's defensive strategy worked. Although the enemy's advance guard had come within eighty yards of their line, the Texians' guns had taken a terrible toll; the outnumbered defenders repulsed their attackers. Even without Sam Houston, they had prevailed.

In contrast to the Texian losses (one wounded, one dying, a few horses lost), downed Mexicans lay across the field of battle. At least sixteen were dead or dying; perhaps twice as many had been wounded.

That afternoon, the parish priest arrived from San Antonio, and after a parley with Austin, a long line of wagons and attendants carted the Mexican dead and wounded back to the town. In the evening, the Texians buried Dick Andrews. Over his grave, located at the foot of a pecan tree, they fired a rifle volley, as well as a cannon salute—using the captured Mexican cannon.

The difference between the kinds of guns used by the two sides had been one deciding factor in the battle. The Mexican smoothbore muskets had an effective range of roughly seventy-five yards; that was perfectly adequate for a European-style battle in which two armies marched toward each other in battle formation on open ground. But General Cos's infantry had marched on a largely hidden enemy, one armed with long rifles with more than double the effective range of the muskets the Mexicans carried.

In the hours after the battle, the Texians discovered they had possessed another—and unexpected—strategic advantage. As they helped themselves to the cartridges and cartridge boxes abandoned by fleeing Mexicans on the field, they examined the salvaged ammunition. To their surprise, they found the enemy had been using "by far the poorest powder" they'd ever seen. As one soldier reported, "Compared with the double Dupont, with which we had been furnished, it was evident that we had vastly the advantage over our enemy in this particular. We therefore emptied all the [Mexican] cartridges, and saved only the bullets."[24] The discovery explained why so many enemy musket balls had fallen well short of the Texian line.

Texian marksmanship and poor Mexican powder helped win the day, but so had their tactics. Having positioned his men wisely, Bowie's order to attack the Mexican artillery position could not have been better timed.

Despite his sleepless night and frustration at Bowie's insubordination, Austin admired the accomplishments of Bowie and Fannin's band

and reported proudly to the conventioneers at San Felipe on the "brilliancy of the victory gained."[25] Perhaps more than anyone else in the Texian camp, Austin also understood the larger military calculus. Whatever their success that Wednesday morning, the rebels remained clear underdogs.

Yet he and his expatriate Americans also knew precisely what they were fighting for. They were raised on the stories of the revolutionary generation. Austin and his Texians were colonists, too, resentful of taxes and other restrictions imposed by European masters. The success at Concepción only served to boost their confidence.

If they had to reprise the War of Independence right there in Texas, then so be it.

FIVE

A Slow Siege at the Alamo

This force, it is known to all, is but undisciplined militia and in some respects of very discordant materials.

—STEPHEN AUSTIN, NOVEMBER 4, 1835

General Martín Perfecto de Cos possessed what General Stephen F. Austin wanted: The Mexicans occupied the town of San Antonio. Cos had roughly twice the men Austin did plus a dozen-odd cannons with which to defend the town. Quite simply, if Austin wanted San Antonio de Béxar, he would have to come and take it.

From his encampment north of San Antonio, Austin eyed the village of some two thousand people just downstream on the west bank of the lazy San Antonio River. The provincial capital consisted of a small grid of streets that radiated from the San Fernando church and the Plaza de Armas and Plaza de las Islas, the military and main squares on either side of the church. Stone buildings surrounded the two squares, but quickly gave way to flat-roofed adobe and mud huts. Where the dwellings ended, fertile fields of corn began.

From his vantage, Austin could also see the single bridge that crossed the shallow and meandering river, linking the town to an array of crumbling structures on the other side. The Mission San Antonio de Valero had been home for much of the previous century to Franciscan missionaries and their Native American converts. More recently, its abandoned church, now occupied by Mexican troops, and a walled courtyard had been armed with cannons now pointing north at Austin and his men. It had also gained the name *El Alamo*, after the Coahuila town that was home to some of the first soldiers stationed there. It looked like whoever held the Alamo would hold the town.

When General Cos looked out from San Antonio, he could see the Old White Mill surrounded by the sprawling encampment of Texian troops, roughly a mile away. To the south of San Antonio, Bowie and Fannin remained in place with a smaller force near Mission Concepción.

From the safety of the Alamo, the Mexicans watched as two hundred fresh volunteers arrived from Nacogdoches, passing within sight of San Antonio; these East Texas "Redlanders," commanded by a South Carolina–born Texian named Thomas Jefferson Rusk, brought the troop count in Austin's camp to six hundred. Cos's spies reported on a dozen supply wagons that arrived from Goliad, carrying much-needed foodstuffs, including forty-three barrels of flour, six sacks of salt, two boxes of sugar, and coffee, as well as soap, candles, and tobacco.[1] Another early November delivery added three light artillery to Austin's small array of cannons.

Austin's first gambit that November was to send two colonels under a flag of truce to invite General Cos to surrender. The Mexican commander refused, sending the town priest, Padre Garza, to explain that his orders required him "to defend the place until he died."[2] Any talk of peace, Cos said, was entirely pointless.

During the early days of the month, the Mexican artillery at the Alamo fired upon the Texian camp; though the Texians fired back, Austin and his gunners soon decided that the effect on the walls of the mission accomplished little beyond sending clouds of dust into the air.

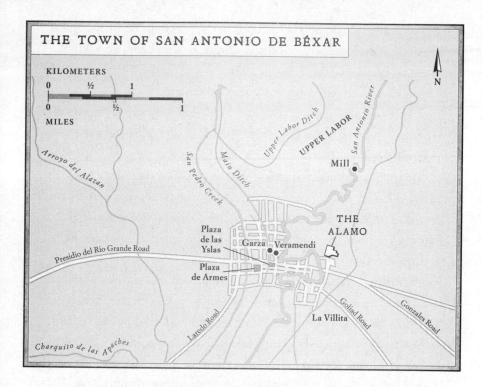

Occasional firings would continue throughout the month, but Austin understood that the Texians needed to soften up the town with bigger guns—an eighteen-pounder was on the way—before attempting a land assault.

Both sides scouted the other, with Austin's cavalry circling the town daily, and one small skirmish did accomplish something. On November 8, a former militiaman named William Barret Travis rode south at the head of a small company of Texian cavalry. A sometime lawyer who had also founded a newspaper back in the Alabama Territory, Travis had come west after his marriage collapsed; at twenty-one he left his son and cheating wife behind, becoming another of Texas's second-chance men. On this day, as he and his men rode along the Laredo road, Colonel Travis spotted what he had been looking for: unmistakable evidence of a large herd of horses. These had to be the Mexicans' surplus animals that, according to a source inside San Antonio, were being driven to the safety of Laredo. General Austin wanted—and needed—these animals for the cavalry, to pull wagons, to position cannons.

Picking up their pace, Travis and his dozen men set off in pursuit. The trail grew fresher as they found first one, then a second campsite. As they closed on their still unseen target, Travis deployed his men for an attack, but darkness fell rapidly and forced Travis to order a halt. He worried his force might be outnumbered by the enemy and didn't want to risk stampeding the horses in the dark. With no fire to warm them nor shelter from the cold rain, Travis's team spent a miserable night waiting for dawn.

At first light, they made a stealthy approach. Seeing two Mexican riders well away from their camp rounding up stray horses, Travis ordered a charge. The surprised Mexicans, outnumbered by the Texians, surrendered without a shot being fired. Five enemy soldiers were taken prisoner, though the two riders rounding up the horses escaped. But Travis reported a haul that included six muskets, two swords, and "300 head of gentle Spanish horses including ten mules."[3]

Travis's success was welcome. "I have to thank you and express my approbation of your conduct and that of your men in this affair," Austin told him. "It has been creditable to yourselves and useful to the service."[4] But the victory proved a small one since the captured horses, underfed and in poor condition, had to be put out to graze before they could be put into daily use.

November would not be a month of big victories, and Austin struggled to maintain discipline in his camp as he waited for the right moment to attack. Some volunteers, unhappy with the weeks of inaction or worried about their farms and families back home, simply packed up and headed for home. His men's behavior could be troublesome, especially when they were drinking, Austin admitted, writing to San Felipe and requesting, "In the name of Almighty God . . . send no more ardent spirits to the camp." The last thing his army needed was more "whysky."[5]

What the Texians *did* need was a little spontaneous leadership—and in the persons of "Deaf" Smith and Old Ben Milam, they would soon find it.

WHEN THE RUMORS of revolution reached him back in September, Erastus Smith wanted no part in the fight. Known as "Deaf" (he'd been hard of hearing since childhood), the red-headed Smith had spent years wandering and tended to keep to himself.

Born in New York's Hudson Valley, he lived in Mississippi before coming to Texas, in 1821, where he married a Mexican widow. For years he had lived a happily settled life in San Antonio with Guadalupe and a family that now included four children. But on his return from a hunting trip early that October, the forty-eight-year-old Smith experienced an event that prompted a change of heart.

One of General Cos's officers stopped him at the edge of town. As the two men talked, Smith observed a group of other soldiers approaching quickly. Smith grew instantly suspicious: In a town of divided allegiances, he had tried to keep his head down, but these men seemed to be coming for him. Then the officer grabbed for the bridle of his horse; Smith reacted, wheeling his horse, but, before he could spur his mount to escape, the officer raised his saber and swung. Smith took a glancing blow to the head.

His hat gone and his head bloodied by the blow, Smith broke for the Texian line. Pursued by Mexican troopers, a storm of shotgun pellets peppering him, Smith returned fire over his shoulder. He won the race and, a mile later, his red hair and unshaven cheeks stained with blood, an angry Deaf Smith presented himself to General Austin.

"I told you that I would not take sides in this war," he explained. "But, Sir, I now tender you my services as the Mexicans acted rascally with me."[6] Like Ben Milam, Austin himself, and others, Smith's sense of justice had been pushed beyond endurance. He, too, would take up arms in this fight.

A GENERAL FADES AWAY

As November passed, Austin's days as a general also neared an end. From the start, he had resisted becoming commander in chief; he was not a natural military leader and had accepted the role only because as the senior leader of the colony he hoped he could be a unifying figure among the motley mix of Texian volunteers. Now with the fight stalled and his health still poor, he dispatched an express rider to San Felipe carrying a note to the Consultation.

He made two plainly stated requests. First, he asked yet again that more artillery and ammunition be sent to the front, along with blankets, shoes, socks, and appropriate clothing for his men now that nighttime temperatures dipped into the forties.

Second, he asked to be relieved of duty. He urged the council "earnestly and pressingly" to organize "a *regular army* and invit[e] a Military man of known and tried Talents to command it."[7]

Now that they had a quorum with Houston and the delegates he had taken with him a few weeks before, the Consultation faced many pressing matters, including whether or not to issue a declaration of independence. (They decided against, settling instead on a pledge to create a provisional state government within the nation of Mexico; to do otherwise, they reasoned, would risk turning Tejano allies against the rebels.)

The nearly sixty delegates moved on to authorize the organization of a civil administration for Texas. They chose a governor (Kentuckian Henry Smith, an early Texas settler) and a legislative body, the General Council, to be manned by one delegate from each district.

Finally, they acted on Austin's recommendation, resolving to establish a "regular army," one modeled on the rulebook of the U.S. military. But they made no provision for the existing volunteer army; they chose a commander for the new army, which then existed only on paper. And they named Sam Houston to be its major general.

Houston had been lobbying for a change to Texian military plans ever since he'd arrived in San Felipe in October. This had less to do with his personal feelings toward Austin and much more to do with his strongly held opinion that the Army of Texas should abandon the siege of San Antonio until spring. So convinced was he that the siege was a mistake that he had even worked to influence his friend Jim Bowie and others under Austin's command to argue with their commander.[8]

Houston's well-known opinions probably contributed to the Consultation's choice of him as general, but it's likely they would have selected him anyway. There was something reminiscent of George Washington's appearance at the 1775 Continental Congress in Houston's presentation of himself for service. His imposing stature, his military service in the War of 1812, his generalship of the Tennessee militia, and his status as a well-known former Tennessee governor made him an easy choice.

Now Texas had two armies and little meeting of the minds: Austin, at least for the present, headed the citizen militia, while Houston was charged with creating an official force.

But the Consultation had a plan for Texas's elder statesman once he left his command. They named Austin the new government's emissary to the United States, instructing him to negotiate a million-dollar loan to get the new state up and running.

As for Austin, he had one more military maneuver left in him.

· · ·

WHEN INFORMED OF HIS NEW, nonmilitary role, on November 18, Austin chose to keep the news to himself. Four days later, he ordered his officers to prepare their men for a dawn attack the next morning. Although officially he had been relieved of duty, no one had arrived to take his place—and Austin wanted to capture San Antonio before his generalship ended.

Austin's wish would not come true, but not because of any failure on his part. At 1:00 A.M. that night, one of his divisional commanders awakened him. He reported that his officers and men refused to obey orders. Some of them, undoubtedly influenced by Houston, opposed the order of attack and were "unwilling to attempt it." Though "greatly astonished and mortified," Austin had little choice but to withdraw the command.[9] There would be no November assault on San Antonio.

The day after, a disappointed Stephen Austin took his leave. He bade the troops farewell, urging them to be "true to Texas and obedient to their commander."[10] Austin would not miss the challenge of instilling discipline among this wild bunch of independent men. He did not question the frontiersmen's toughness, but he felt frustrated by their unwillingness to submit to normal military discipline. It was apparent even at reveille. As one recent recruit reported, the troops at morning roll call stood before their sergeant half-dressed, most without their guns. Some didn't join the ranks at all but remained at nearby fires preparing their breakfasts. "Once a sleeping 'here!,'" the newcomer reported, "[coming] from under the canvass of tent, caused a hearty laugh among the men."[11] Despite the call to attention, the man couldn't be bothered to rise from his bed. This assemblage of Texians could barely be called an army. It survived on rationed supplies, fought for no pay, and lived in the cold. That very morning the temperature had dropped to thirty-one degrees.

Yet as he took his leave, the volunteers understood that Austin, whatever their doubts about his generalship, was one of Texas's finest. "The men came up and shook hands with him in tears and silence," his nephew and aide Moses Austin Bryan reported, "for many thought they would never see him more."[12]

With Houston off raising the new official army, a Texian named Edward Burleson was elected general of the militia. Like Houston, he had fought in the War of 1812, and the troops identified with his personal history. His family had moved from North Carolina to Alabama during his childhood; after his marriage, he'd taken his own family to Missouri and Tennessee before coming to Texas, in 1829. He, too, was a second-chance man. With Burleson now in charge, Austin, together with his nephew and a manservant, headed out for San Felipe de Austin, the first step in his journey back to the United States.

THE GRASS FIGHT

When Deaf Smith had come into camp, Austin recognized he was a natural scout. He was a skilled horseman. He knew the region well, and the solitary nature of the task suited him. His neighbors reported that Smith was afraid of nothing. Austin sent him on regular patrols, since the Texians needed intelligence regarding Mexican supplies and troop movements. He had become "the eyes of the army."

Smith, Bowie, and Burleson, in small bands or, sometimes, in mounted companies of fifty or a hundred men or more, looked to intercept Mexican dispatches, disrupt convoys, and drive off Mexican reinforcements coming from the Rio Grande. Teams of Texians lit prairie fires to burn off grasses that the Mexicans might use for forage to feed their animals. The result of these November forays had been a series of small skirmishes, but the fighting, mostly limited to small-arms fire, did little harm to either side. On several occasions, large bands of Texians tested the Mexicans, advancing to within a quarter mile of the town, but Cos refused to be drawn out into the open.

Then, at 10:00 A.M. on November 26, Deaf Smith returned to the main encampment at a full gallop. He brought news: A Mexican cavalry column, roughly five miles southwest of San Antonio, was headed toward the town. Smith's sighting, coupled with recent rumors of a shipment of silver coin for an overdue Mexican payroll, got everyone's attention. The new camp commander, General Burleson, ordered Jim Bowie and a squad of forty men to saddle up and intercept the Mexican troops. In minutes they rode out of camp, followed by one hundred infantrymen on foot.

The Texian cavalry caught up with the 150 Mexicans a mile from San Antonio as they crossed a dry creek bed. Among the volunteers were both Deaf Smith and Henry Karnes, the picket who first spied the Mexican attackers at Concepción.

Despite unfavorable numbers, Bowie charged into the midst of the enemy, guns blazing. The return fire was intense, but Bowie drove his men into the enemy ranks a second and a third time before both sides took cover in "Muskeet Bushes."[13] Bowie and the Texians kept up their fire, awaiting the arrival of the infantry.

Then the Mexicans attacked. The Texians, now able to aim their long rifles with precision at the uniformed men surging toward them, forced the Mexicans to retreat. An enemy wave came again, but the Texian infantry, moving in double-quick time, arrived, and the Mexican attackers were driven back.

An enemy relief party arrived from the town towing a single cannon. The field piece was quickly positioned, its barrel aimed at the Texians. But the grape and canister shot that arced its way toward Bowie's line did little harm.

Within the larger confusion of battle, several skirmishes were fought.

In one, James Burleson, the general's father, led a cavalry charge, urging his men, "Boys, we have but once to die!"[14] The momentum of the battle favored the Texians, and after repeated cannon firings failed to dislodge the Texians, the Mexicans, under covering artillery fire, retreated to the town. Except for a few cannon booms and sporadic musket and rifle fire, the fight was over.

For the Mexicans, the price had been high. Burleson claimed fifteen dead Mexicans lay in the creek bed and that other casualties had been carried from the field; Bowie estimated the Mexican losses at more than fifty.[15] The price for the Texians was much smaller, amounting to several wounded, none seriously.

In their hasty retreat, the Mexicans had also abandoned a pack train of forty heavily laden mules and horses. In the quiet after the tumult of battle, the Texians examined their captured spoils, hoping to find a wealth of silver. Or perhaps ammunition and food. They found nothing so precious. Rather than silver—or even flour, sugar, and salt—the Texians discovered they had fought for fodder. The animals carried only fresh-cut grass, gathered to feed the horses within the besieged town.

The fight—a "ludicrous affair," in the judgment of one soldier—was mockingly called the "Grass Fight," but Burleson's men had fought well.[16] Finally they had managed to confront a contingent of Cos's men outside of San Antonio. But the anticlimactic battle over grass cuttings seemed oddly apt: The month of November, which opened with Austin's high hopes for capturing San Antonio, drew to a quiet close.

DECEMBER

Far from the front and looking to find recruits for Texas's new regular army, Houston still grumbled; he remained convinced the Texian militia would never take San Antonio without larger cannons. He pressed for withdrawal, trying to enlist Bowie and others in opposing an attack. *Why not wait?* he argued. As he wrote to James Fannin, "Remember our Maxim, it is better to do well, *late:* than never!"[17]

On the night of December 3, the tide looked to be turning Houston's way.

That day three Anglo Texians fresh from San Antonio had brought both encouraging news and invaluable intelligence. Mexican morale was low, they said, and they were able to map out the city's gun placements and the locations of the Mexican troops. The storming of San Antonio seemed suddenly feasible. Armed with this knowledge, at first General Burleson ordered the troops to be ready at 4:00 A.M. for an attack to begin at dawn. Then, at midnight, a shadowy figure was reported near the Texian lines, crossing to speak to a Mexican sentry.

Had he been a spy? Did Cos now know they were coming?

Fearing his plans had been discovered, Burleson, as Houston himself would have wished, withdrew his orders. Seeing the wisdom of waiting until they had full strength, the Texian leadership supported him. His officers, almost to a man, had voted at a council of war against moving on San Antonio.

The reaction was different among the rank-and-file volunteers. These men were exhausted by the seven-week siege, wound tight by waiting for the fight, and staying constantly ready to risk their lives. As they got word that there would be no fight, their tense quiet gave way to a clamor of outraged shouts. Some indignant volunteers openly cursed their leaders.

These settlers had come to fight for their adopted homeland: "[We] preferred Death in the cause," one soldier wrote to his brother and sister, "than such a disgraceful defeat."[18] Marching for a winter camp—at Gonzales, at Goliad, it didn't matter—made no sense to them. That would be to retreat. "All day we [got] more and more dejected," one Texian wrote in his diary.[19]

Furious at having their time wasted and not willing to stay and serve as winter came on, disgruntled groups of weary and frustrated Texians collected their gear and headed for home. By one count, between 250 and 300 men marched out of camp.

Looking to stem the flow of departures, Burleson mustered the men. As the commander prepared to issue orders to abandon camp and march for Goliad, big Ben Milam returned from a scouting mission south of San Antonio. He read the faces around him—the anger, the disappointment—and decided immediately that this humiliation was wrong. He wasn't a man to give up.

As the troops gathered, Milam stepped forward and offered a challenge.

"Boys, who will follow Ben Milam into San Antonio—let all who will form a line right here."[20]

A thunderous chorus of voices responded: *I will! . . . I will! . . . I will!* Deaf Smith was among the first to step up, but many other men followed. Though most were Texians, more than a hundred were members of the New Orleans Greys, one of the first companies of troops from the United States, who had marched into camp two weeks earlier. The men in the fresh gray uniforms arrived well armed and well supplied, thanks to generous citizens back in the Crescent City. These soldiers were a mix, with more than two dozen Americans from the North plus men who were French, Canadian, German, English, and Irish. They quickly melded into the three-hundred-man army of self-selected men. With the unexpected demonstration of a willingness to fight, Burleson made the case to the remaining volunteers, several hundred in number, to remain at the White Mill as a reserve force.

Milam laid out a bold but simple attack. First, a small company of gunners would, under the cover of night, position their cannons within range of the Alamo. At 5:00 A.M. they would begin firing, bombarding the mission buildings. Milam expected the Mexicans to rally. They would seek to defend the Alamo—but against an anticipated onslaught from the east that would not materialize.

The shelling would be a classic diversion: Milam's real objective was the town itself. The new arrivals from San Antonio had offered an invaluable tactical fact: A number of buildings at the edge of town stood unoccupied. Milam's plan called for the Texian invaders to breach the village perimeter from the northwest. If they could gain a foothold in the empty houses, they could move on the squares at the heart of the city. With Mexican defenders otherwise occupied on the other side of town with the incoming salvos, many fewer men would be in position to oppose the assault.

The plan made sense, and in a few hours the long-awaited attack would begin. An entirely new mood suddenly prevailed among the Texians. Milam's bold leadership lifted morale: These men had come to fight, not to run, despite Houston's cautions. As they waited for the order to march, according to one fifteen-year-old soldier, "the boys were as joyous as if waiting a festive affair."[21]

A QUIET NIGHT, INTERRUPTED

In the predawn quiet, the rebels moved through the corn stubble north of San Antonio. Forbidden by their officers to speak, the two divisions of men listened to the whistle of a cruel north wind and the routine shouts of "All is well!" that echoed along the line of Mexican sentries. So far, the town's defenders knew nothing.

The artillery crew, escorted by a small band of infantrymen, positioned, loaded, and primed a field piece within range of the Alamo.

Across the river, at the head of one division, Milam brought his hundred-odd troops to a halt. He hoped to enter the town via a quiet back street, leading his half dozen companies toward an empty house within musket range of the town square. The other division, guided by Deaf Smith, would follow the river to Soledad Street and occupy the empty Veramendi house, once the home of Jim Bowie's wife and in-laws, all taken by cholera.

A fog rose off the river as daylight approached, offering a welcome shroud for the break-of-day surprise to come.

When the boom of the single cannon fractured the silence at 5:00 A.M., the waiting Texians listened. Within moments they heard "the brisk rattling of drums and the shrill blast of bugles."[22] Judging by the direction of the trampling feet, many Mexicans soldiers were headed toward the river to help defend the Alamo. "Our friends," said one of the New Orleans Greys of the gunners, "had done the trick."[23]

Then came the firm but quiet order to march. "Forward, boys! We're going to town."[24]

The Texians closed on San Antonio as planned, and Milam's men reached their objective without incident. But a Mexican sentry spotted Deaf Smith as his team approached Casa Veramendi. The enemy picket fired once before Smith silenced him, but the report of the gunshots led to a general alarm. The artillery diversion had worked, getting Milam and his men close to the central plazas without a single casualty. But now the enemy knew they were there.

Suddenly the world was shooting at them as a storm of musket fire came their way. The main plaza at the town center had been closed off with barricading, and the muzzles of cannons protruding through port-holes were soon spitting fire, too. With the narrow streets raked with canister shot, the invaders turned to the nearest houses, breaking through their doors to find cover. Some of the homes they entered were very much occupied. "Men, women and children began to run out," reported one of the invaders, "in their night clothes and unarmed."[25]

When and where they could, the Texians returned fire. Again their Kentucky long rifles and superior powder proved lethal, effective at

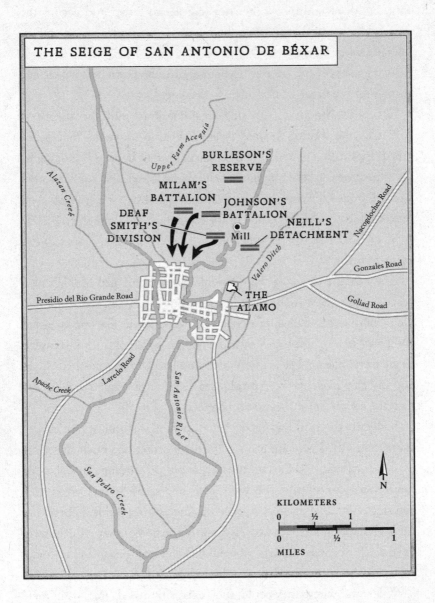

THE SEIGE OF SAN ANTONIO DE BÉXAR

Upper Farm Acequia

BURLESON'S
RESERVE

MILAM'S
BATTALION

JOHNSON'S
BATTALION

DEAF
SMITH'S
DIVISION

NEILL'S
DETACHMENT

Mill

Alazan Creek

Nacogdoches Road

Valero Ditch

Presidio del Rio Grande Road

Gonzales Road

Goliad Road

THE
ALAMO

Apache Creek

Laredo Road

San Antonio River

San Pedro Creek

N

KILOMETERS

0   ½   1

0   ½   1

MILES

two hundred yards. "No sooner did a head appear above the walls than it served as a target for a dozen hunting rifles, and there was always another dead Mexican."[26] But as the sun rose, the "heavy cannonading from the town was seconded by a well directed fire from the Alamo."[27] General Cos, no longer deceived by the lone gun firing from the east—which the Texians had already withdrawn—had pivoted his array of cannons to bombard the rebel position in the town.

At midday the firing slowed as both sides considered the new terms of the fight. The two field pieces the invaders had brought with them had been of little value; although the Texians had finally taken the fight to the streets of San Antonio, the Mexicans, after weeks of preparation, still held a strong defensive position. Pinned down, the invading force of Texians could clearly see that unlike their battlefield successes at Gonzales and Concepción, this fight wouldn't be over in a matter of minutes or even hours.

From their new headquarters, in town but also inside a set of Spanish-style houses, the rebels would face five days of overcoming the enemy's "obstinate resistance" to decide this first battle for San Antonio.[28]

DOWNTOWN SAN ANTONIO

Out of fear of Indian attack, the founders of San Antonio de Béxar had arranged their streets for easy defense. The town's homes were fortress-like, consisting of thick adobe or limestone walls with iron grates on the windows and solid oak doors. The Texians, once inside the dwellings, set about further adapting them to their purposes. "With crow bars we perforated the walls of the houses," remembered physician Joseph Field, "making port holes, through which we kept up a constant fire."[29]

The sightlines weren't perfect, so ten of the Texians, led by Deaf Smith, climbed to the roof of the Veramendi house. They made their way to the parapet that surrounded the roof but were quickly spotted by Mexicans in the tower of the San Fernando church. The Texians soon paid a heavy price. Half the men were hit, including Smith. His wound was serious enough that a hole had to be chopped in the earthen roof so that he could be lowered back into the house using an improvised sling made of blanket.

To ease communications between their two divisions, the Texians had spent the night hours trenching the nearby street. Using the excavated dirt, they raised a breastwork of dirt, stone, and sandbags. Meanwhile, Burleson consolidated the reserves back at the White Mill and dispatched a messenger to San Felipe, urgently requesting more troops and ammunition. "Considerable reinforcements" were said to be on the way to aid the Mexicans—and the Texians needed all the help they could get.[30] Artillery at the Alamo was steadily firing into their midst, and the Mexican small-arms fire persisted.

When day two of the fight ended with no notable gains, the Texians realized that if they wanted to more than hold their ground, they needed to dislodge the well-entrenched Mexicans; in short, they needed to advance on the square where they could mount a direct offensive. At midday on day three, December 7, Henry Karnes led one such raid.

Eyeing a large stone house across the street, Karnes instructed his fellow soldiers, "Boys, load your guns and be ready." Indicating his destination, he explained, "I am going to break open that door, and I want you to pour a steady hot fire into those fellows on the roof and hold their attention. . . . When I break [the door] in I want you boys to make a clear dash for that house."[31]

With an iron bar in one hand, his rifle in the other, he sprinted across to the doorway and made short work of bashing in the door. When he and his company burst in, they saw Mexicans escaping into another room. Some Mexicans fired back, but the invaders knew what they had to do. Using bars and axes, they pounded through interior walls, moving room by room, gradually getting closer to the square.

The Texians scavenged food where they could, including slaughtering and butchering an ox and cooking it over open fires. But the Mexicans peppered their fires with musket fire, making food preparation a dangerous occupation.

Late on the afternoon of December 7, the Texians sustained a major loss.

Their leaders met at Casa Veramendi to lay out the plan of attack. Colonel Ben Milam crossed Soledad Street to join the conference, where he and the others sat down to plot out an after-dark surprise attack on the Mexican position on the plaza. In order to better understand the topography, Milam stepped out into the courtyard of the Veramendi house. All day gunfire had echoed around the square, but Milam ignored it. Protected by the garden wall, he wanted to get a better view of the enemy guns and command post.

Before departing two weeks earlier, Stephen Austin had given Milam a field glass. The big man held the telescopic lenses to his eyes, scanning the enemy stronghold. As he took in the view, planning the Texians' next step, he caught the attention of a Mexican positioned in a tree by the river. The Mexican aimed. He fired. And Ben Milam collapsed to hard ground. The ball that entered his brain killed him on the spot.

One soldier who turned in the direction from which the shot had been fired saw a telltale puff of smoke amid the thick greenery of a cypress tree near the river. Texian rifles were quickly readied, aimed, and fired; the report of the rifles was followed by the fall of another corpse, as the rifleman tumbled through the evergreen branches before crashing to the ground and rolling into the San Antonio River.[32]

The day's casualty list for Texians was small—one dead, two slightly wounded—but the loss of Milam weighed heavily on Texian morale. He had inspired this assault on the town; now he was dead. Adding to a sense of alarm, the enemy raised a black flag.[33] Though this was the rebels' first sighting of the dreaded pennant, they knew its message. The enemy would give no quarter; the Mexicans would offer no mercy and take no prisoners. To be captured would likely mean being put to death. This was Santa Anna's way.

Everyone knew, as one captain put it, "This army is in danger—Texas is in danger."[34]

"THE ENEMY GAVE WAY INCH BY INCH"[35]

The battle had become a struggle for survival. The dogged, rugged fighting continued on the streets, but, out of reach of the raking musket and cannon fire, the rebels advanced, house by house. Like moles tunneling unseen, the Texians broke through the interior adobe walls that separated one house from the next. "Using battering-rams made out of logs ten or twelve feet long . . . stout men would punch . . . holes in the walls through which we passed."[36]

They worked toward the plaza, but time was tight with the arrival that day of a convoy of Mexican troops, which had eluded Burleson's scouting parties, and the prospect of more. The Mexican reinforcements were a mixed bunch, experienced infantry, cavalry, and artillery men, along with untrained conscripts and even convicts. One Texian soldier expressed his worry: He reported that he and his fellow fighters feared that they would be "sweap of [swept off] by a general charge."[37] The new arrivals—they numbered about six hundred—could tip the balance.

Then, during the night of December 8, the Texians captured an important prize: They gained control of the priest's house; from there rebel riflemen could sweep the Plaza de las Islas—and the Mexican gun emplacements—with direct and deadly fire. They set about cutting portholes to make the most of this commanding vantage. Despite the loss of Milam, this new development gave hope to the tired men.

Even before firing could begin at first light, the Mexicans recognized they had no choice but to pull back. In the middle of the night, hundreds of soldiers began hauling nine of the ten artillery pieces, munitions, wounded soldiers, and everything of value to the Alamo. The sudden retreat inspired numerous officers and their companies— some two hundred Mexicans—to set out in the direction of the Rio Grande. They deserted rather than stay and face defeat.

The Mexicans had managed to get out of the town, but the scene across the river at the Alamo was chaotic. The mission enclosure was simply too small to accommodate all the men, along with the women and children, not to mention the horses.

Cos was in deep trouble and he knew it. His supply line had long since dried up; the six hundred arrivals had brought no supplies, only more hungry mouths to feed. There was insufficient firewood and water inside the Alamo, and replenishing the supplies required venturing out to face Texian rifle fire. The days of fighting had taken a toll, too, with wounded officers and men to care for. And the cannoneers were running short on ammunition.

At 6:00 A.M., General Cos, still in his bed, rose to a sitting position and issued the order to surrender. "I authorize you to approach the enemy and exact of him whatever may be possible."[38] Three officers, accompanied by a trumpeter, rode into town.

The trumpeter sounded the call for a parley; the Texians did not reply. They now occupied all the houses that lined the north side of the plaza, and their rifle barrels were visible protruding through windows and holes cut into the walls. Cos's emissaries resorted to a handkerchief, mounted on a pole. Raising the white flag got a reaction: Thirty Texians emerged from the priest's house. The Mexican officers asked to see the Texian commander; Burleson was duly summoned. After a delay, he arrived and immediately agreed to a suspension of fighting.

Only the terms of the surrender remained to be settled; the fight for San Antonio de Béxar was over. Unlike the Mexicans and their flag of no quarter, however, the Texians would be fair and merciful. An honorable fight would conclude with honorable terms.

THE END OF THE BEGINNING

More than a dozen hours of negotiation concluded, at 2:00 A.M., Thursday, December 10, 1835. The terms of surrender permitted the defeated army to depart with arms and private property. They would take one cannon, a four-pounder, for protection in the event of Indian attack. The sick and wounded would remain and be cared for. Most important, General Cos and his officers gave their word of honor that they would not "in any way oppose the reestablishment of the federal constitution of 1824."[39] They were not to rejoin the fight to suppress the uprising.

Not every Texian was happy with the terms of surrender. Many thought the Mexicans had been let off easy. Lieutenant William R. Carey probably spoke for many when he called it a "disgraceful treaty" and a "childs bargain."[40]

Nonetheless, on December 14, General Cos led an ignominious march toward the Rio Grande. He departed with 1,105 men, a count that did not include hundreds of troops who had deserted the day before or the wounded who remained in San Antonio. They left to the victors twenty-one artillery pieces, five hundred muskets, and other supplies.

The Texians had defeated a well-entrenched foe with substantially more manpower. The cost had been the life of Ben Milam, buried with his boots on in the dooryard of Casa Veramendi. Another five rebels died; though one man lost an eye and another a leg, fewer than three dozen were wounded. That seemed a small price to pay for a large prize in the fight for freedom. The Mexican losses were harder to calculate, but their casualty count was in the hundreds.

This felt like victory. When, on Christmas Day 1835, Cos and his army arrived at the Rio Grande, they were the last Mexican troops in Texas. They had vowed never to serve again against the rights of the Texians, and most of the Texian fighters felt safe in returning to their homes and families, where they could bask in the glory of their accomplishments. As the Texas General Council proclaimed, "You are the brave sons of Washington and freedom."[41]

The victory at San Antonio appeared to be a giant step closer to independence. The capture of the Alamo was a triumph, and the retreat of the Mexican force cause for great rejoicing. Could the war even be over? Sam Houston didn't think so. He suspected it was a fight they should not have had, and the Alamo a fort that could not be held: Preparing for the worst, he kept busy trying to raise an army, offering a cash bonus, eight hundred acres of land, and immediate Texas citizenship to fresh volunteers.

Yes, the Texians had proven themselves on some level, but now they would have to confront a profoundly angry and vengeful enemy in the person of His Excellency Santa Anna. Houston would see that they were prepared.

SIX

The Defenders

[We have] no remedy but one, which is an immediate declaration of independence.

—STEPHEN AUSTIN, JANUARY 7, 1836

The new year brought bad news. On January 4, 1836, the *Telegraph and Texas Register*, the San Felipe newspaper launched three months before as "a faithful register of passing events," published a chilling warning. President Santa Anna, along with a reported ten thousand troops, was bound for Texas to do battle with the rebels, to avenge their victory over General Cos. His stated intention? To leave nothing of the rebels "but the recollection [they] once existed."[1]

Major General Sam Houston felt ready to seize the moment. Focused on his duties in Texas's newly designated capital, Washington-on-the-Brazos, the usually hard-drinking commander in chief had even set aside liquor. "I am most miserably cool and sober," he assured a member of the General Council, "instead of Egg-nog; I eat roasted Eggs in my office."[2] He ordered clothes sent from Nacogdoches to his new headquarters, now located in Washington-on-the-Brazos. His personal library came, too, including Thucydides' *History of the Peloponnesian*

War, a history of Texas, and a volume of army regulations. He would need all the knowledge and wisdom he could find as he confronted the many obstacles facing the Texian army.

The deeply divided provisional government of Texas posed one large challenge. Governor Henry Smith and the General Council seemed unable to agree on anything, including the very goal of the present war: Was Texas fighting to be a Mexican state or a "*free,* sovreign" republic?³ The two branches of the young government differed on military matters, too, starting with whether Houston was commander in chief. Governor Smith thought he was, but the General Council regularly ignored the chain of command, issuing orders directly to various officers in the field.

By mid-January, the divide was so great that the governor proclaimed the General Council dissolved (he called its members "scoundrels") and the council, dismissing him as a "tyrant," impeached Smith.⁴ That left Texas governance effectively paralyzed until the next meeting of Texas's delegates, scheduled to convene on March 1.

Caught in this political crossfire, Sam Houston looked for the best strategy to defend Texas. But the military situation was no less chaotic.

In the weeks after the capture of San Antonio, the Army of Texas splintered. Many Texians headed home, thinking the war had been won. Then, on January 3, 1836, two hundred of those who stayed to defend San Antonio packed their bedrolls, grabbed their guns, and headed for Goliad. The General Council, ignoring Houston, had decided to take the fight to the border; headed for Matamoros, Mexico, they hoped that by capturing the port town on the south bank of the Rio Grande, they might take the action out of Texas and into Mexico. James Fannin, veteran of the successful fight at Concepción, worked to raise an auxiliary corps for an expedition to "reduce Matamoros." With no money in the treasury, the Texian soldiers were promised they could ravage the town if they took it, collecting "the first spoils taken from the enemy."[5] Fannin and his men departed with the bulk of the provisions, horses, and medicines, leaving a mere 104 soldiers at the Alamo. The Texians who stayed, some of them sick and wounded, faced "all the hardships of winter"—*and* the task of defending the town.[6]

"Oh, save our poor country!" Houston exclaimed when he heard what had happened. "[We must] send supplies to the wounded, the sick, the naked, and hungry, for God's sake!"[7]

He recognized the Matamoros plan for what it was—an "absurdity."[8] He regarded the Texas Revolution as a fight for right, and to give the men license to loot the Mexican town? That would make the Texians pirates and predators.[9] The planners believed that the Mexican inhabitants of the town would rise up, embrace the invaders, and join their rebel ranks, but that sounded like wishful thinking to Houston. So he set off to meet the men at Goliad, hoping to lead the army in a different direction.

When he got there, on January 14, Fannin was off recruiting soldiers. In his place, Houston found a pretender to his own role, a man named Dr. James Grant, who styled himself "Acting Commander-in-Chief." Wounded in the fight at San Antonio, the educated Scotsman had won the respect and admiration of many of the soldiers as a man who had fought for Texas, something Houston had yet to do.

Houston thought the plan was bad, but he now saw the motivations were even worse: Grant's main interest was to use the volunteer army to fight for *his* personal land claims south of the Rio Grande. Plus the proposed invasion of Matamoros, now discussed publicly for a month, was no longer a Texas secret. "The Mexicans," as one soldier in the little army noted, "aware of our plans, were strengthening the defenses of their city and every day making it more nearly impregnable."[10] *And* Santa Anna and his men, though still far away in central Mexico, were mile by mile making their way north.

Two decades before, Houston had selflessly thrown himself into battle, risking his life at Horseshoe Bend. For that, he paid dearly, sustaining devastating wounds to his shoulder and upper thigh that still tormented him more than twenty years later. This time, Houston counseled caution.

He spent several days with the army as it marched to Mission Refugio, listening, getting to know the men, and getting known by them. As they talked, Houston, older and wiser at age forty-three than most of the troops, made a lawyerly case for holding back. Then, on arrival in Refugio, he addressed the assembled troops. After years spent under Andrew Jackson's tutelage, he knew how to work a crowd of soldiers.

"We must act together," he told the Army of Texas—"*United we stand divided we fall.*"

He argued that to invade Mexico was pure folly. "[Though] I praise your courage," he told them candidly, "my friends, I do not approve of your plans."[11]

Houston believed the Texian army might be destroyed in such a fight. Just two hundred men, marching two hundred miles through strange and potentially unfriendly territory? "A city containing twelve thousand souls," he believed, "will not be taken by a handful of men who have marched twenty-two days without bread-stuffs, or necessary supplies for an army. If there ever was a time when Matamoras could have been taken by a few men, that time has passed by."[12] With that, Houston again mounted his horse and rode away. As head of the regular army, he could not order these militiamen; he could only plant doubts in their minds.

But he departed disheartened. He worried about the cause of Texas and, seeing him lost in thought, Houston's staff left him to his thoughts as they headed north.

That night and the next day, Houston pondered. He later admitted he considered "withdraw[ing] once more from the treacheries and persecutions of the world" to return to the Cherokee to "bury [myself] deep in the solitude of nature, and pass a life of communion with the Great Spirit."[13] And, very likely, once again drink deeply from the "flowing bowl."

When Houston and company reached San Felipe de Austin, Governor Smith, trying vainly to hold on to power, granted the unhappy Houston a few weeks' furlough to carry out an assignment. The task would take him back to the Cherokee, but very much in service to the Texian cause. Houston would become an ambassador for Texas. He would stay true to the cause, since Governor Smith wanted to be sure that a large band of some four hundred Cherokee in East Texas remained peaceable—the last thing the Texians needed was a second formidable enemy. Houston headed east to make peace at the council fire of Chief Bowl, warlord of the Texas Cherokee, hoping to return with a treaty in time for the next gathering of delegates. With a new duty, he again aimed his gaze "with enthusiasm upon the future prospects of Texas."[14]

During Houston's weeks of absence, the Texian plan to move on Matamoros collapsed, in part because Houston's words had persuaded many soldiers such an attack would be a fool's errand. Instead, the next Texian fight would unfold back in San Antonio. Only this time, the roles were reversed: The Texians, now inside the Alamo, would face a siege by the Mexican army now making its way north.

FIGHT OR FLIGHT?

On January 18, Jim Bowie rode hard for the Alamo. After a long day in the saddle—he and his thirty men covered more than seventy miles—he saw a bittersweet sight. In the middle distance he spied the silhouettes of the mission and the bell tower of the San Fernando church.

They would never fail to bring to mind his wife and children, now more than two years dead.

For Bowie, San Antonio de Béxar remained a place of homecoming, but this time he arrived with a purpose. Sam Houston admired the man's "promptitude and manliness" and respected his "forecast, prudence and valor."[15] Just the day before, freshly back from his mission to the Cherokee, he'd entrusted Bowie with orders for the garrison at San Antonio.

In recent weeks, the Texian commandant in San Antonio, Lieutenant Colonel James Clinton Neill, had written repeatedly to the government, pleading for reinforcements. Like Houston, he had fought and been wounded in the Battle of Horseshoe Bend. Like the men around him, he saw this fight as an extension of his father's and grandfather's fight back in North Carolina in the Revolution.

On arrival, Bowie saw an undernourished, ill-clad, and unpaid garrison. In the new year, Neill's company had continued to dwindle, falling to 114 men, three dozen of them sick or recovering from wounds. And this contingent was supposed to fight off a thousand-man Mexican force that, according to Neill, was already "destined for this place" from central Mexico?[16]

Yet morale remained surprisingly high, further buoyed by the sight of braveheart Bowie and his men. But the situation was not as it at first seemed to Colonel Neill. When he read Houston's written directive, Neill found Bowie hadn't come to fight Mexicans: Houston's orders called for dismantling the San Antonio outpost. The commander in chief instructed that the barricades in the streets of San Antonio be destroyed; the Alamo blown up, demolished, rendered unusable; and the artillery and stores removed to Gonzales. He didn't want to lose good men fighting to hold a fort he believed they couldn't defend.

Colonel Neill had requested relief—and this notion of abandoning and obliterating San Antonio was something else altogether. Like Ben Milam's back in December, Neill's first instinct was to rebel.

He was an artillery officer by training, and together with one of his junior officers, Lieutenant Almeron Dickinson, Neill had fired the first cannon at Gonzales. As they absorbed Houston's orders, Neill and Dickinson quickly realized that removing the artillery and ammunition simply was not possible. When Dr. Grant departed in December with the bulk of the troops, he had taken virtually all the horses and wagons; without draft animals, the array of captured cannons, many of which were in good firing condition, were going nowhere. To the cannoneers, the notion of abandoning the guns, the largest array of Texian artillery, made no sense at all.

Houston's orders arrived without President Smith's authorization, so the men in Neill's command decided to carry on with the work of stiffening the defenses at the Alamo; they would await confirmation. As he waited, Bowie began to weaken in his commitment to Houston. After all, Bowie recognized a good defensive position when he saw one, and here was a town that had been his home and that was defended by men whose bravery and commitment were contagious. Unable to resist helping, Bowie pitched in with the rebuilding, "laboring night and day."

Bowie soon communicated his change of mind to the Texian government. "I cannot eulogise the conduct & character of Col Neill too highly," he wrote to Governor Smith two weeks after his return to San Antonio. "No other man in the army could have kept men at this post, under the neglect they have experienced."[17]

Jim Bowie, widower and wheeler-dealer, fortune hunter and fighter, also confided how much the forthcoming fight at the Alamo now meant to him. An uncomplicated man, Bowie, together with Neill, had reached a joint resolution.

He wished to help the people of San Antonio. "We will rather die in these ditches than give it up to the enemy."[18]

But if they were going to keep the Alamo in Texian hands, they were going to need more help.

WILLIAM BARRET TRAVIS

For a man of twenty-six, Lieutenant Colonel William Barret Travis brought wide experience to the fight for Texas. A teacher, lawyer, and militia officer, he appeared to many as a fine man and good citizen, despite rumors of a checkered past. Travis was said to have blown up his promising law career when at age twenty-one he suspected his wife of infidelity and murdered the man he thought was her lover.

Having settled in Texas in 1831, Travis officially became a landowner and Texas settler, making a new home in the land of men looking for second chances. He practiced law in San Felipe de Austin and lived alone in a rooming house. His success permitted him to hire a law clerk and own several horses. A literate man, he read widely, noting in his diary the borrowed books of Greek and English history, as well as fiction.

By 1835, he wanted a more settled life. He had found a woman he wished to make his second wife, and to make that possible, a formal divorce from his first wife was begun. Travis also addressed the matter of the children left behind in Alabama when, in May 1835, he signed his last will and testament. He designated Charles Edward, five years of age, and Susan Isabella, the daughter he had never seen, as his sole heirs.[19]

When the Texas rebellion began, Travis immediately committed himself to the fight. He remained with Austin during the siege at San

Antonio, proving himself both as a scout and as a field commander in the skirmish where he and his men captured the Mexican horses in November 1835. He offered detailed advice to the governor and the council, giving them recommendations regarding the organization of the new army. His reward, on December 21, 1835, was elevation to the rank of lieutenant colonel, commandant of the cavalry.

Then, on February 3, 1836, Lieutenant Colonel Travis, dressed in homemade Texas jeans (a formal uniform he'd ordered hadn't arrived), crossed the San Antonio River. In response to Neill's repeated pleas for help from San Antonio, the governor had ordered Travis to the town's defense.

Along with his platoon of thirty men, Travis brought the total defenders to barely 150.

FORTRESS ALAMO

"You can plainly see," observed Ensign Green B. Jameson, "that the Alamo never was built by a military for a fortress."[20] Jameson, the chief engineer at the Alamo, spoke truly as the mission, established in 1718 and after, began as a place of faith, where Franciscan friars taught Native Americans the tenets of Roman Catholicism.

The Franciscans chose the site of their church with care. The little community required a reliable source of water, fuel for warmth and cooking, and surrounding acreage for grazing and cultivation. Over the decades, the church with its enclosed village developed, rectangular in shape, with tall walls of rough stone that bounded an open plaza on three sides. Lining the enclosure were rambling adobe living quarters for Indians, soldiers, and servants, as well as kitchens and shops, all of which faced into the courtyard.

Green Jameson wanted to transform the rambling structures into

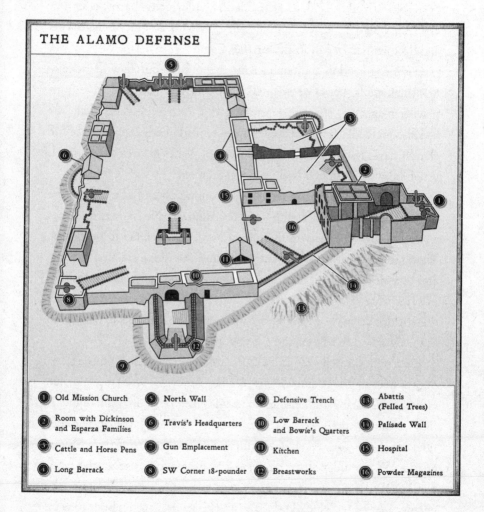

THE ALAMO DEFENSE

① Old Mission Church	⑤ North Wall	⑨ Defensive Trench	⑬ Abattis (Felled Trees)
② Room with Dickinson and Esparza Families	⑥ Travis's Headquarters	⑩ Low Barrack and Bowie's Quarters	⑭ Palisade Wall
③ Cattle and Horse Pens	⑦ Gun Emplacement	⑪ Kitchen	⑮ Hospital
④ Long Barrack	⑧ SW Corner 18-pounder	⑫ Breastworks	⑯ Powder Magazines

what he thought of as "Fortress Alamo." He hadn't trained as an engineer—just weeks earlier he had been practicing law in San Felipe de Austin—but he drew a rough plan of the Alamo. The church had been secularized in 1793, and the mission had become barracks for the Spanish, then the Mexican military. The previous autumn General Cos and his men had begun fortifying the Alamo.

Cos recognized that, though a ruin, the former church, with its four-foot-thick walls, could be adapted for military purposes, with a gunpowder magazine, officers' quarters, and a storehouse. The Mexicans had also erected a ramp of rubble that extended nearly the length of the church nave, rising from the entrance to a platform over the chancel, which became an improvised gun emplacement.

Now, however, Jameson faced the daunting task of completing the fortifications and doing it with limited manpower. Near the church was a yawning fifty-yard gap in the mission wall that needed to be closed. There were no parapets atop the walls, and the Mexicans had left several unfinished semicircular earthen batteries at intervals around the exterior walls. Jameson wanted perimeter ditches dug, too, one with a drawbridge across it. Most important, there were cannons to install "so as to command the Town and the country around."[21]

Even with limited time and labor, Jameson was bullish on the prospect of making the Alamo defensible. The rumored "1000 to 1500 men of the enemy being on their march to this place" left him undaunted. If they continued their work of fortifying the Alamo, Jameson felt confident that the Texians would "whip [the Mexicans] 10 to 1 with our artillery."[22] Confidence (or was it overconfidence?) rose as the work continued, despite the fact that no one knew the whereabouts of the enemy, near or far. Nor did the Texians know they were about to get a much needed boost to their morale.

COLONEL CROCKETT

Back in early November, a Tennessean in a coonskin cap headed for Texas. For the next three months, walking all the way, David Crockett got the lay of the land in rebellious Texas.

He was another of the many lured by the fight for liberty. Word of the conflict had reached Boston, New York, and Philadelphia. Crowds gathered in Mobile, Macon, New Orleans, and Nashville to raise their voices and raise money for the cause. Men from Pennsylvania, Virginia, Alabama, Kentucky, and Louisiana, inspired by rousing speeches, went west. Like many who had gone to Texas in previous years, these volunteers could be called second-chance men. Certainly Crockett, not so many months from his fiftieth birthday, was looking to start again.

Born on the Virginia frontier in 1786, he spent most of his teenage years away from his perennially penniless family (he had eight siblings), sometimes to avoid his father's beatings, at other times to work off his father's debts.[23] Married at nineteen, David soon fathered three children of his own and migrated west, reaching West Tennessee. He built a log cabin and set out to make a life for himself and his family.

With the outbreak of the War of 1812, he joined up to fight the Creek Indians, serving as a scout for Andrew Jackson. Though a mere private, he once met with the general in person and left the encounter impressed. On witnessing Old Hickory's resolution of a dispute, Crockett adapted Jackson's words, which became the frontiersman's motto: "Be always sure you are right then Go, ahead."[24]

The necessities of backwoods life made hunters of many men, but Crockett "got to be mighty fond of the rifle" and gained superb skills as a marksman and tracker.[25] He regularly won shooting matches and at times made his living as a hunter. Once he shot forty-seven bears in a single month; he killed another on a moonless night by stabbing the animal in the heart. People said he could "whip his weight in wildcats, and was so tough he could climb a thorn tree with a panther under each arm."[26] By his own account his eyes were "as keen as a lizard's."[27]

When his first wife died, he remarried and moved to Tennessee's Alabama border. Likable and entertaining, Crockett leveraged his local popularity into an appointment to serve as magistrate, a position where he continued to display the homespun humor and straightforwardness for which he was beloved. In executing his judicial responsibilities, he said, "I gave my decisions on the principles of common justice and honesty between man and man, and relied on natural born sense . . . for I had never read a page in a law book in all my life."

His neighbors approved, sending him to the Tennessee General Assembly, where he displayed a deep distrust of "ready money men." These speculators, with cash in their pockets, would buy lands that Crockett thought ought to be distributed to "poor people" who would establish homesteads.[28] Helping people with very little was a theme he would return to throughout his political life and, whatever his circumstances—over the next decade his fortunes rose and fell— Crockett always thought of himself as "a poor man." That status brought with it a sympathy for others in need. "Whenever I had any thing," he would write late in his life, "and saw a fellow being suffering, I was more anxious to relieve him than to benefit myself. . . . It is my way."[29]

By December 1827, he was on his way to Washington City, where he served for three terms in the U.S. House of Representatives. Despite an unremarkable record as a legislator, he emerged as a national character. More than a few politicians resented his candor, sharp tongue, and independence. One of those was Andrew Jackson, and Crockett, defying both President Jackson and his party, lost his reelection campaign in 1831, only to regain his seat in 1833. Then, in 1835, when he faced another close race—and the very determined opposition of Jackson—he offered a plainspoken platform. "I told the people of my district that I would serve them as faithfully as I had done; but if not, they might go to hell, and I would go to Texas."[30] After losing by 252 votes, Crockett, true to his word, lit out on the Southwest Trail.

On his trek across Texas, the famous hunter, raconteur, congress-man, and author had been fêted at every stop. Cannons were fired in his honor; he was toasted at banquets.

He was a folksy man of the people who spoke truth to power but on leaving home the previous November, he claimed no commitment to the cause of Texas, saying only, "I want to explore the Texes well before I return."[31] But by January, he reported, "I must say that as to what I have seen of Texas it is the garden spot of the world [with] . . . the best land and best prospects of health I ever saw." And he ended his letter with a few words of reassurance. "Do not be uneasy about me," he wrote. "I am among friends."[32]

When Crockett came through the Alamo gates, on February 8, 1836, he led a merry band of a dozen soldiers. He called them the Tennessee Company of Mounted Volunteers, although just three of them had begun the trip with him back in Tennessee. The men in the old mission certainly welcomed any and all volunteers—but a man like Crockett doubly so.

Crockett's fame preceded him and the defenders of the Alamo called upon the new arrival to give a speech. Climbing atop a wooden box, Crockett happily obliged the cheering crowd. As one Texan lad recalled, Crockett, at age forty-nine, remained "stout and muscular, about six feet in height, and weighing 180 to 200 pounds." Though his florid complexion suggested his fondness for drink, he "had an ease and grace about him which . . . rendered him irresistible."[33]

No one told a story like Crockett, who had published a memoir that had partly been key to his fame, and he regaled the men with his best stories, events from his own life, quickly winning their rapt attention. There were hunting yarns and stories of highfalutin politicians whom

Crockett expertly humbled. He told them of his promise to his constituents in Tennessee, that if they didn't want him to represent them in Washington, he would go to Texas. And here he was!

As if he hadn't already won their admiration and respect, Crockett refused an offer of an officer's commission; despite his military experience and seniority, he was content to be a simple soldier: "[A]ll the honor that I desire," he told them, "is that of defending as a high private . . . the liberties of our common country."[34]

Crockett would be a welcome soldier, valued for his wit, as well as his fiddle playing, and counted upon for the deadly accuracy of his famous rifle, Betsy. He was doubly welcome because he wasn't above picking up a shovel, working to improve the Alamo's defenses.

WHO'S IN CHARGE HERE?

No one sat still at the Alamo. Following the orders of engineer Green Jameson, men worked at getting the twenty-odd cannons mounted on the parapets, and by midmonth Almeron Dickinson and the other artillerymen had positioned all but three.

Colonel Neill watched the work—and waited for reinforcements. One by one, Jim Bowie, William Travis, and David Crockett had arrived, each accompanied by his own squadron. Even with the added troops, counted only in the dozens, the total number of ready fighters still remained at fewer than roughly 150. With Tejano volunteers, the defenders reached barely 175 men.

When, on February 11, Neill departed unexpectedly—an urgent summons prompted by a family illness led him to take a leave—the chaotic divide in the new Texian government began to play out in San Antonio, too. Before leaving, Neill asked Travis, whose rank made him the obvious choice, to take command of the post. But volunteer Texians, as Austin had found to his frustration the previous fall, insisted upon voting their preferences. Travis had no choice but to permit an election and Travis, as the newcomer, got fewer votes than Jim Bowie, who, despite his lack of a formal officer's commission, had led many of these men at Concepción. Lieutenant Colonel Travis might have the ear of the governor and the authority of the commander in chief, Sam Houston, but the famously daring Jim Bowie remained the volunteers' favorite. There was no firm hand to settle the dispute since Houston, still far afield conversing with the Cherokee, was in no position to intervene.

Worried about the chain of command, Travis dispatched a private letter to Governor Smith. "Since his election [Bowie] has been roaring drunk all the time . . . turning everything topsy turvey."[35] But soon Bowie, sobering up after a two-day binge, apologized to Travis, and the two came to an understanding. They would sign orders jointly, with Bowie in charge of the volunteers and Travis commanding the regulars and the cavalry.

Meanwhile the work of strengthening Fortress Alamo continued, and Travis dispatched men to scour the countryside for provisions. Wells were dug to assure a supply of water within the walls. But the men needed a respite and on the occasion of George Washington's 104th birthday, Travis and Bowie granted their soldiers permission to set aside their work at the Alamo.

On San Antonio's Soledad Street, Texians and Tejanos alike ate tamales and enchiladas. They drank and they danced the fandango with the women of the town, to the accompaniment of fiddles and guitars. The carefree carousing, which extended into the night on February 22, seemed less a celebration of the Founding Father's life than a release of tension built up over weeks of preparation and anticipation.

By the next day, however, the simple pleasures of the celebration returned to worries about the Mexican army. Travis's best guess had been that Santa Anna would not arrive until mid-March, but with too few men to perform too many tasks, he was forced to rely on friendly Tejanos for scouting reports. One Tejano resident of San Antonio, freshly returned from the Rio Grande, reported that the Mexican army, numbering some thirty-five hundred on foot, accompanied by fifteen hundred cavalrymen, was crossing the river. If true, that meant the estimated time of arrival was a matter of days. But some Texians scoffed at the Mexican intelligence.

Travis took a wait-and-watch approach, until the afternoon of February 23, when he heard five ominous words: *"The enemy is in view!"*[36]

Accompanied by the pealing of bells, the voice came from a lookout, high in the belfry of the San Fernando church. A crowd gathered as several soldiers quickly ascended the bell tower. But they saw no enemy army. They "halloed down that it was a 'false alarm.'"

The crowd dispersed, but Travis wanted to be certain that the Mexicans weren't simply hiding "behind a row of brushwood," as the sentinel who'd seen them insisted. He dispatched two men on horseback to investigate, instructing them to return at speed if they spied the enemy. Travis himself then climbed the tower stairs to watch as Dr. John Sutherland and another scout, John W. Smith, departed.

The men rode out on the Laredo road, which was muddy and slick from recent rainfall. And minutes later Lieutenant Colonel Travis got his answer: Barely a mile from the town, topping a low rise in the terrain, the scouts wheeled, spurred their horses, and made for the fort. They had seen the glint of armor of what they guessed to be fifteen hundred men on horseback.

Sutherland's horse lost its footing on the sloppy track, throwing its rider to the ground. But the doctor's companion helped him back into the saddle, and together they galloped back to San Antonio. There, when Sutherland dismounted, his knee gave way beneath him, and he needed David Crockett's shoulder to lean on as he reported to Travis.

Sutherland and Smith told Travis what they had seen—and at the speed of sound the news spread around the town. By three o'clock, on February 23, Commandant Travis had penned a short but imperative dispatch. Dr. Sutherland, despite his painful knee, could still ride a horse; since he would be little use as a defender, the doctor played the messenger, carrying the news of Santa Anna's arrival to Gonzales.

The note, in Travis's script, put the situation plainly.

> *The enemy in large force is in sight. We want men and provisions. Send them to us. We have 150 men and are determined to defend the Alamo to the last. Give us assistance.*[37]

The countdown had begun.

SEVEN

Twelve Days of Uncertainty

You know that in this war there are no prisoners.

—General Antonio López de Santa Anna, February 27, 1836

El Presidente—General Antonio López de Santa Anna—mounted his horse. He led from the front, mimicking a portrait he once saw of his idol, Napoléon Bonaparte, at the head of his troops. This time Santa Anna's advance corps consisted of staff officers, three companies each of light infantry and grenadiers, and artillerymen with two mortars. As the line of march snaked out from behind the low San Alazán Hills, the sun glinted off the Mexicans' silver helmets and breastplates. Less than two miles away, Texian lookouts watched from San Antonio.

Tall for his time—he stood five-foot-ten—Santa Anna looked lean and hungry. At forty-two, his hair remained dark, his skin olive toned. A man of little education, he spoke only Spanish, but his manners were practiced, and he had the carriage of a nobleman. He was here to put down a rebellion, but his greatest desires remained money and luxury. He flaunted a gold snuffbox and wore epaulets fringed with silver. He reveled in the attention and admiration of his people. A man of no fixed principles, his politics remained fluid—after fighting for Spain, then for Mexican independence, he fought now for himself, his comforts, and his own wealth and power.

Santa Anna did not reserve his cruelty for the enemy. Though he slept in a luxurious tent and dined on monogrammed china, his two-month march north had been an ongoing ordeal for the troops, with frigid rivers to cross and a shortage of food and water. Santa Anna himself had spent two weeks sick in bed en route, but he was luckier than many. His army lost about a man a mile, with more than four hundred of his 6,119-man force dying of dysentery, fevers, and exposure to cold and snowfalls of a foot and more. Occasional Indian raids also took a toll.

He arrived with a mission. Ten weeks before, the honor of his country had been sullied, at this very place, by the surrender of General Cos. For that, he would punish the Texians at Gonzales, Goliad, and Concepción.

He wasn't intimidated by the rebels. To Santa Anna, the Alamo was no more than "an irregular fortification hardly worthy of the name." He saw opportunity: Capturing the dilapidated mission would, he believed, "infuse our soldiers with that enthusiasm of the first triumph that would make them superior in the future to those of the enemy."[1] He anticipated only weak opposition, merely "mountaineers of Kentucky and the hunters of Missouri . . . an army ignorant of the art of war, incapable of discipline."[2]

He was a cruel and driven man, yet women found this man attractive, despite the fact that he rarely smiled, his expression perpetually unhappy, even gloomy. That inscrutability left some people wondering, but as one lady of the day would soon say of him, "It is strange . . . how frequently this expression . . . of placid sadness is to be remarked on the countenances of the most cunning, the deepest, most ambitious, most designing and most dangerous statesmen."[3]

The men of the Alamo would soon discover how utterly ruthless Santa Anna could be.

THE ENEMY APPROACHES

This time, no one doubted the meaning of the clanging bell. On Tuesday, February 23, the lethargy of a morning-after in San Antonio quickly gave way to furious activity as the bell tolled. Travis ordered the soldiers to withdraw to the Alamo, and double-quick the Texian fighters grabbed their guns, ammunition, whatever they could carry, and headed for the bridge.

Time was tight: Mexican troops, now in full sight and less than two miles away, marched toward them. No one knew when the first shots would be fired, but the Texians corralled the horses, penning them in what, during the Alamo's days as a mission, had been the convent garden. Still in the town, Jim Bowie went about San Antonio, searching for foodstuffs, ransacking deserted houses. He found some of what he was looking for, and the stores of corn at the Alamo went from three bushels to more than eighty.[4] Other defenders confiscated a herd of thirty beef cattle and drove the animals into a pen within the mission walls. Wounded and sick men were transferred to the safety of the walled compound.

The Texians' refuge, consisting of about four acres enclosed by the makeshift ramparts, became home to not only the men sworn to defend the Alamo but a mix of Anglo and Tejano families. Bowie collected members of the Veramendi clan, including his late wife's sister and her husband. In the hustle and bustle of the evacuation, Captain Almeron Dickinson reacted not as an artillery officer but as a husband and father.

Riding bareback, he galloped to the house he shared with wife Susanna at the corner of Commerce Street and the main plaza. Without dismounting, he called to her, "Give me the baby! Jump on behind and ask me no questions." With fifteen-month-old Angelina cradled in one arm, he helped swing Susanna up behind him.

There would be no fight this day: The Texians conceded the town as indefensible and, by late afternoon, the Mexicans took possession of San Antonio. Mounted grenadiers and foot soldiers dispersed to scout the nearly deserted streets. A Tejano boy of the town who had been playing nearby watched as Santa Anna and his staff dismounted near the church. For twelve-year-old Enrique Esparza, the sight of the general was indelible. "He had a very broad face and high cheekbones. He had a hard and cruel look and his countenance was a very sinister one."[5]

As the Texians watched from behind the Alamo's west wall, a distance of less than a half mile, a flag rose above the bell tower of the San Fernando church, previously the site of a Texian lookout post. Once again, Santa Anna's men would take no prisoners and show no mercy in dealing with these rebels.

But the Texians would not be intimidated: In response, they fired their biggest cannon, an eighteen-pounder, with a great, resounding boom.

After the Mexicans returned fire, lobbing a few shells from their field pieces, the guns on both sides went quiet. When a white flag was raised, the Texians sent messengers under a flag of peace to parley. With the odds as they were, an honorable retreat like the one Neill had granted to General Cos in December might be worth considering. But Santa Anna refused to negotiate. An aide, responding on his behalf, stated that "according to the order of His Excellency, the Mexican army cannot come to terms under any conditions with rebellious foreigners."[6]

The flag of no quarter and Santa Anna's unwillingness to talk left the Texians with no alternative. Travis and Bowie drafted a joint letter to Colonel Fannin, pleading for help. The commander of Goliad seemed their best hope—Fannin and his four hundred troops weren't so far away, a hundred miles distant. The two Alamo commanders told Fannin that their garrison, as of that morning's muster, amounted to just 146 effectives. They urged Fannin to send help—and assured him that they remained "determined *never to retreat*."[7]

As for Santa Anna, he received no plea from the Alamo. Travis gathered the men of the Alamo; they agreed to swear a collective oath to "resist to the last."[8] That day the Texians responded to Santa Anna's threats with gunfire, as the report of their biggest gun once more echoed over San Antonio. The rebels would stand their ground.

THE SIEGE

The concussion of cannon blasts was almost constant. A five-inch howitzer and several field pieces bombarded the Alamo throughout the day. Though the cannonballs and shards of flying stone injured no one, the Texians did find themselves one man down when Jim Bowie fell ill, deathly ill.

Bowie's sister-in-law, Juana, cared for the fevered man in an upstairs room in the Alamo chapel. But the nature of his ailment could only be guessed. Cholera or typhoid? Pneumonia? Perhaps some long-lingering ailment like tuberculosis that had grown suddenly grave? Whatever it was, it was serious, keeping Bowie confined to a cot that, some feared, might become his deathbed.

The illness meant that Bowie, weak and delirious, could no longer lead the volunteers. That put William Travis in charge of both Bowie's men and the regulars. The responsibility for saving the lives of those around him, much less winning a battle against Santa Anna's vastly larger army, had become Travis's heavy burden.

He considered the situation. Sam Houston's worst fears seemed to be coming true. The enemy was near—but help far away. Windswept San Antonio sat amid a Texas wilderness. No help would come from

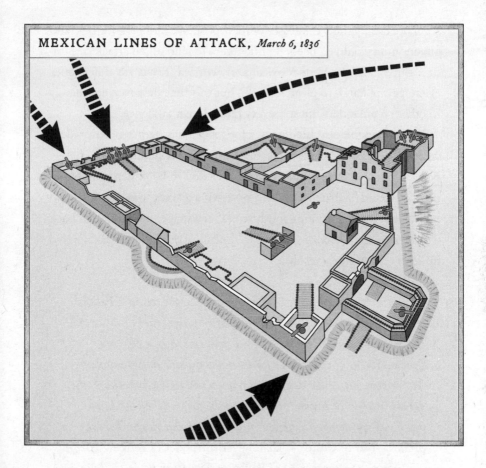

MEXICAN LINES OF ATTACK, *March 6, 1836*

the north, where the hills and plains were home to few settlers and many unfriendly Indians. Travis hoped reinforcements would arrive from Gonzales to the east and Goliad to the south, but the enemy now entirely controlled the territory west of the city. Santa Anna and his men occupied the nearby streetscapes, and scouting reports warned of other large Mexican forces on the march.

Although the Texians had worked for weeks to make the Alamo battle-ready, the defenders, now withdrawn inside the fort's walls, could see more clearly the weaknesses of their position. More men, rifles, and ammunition would be needed if they were to fend off an attack by hundreds upon hundreds of Mexicans. A worried Travis sat down once again, pen in hand, to plead for help, but this time he wrote not merely to other commanders but for a very much larger audience.

Two weeks before, his instinct for leadership hadn't been evident when he and Bowie bickered over which of them should be in charge. Now as the sole commander, suddenly boxed in by a merciless opponent, he found his true voice. He possessed a gift for words, one he had polished in his days writing for the small newspaper he'd founded back in Alabama, the *Claiborne Herald*. In drafting a public letter, he blended his fears with a steely resolve.

> *To the People of Texas & all Americans in the world—Fellow citizens & compatriots—I am besieged, by a thousand or more of the Mexicans under Santa Anna—I have sustained a continual Bombardment & cannonade for 24 hours & have not lost a man— The enemy has demanded a surrender at discretion, otherwise, the garrison are to be put to the sword, if the fort is taken—I have answered the demand with a cannon shot, & our flag still waves proudly from the walls—*I shall never surrender or retreat. *Then, I call on you in the name of Liberty, of patriotism & every thing dear to the American character, to come to our aid with all dispatch—The enemy is receiving reinforcements daily & will no doubt increase to three or four thousand in four or five days.*
>
> *If this call is neglected, I am determined to sustain myself as long as possible & die like a soldier who never forgets what is due to his own honor & that of his country—*VICTORY OR DEATH.
>
> *William Barret Travis*
> *Lt. Col. comdt*[9]

Travis knew that he and the men around him, captive as they were, faced the fight of their lives. He understood, too, that defending the Alamo represented something larger. He and his Texians might occupy an obscure frontier town, but he wrote as if their story, their cause, transcended time and place, his a voice for the cause of liberty everywhere.

THURSDAY, FEBRUARY 25, 1836

No friend of liberty, Santa Anna tested his tactics. In the night his men planted batteries north and south of the mission, roughly four hundred yards from the Alamo. From these new positions, they maintained their fire.

Conserving their powder, the Texians fired back only intermittently.

From his headquarters, Santa Anna supervised the distribution of shoes. He left the town to scout with a cavalry unit. Then, at ten o'clock that Thursday morning, he ordered a force of more than two hundred Mexicans to march on the Alamo. The uniformed men crossed the shallow river and marched toward the scattering of nearby buildings south of the Alamo's main gate.

The Texians held their fire until the enemy arrived "within point blank shot." Then the Alamo's defenders opened with a full fusillade, their cannons unleashing grape and cannon shot. The Texians' long rifles—with David Crockett cheering his boys on—and the artillery took a deadly toll on the approaching fighters. The Mexicans still standing scrambled back into the shelter of the abandoned houses, and the two sides exchanged fire for two hours before the Mexicans finally withdrew. When they retreated, they carted with them at least eight dead and wounded.

Travis reported on the morning's action, writing to Major General

Sam Houston. Houston was far away, still on his journey to and from the Cherokee, blithely unaware of the turn of events at the Alamo, having ordered its evacuation the month before.

"Many of the enemy were wounded," Travis wrote, "while we, on our part, have not lost a man. . . . I take great pleasure in stating that both officers and men have conducted themselves with firmness and bravery." He cited Captain Dickinson in particular for his gallantry, as well as "the Hon. David Crockett" for "animating the men to do their duty."

Proud as he was of the first exchange of fire, Travis remained deeply worried. "Do hasten on aid to me as rapidly as possible, as from the superior number of the enemy, it will be impossible for us to keep them out much longer."

Without apology, Travis also spelled out the stakes once more: "If they overpower us, we fall a sacrifice at the shrine of our country."[10]

TRAVIS'S CALL FOR HELP had reached Colonel James Fannin. Goliad's commander speedily divided his garrison, ordering all but one hundred of his four-hundred-some men to prepare to march. As they readied for departure, Fannin reported via letter to army headquarters in Washington-on-the-Brazos that he felt a brotherly obligation. "The appeals of Cols. Travis & Bowie cannot . . . pass unnoticed—particularly by troops now on the field—Sanguine, chivalrous volunteers—Much must be risked to relieve the besieged."[11]

Fannin and company headed out for San Antonio, a hundred miles away, that very afternoon. But then, just two hundred yards from Goliad's gate, they faced their first obstacle. A wagon broke down.

After a delay, with pairs of yoked oxen pulling each cannon, Fannin and his men managed to cross a nearby river. But, as more wagons failed in the process, their progress slowed again. With darkness falling, the little army made camp for the night, still within sight of the Goliad mission.

In the morning, Fannin's officers requested a council of war. They were having second thoughts about their immediate urge to go to the aid of their fellow Texians. The three-hundred-man contingent had no bread or beef and little rice; as Fannin's aide-de-camp Captain Brooks put it, "We are almost naked and without provisions and very little ammunition." Fannin himself now doubted whether the artillery could be gotten to the Alamo. Others expressed concern that the hundred men left behind would be unable to defend Goliad, the place they had recently renamed Fort Defiance. And even if Fannin's contingent made it to the Alamo, wasn't the mission likely to fail? In Captain Brooks's words, "We can not therefore calculate very sanguinely upon victory."[12]

Fannin, Brooks, and the other commissioned officers deliberated before reaching a unanimous decision. As Fannin, seeming to forget that he had just said that much should be risked for the sake of the Alamo, soon decided, "It was deemed expedient to return to [Goliad] and complete the fortifications."[13]

Travis's request that Fannin send men would go unanswered. Fannin's resolve had wavered and broken; the proposed mission to aid the Alamo had come to nothing.

A STRONG WIND came up that evening, but Santa Anna and his men ignored the temperature as it dropped below forty degrees. The Mexican guns not only maintained their fire, but the Texians awoke to the sight of cavalry encamped on the hills east of the Alamo. The enemy was now poised to block a retreat or to intercept reinforcements from Gonzales. The noose was tightening.

In the night, a small band of Texians had quietly left the Alamo and set fire to the houses close by. The shanties, which had provided the enemy cover during the previous day's skirmish, went up in smoke. Burned to the ground, the ash and rubble of the humble buildings left an open field for the men with long rifles.

The terms of the battle grew clearer. From the safety of Fortress Alamo, the Texians could hold off a much larger army, with their artillery and rifles throwing lead at any attackers who approached within two hundred yards. If the enemy chose to make an all-out assault, Travis felt confident that his gunners and riflemen would inflict staggering casualties. Santa Anna might risk such a bloodbath—and with his superior numbers, he could prevail—but surely His Excellency recognized that such a victory would seem more costly than a defeat?

On the other hand, the Alamo enclosure, Travis knew well, was simply too large for his 150 men to defend indefinitely in the face of constant artillery fire. Not that he had a choice: Until more Texians came to their aid, the Alamo defenders would have to occupy themselves with improving their fort. That wasn't easy: Moving about the Alamo, they had to be constantly wary, dodging shells and cannonballs that regularly whistled in from the sky.

LONG DAYS, LONGER NIGHTS

Travis ordered more sorties to demolish all the remaining shacks near enough to the Alamo to provide enemy cover. In the process, his men salvaged bits and pieces for firewood, an increasingly precious commodity.

Engineer Green Jameson and his construction detail dug trenches; one shovelful at a time, the excavated earth added to the bulk of the walls and shaped parapets atop them.

Riflemen found the best spots from which to pick off any Mexican foolish enough to raise his head within range. From the opposite side of the line, a Mexican captain observed one shooter whose flowing hair distinguished him from the rest. The tall man fired from a favored spot, dressed in a buckskin suit and patterned cape.

"This man," Rafael Soldana reported, "would kneel or lie down behind the low parapet, rest his long gun and fire, and we all learned to keep at a good distance when he was seen to make ready to shoot. He rarely missed his mark, and when he fired he always rose to his feet and calmly reloaded his gun seemingly indifferent to the shots fired at him by our own men."

The independent figure sometimes crowed over his well-aimed shots, taunting the enemy in "a strong, resonant voice." The Spanish-speaking Mexicans could not understand his words, spoken in English, but would later learn his identity. As they rendered his name, he was "Kwockey."[14] To the Americans, he was the man known as Crockett, who was defending the biggest gap in the Alamo's perimeter, where, on the south side, the wall ended short of the chapel. Although the space was now lined with a palisade of sharpened stakes angled toward potential attackers, it remained a likely Mexican route of assault.

General Santa Anna, on the outside looking in, bided his time. He would wait for an oncoming brigade to add to his forces, but he harbored no doubts as to the outcome of the eventual fight.

"After taking Fort Alamo," he wrote confidently to his minister of war, "I shall continue my operations against Goliad and the other fortified places, so that before the rains set in, the campaign shall be absolutely terminated up to the Sabine River, which serves as the boundary line between our republic and the one of the North."[15]

He ordered the installation that night of another gun battery, this one near the old mill. With first light, cannonballs began to rain in from yet another direction, almost due north of the Alamo. When one of his scouts reported, on February 29, that a two-hundred-man Texian force was on the road from the Presidio La Bahía, the fortress at

Goliad, Santa Anna ordered one of his generals to lead a force of cavalry and infantry to intercept the Goliad men. When they found no sign of a Texian force, they returned to Santa Anna's camp at San Antonio.

Wondering at the whereabouts of Fannin and company, Travis asked Austin's old friend Juan Seguín, a trusted Tejano, to carry another plea for help to the outside world. Needing a good horse for the mission, he went to ask the bedridden Bowie if he might borrow his.

Seguín found the aging fighter "so ill that he hardly recognized the borrower."[16] But Bowie agreed to lend his mount, and the messenger left that night through the north gate.

Nearing the Mexican cavalry camp, he approached at a leisurely pace as if reporting in. He spoke Spanish, lulling the Mexican sentinels into lowering their guard—but, as he neared, he suddenly spurred his horse and dashed past, disappearing into the night before the dragoons could react.

Back at the Alamo, Travis and his men waited and hoped. Crockett distracted them with his fiddle, accompanied by the droning bagpipes of Scotsman John McGregor. These were evenings of drink, of cards and talk, but little seemed to change except the weather. One night Crockett and McGregor faced off in a musical competition to make the most noise; it was a fine distraction as a brutal norther finally blew past, its bitter cold winds giving way to milder air.[17] The Texians welcomed the change—it occurred at a moment when nothing whatever seemed to be going their way.

DON'T SHOOT!

In the early morning hours of March 1, the Alamo sentinel shot first. Noises in the dark, nearby but outside the walls, drew his fire—but no one shot back. Instead the lookout heard voices, hissing in English.

Don't shoot! We're friends!

They were men from Gonzales, the place where, with the second shot heard 'round the world, the war had begun. Their neighbors had come to the aid of Gonzales and, summoned by a Travis alert, they had come here to do the same. Circling north, they had managed to skirt the Mexican dragoons guarding the road.

Ushered into the Alamo, the reinforcements were welcomed with cheers. But the defenders' sense of relief at the newcomers' arrival quickly faded. The company of volunteers, one of them wounded in the foot by the guard's gun, numbered just thirty-two men. That brought the total to 180 fighters; the Mexicans, depending upon which estimate one believed, numbered fifteen hundred. Or twenty-five hundred. Or even six thousand men.

For the rest of the defenders, the arrival on March 1 was a sort of anniversary: One week had passed since the appearance of Santa Anna forced them to withdraw into the Alamo. There had been no major attack. The only thing that seemed to change was still the weather, which was turning cold again, but every man understood the situation could explode at most any time.

WHERE IS SAM HOUSTON?

While the men in the Alamo waited and worried, the missing general reappeared: Houston had returned from Cherokee country, riding into Washington-on-the-Brazos on February 28. He brought good news: He'd signed a treaty of peace with the Cherokee. On arrival, however, he encountered some very bad news, in a just-arrived dispatch addressed to "Sam Houston, Commander-in-Chief of the Army of Texas."

The report, written in Colonel Travis's slanting and hurried hand, was enough to make Houston's head spin. He learned for the first time of Santa Anna's early arrival. He read of the initial skirmish between the desperate defenders of the Alamo and the Mexican army. He didn't have to read the closing line—*"Give me help, oh my Country! Victory or Death"*—to know Travis and troops were in terrible trouble, trouble they might have avoided had they followed Houston's earlier instructions to evacuate the mission.

Houston immediately began planning his response, but before he could take military action, he had to help complete the writing and signing of a Texas declaration of independence, an action that had been a long time in coming.

On March 1, in a makeshift building overlooking the Brazos River, forty-one delegates to a new convention came to order to reorganize revolutionary Texas into a republic.

In a simple structure with cotton cloth and animal skins for doors, the delegates suffered in bitter wind and cold, but they produced what they had come for: "The Unanimous Declaration of Independence made by the Delegates of the People of Texas." One statement summed it up: "We do hereby declare, that our political connection with the Mexican nation has forever ended, and that the people of Texas do now constitute a free, sovereign, and independent republic."[18]

On March 2, which just happened to be Sam Houston's forty-third birthday, the delegates signed the declaration. The day after, the delegates designated him commander in chief, this time with full and absolute authority over all the troops, be they volunteer, regular army, or militia.

Now could he address the task of facing down Santa Anna.

BACK AT THE ALAMO

On Thursday, March 3, a lone rider slipped through the ever-tightening enemy perimeter to enter the Alamo. He told of sixty volunteers en route from San Felipe, with another three hundred to follow. To Travis and his officers, the arithmetic looked suddenly better. With these fighters—along with, they hoped, Goliad's three hundred—Travis's command could grow to eight hundred men. *That* would make for a much fairer fight. But before more Texians could arrive, raucous cries of celebration sounded across the river.

A glance over the west wall revealed the reason. A long ribbon of troops entered San Antonio. There were a thousand or more men marching in from the west, a mix of experienced sappers (military engineers) and fresh conscripts. These new troops raised the total under Santa Anna's immediate command to at least twenty-five hundred men, a force more than a dozen times greater than that inside the Alamo.

Travis could wait and hope for help to arrive from somewhere, from anywhere; or he could try writing yet again. This time he addressed the top man, the president of the Texas convention.

He reported in full, describing the enemy's gradual encroachment, the arrival of the small Gonzales force, and the near doubling of enemy ranks. Despite the fact that "at least two hundred shells have fallen inside of our works," Travis reported proudly, "the spirits of my men are still high." He again appealed for troops, ammunition, and supplies, requesting the immediate dispatch of "at least 500 pounds of cannon powder, 200 rounds of six, nine, twelve, and eighteen-pound balls, ten kegs of rifle powder, and a supply of lead." If they were better equipped for battle, the fight could be "decisive," he promised. His men could be trusted to "fight with desperation and that high-souled courage that characterized the patriot, who is willing to fight in defense of his country's liberty and his own honor."[19] He sealed the letter with wax.

Within hours, however, Travis's hopeful house of cards began to collapse when word came of Fannin's decision to turn back. No help would be forthcoming from Goliad.

With that news, a fatalistic frame of mind came over William Travis.

He understood perhaps better than any in the garrison that, as he ominously admitted, they were probably engaged in their "last struggle." With the call for outgoing mail announced, the messenger readied to depart with the fall of night. He would carry letters from several Alamo defenders, but Travis at this late hour felt the need to scribble down one more note. This he composed as a private citizen, not a commanding officer. It was a letter to his son's schoolteacher.

> *Take Care of my little boy. If the country should be saved, I may make for him a splendid fortune; but if the country be lost and I should perish, he will have nothing but the proud recollection that he is the son of a man who died for his country.*[20]

It would be Lieutenant Colonel William Barret Travis's last letter.

MARCHING ORDERS

As the courier carried his pouch full of letters toward their intended recipients, Santa Anna called a council of war on March 4.

Some of his officers advised patience: The Texians could go nowhere and, with a pair of twelve-pound cannons only two days out, why not wait and reduce Fortress Alamo to rubble? Other generals expressed eagerness to attack right away.

Santa Anna himself had grown impatient. He wanted a plan of attack, an immediate plan for ending the rebel resistance with a direct assault. He ordered one be prepared.

The preliminaries were in place. Just the previous afternoon, the Texians had observed Mexicans, in the plain light of day, sawing and hewing lengths of wood for the legs and rungs of scaling ladders. At varying distances, Santa Anna's men had dug entrenchments and gun batteries on all sides of Fortress Alamo. The most recent, north of the fort, was closest, now firing from within two hundred yards.

At two o'clock on the afternoon of Saturday, March 5, detailed orders from Santa Anna circulated. "The time has come," they began, "to strike a decisive blow upon the enemy occupying the Fortress of the Alamo."[21] The soldiers were to retire at dark, then, at midnight, form into four columns of foot soldiers, each assigned a point of attack—the northwest and northeast corners, the east wall, and the Alamo's most evident vulnerability, the palisade in the gap of the south wall. A cavalry regiment deployed to the east would crush any Texians seeking to escape. A fifth column would lie in wait at the new north battery; commanded by Santa Anna, the reserves could be ordered into battle whenever and wherever the need arose. Everything was to be in readiness by four o'clock on Sunday morning.

Although wholly ignorant of how soon their fate would fall, the Texians would have to endure only one more bitter night, with a wet north wind and temperatures near freezing.

CROSSING THE LINE

On Saturday afternoon, the Mexican cannonade went silent two hours before sunset. In the welcome but unfamiliar quiet, William Travis summoned his men to parade in the Alamo's central plaza. Several soldiers carried Jim Bowie, still on his cot, feverish and on the edge of delirium, from his confinement.

Travis addressed the garrison.

"My soldiers, I am going to meet the fate that becomes me. Those who will stand by me, let them remain, but those who desire to go, let them go."[22]

The men cheered his words.

Travis drew his sword. Using its tip, he scribed a line in the dirt in front of the men in formation. He invited all those who would stand with him, who would die with him, to step across the line.

As one, the able-bodied men stepped forth; Jim Bowie, despite his fevered state, requested that he be helped across. Just one man remained behind; he was permitted to depart. He would survive to recount this story.[23]

Travis and his men worked into the night, further stabilizing the fortifications. Many of the eight hundred muskets and rifles on hand were made ready: With more than one gun per man, the Texians could deliver a rapid initial rate of fire without reloading. The artillerymen had at least five hundred loads of canister and grapeshot.

The commander made one other parting gesture before retiring for what would prove to be an abbreviated night's sleep. Visiting the Alamo church, Travis noticed little Angelina Dickinson. From his finger, Travis removed a ring of hammered gold; it was inset with a large agate stone. He strung it on a loop of string, which he then slipped over the head of the fifteen-month-old like a necklace.

The child's mother, Susanna, stood nearby. She promised Travis that if anything happened to him she would be sure that the keepsake was delivered to Travis's son, Charles.

EIGHT

The Massacre

A desperate contest ensued, in which prodigies of valor were
wrought by this Spartan band.

—MARY AUSTIN HOLLEY, *Texas*

he Texians' day began at 5:30 A.M. with the sound of distant
shouting. As the sun came up, the Alamo defenders heard calls
of *Viva Santa Anna!* and *Viva la republica!*

Blaring bugles then made the attack official, and the Mexican troops,
less than two hundred yards away, leapt to their feet. Having lain quietly for two hours, on their stomachs and unseen in their blue uniforms,
they hoisted their guns and swords and ran toward the Alamo.

At last, on Sunday, March 6, 1836, the real fight began.

For the Alamo's sleeping commandant, insulated by the adobe brick
of his room in the middle of the west wall, his officer of the day put
the news plainly. Banging open the door of Travis's bedchamber, he
shouted, "Colonel Travis! The Mexicans are coming!"

Rising quickly from his bed, Travis grabbed his gun and sword.
He ran out into the open plaza, yelling, "Come on boys, the Mexicans
are upon us and we'll give them *Hell*."[1]

Heading for the gun battery in the Alamo's northwest corner, he could hear his riflemen atop the walls as they began firing at the oncoming Mexicans. The cannon were not yet booming, though Travis needed the big guns to prevent the much larger Mexican force from reaching the Alamo's wall. He sprinted up the ramp that rose to the gun emplacement.

On reaching the top of the rampart, he, too, discharged his shotgun, one barrel first, then the other. Moments later, the cannons at last started firing. Standing nearby, silhouetted by stop-time powder flashes, Travis made a fine target from the darkness below. Some unnamed Mexican sighted in and fired.

Travis took a hit: A lead ball smashed squarely into his forehead. He went down, his hand still clenching his gun, collapsing into a strangely lifelike sitting position. In the opening minutes of the fight for the Alamo, the Texians lost their battle leader, the man whose words would forever frame the events of the fight that was unfolding around his lifeless form.

THE FIRST WAVE

Santa Anna employed Napoléon's tactics. With his overwhelming manpower advantage and little regard for casualties, he threw the four columns of infantry at the four corners of the Alamo. He remained well back, an observer, astride his fine steed.

The general had surprise on his side: After weeks of bombardment, in the wee hours of a Sunday, he caught the Texians unawares and unready. His advance guard had overwhelmed the rebels' pickets on the perimeter, slitting throats or running them through with bayonets before they could sound the alarm.

Inside the Alamo, the surprised Texians moved to their assigned posts as quickly as they could and began delivering a murderous fire at the attackers approaching the Alamo's perimeter walls. Their rifles damaged the Mexican wave, "leaving a wide trail of blood, of wounded, and of dead."[2] Each rifleman, having emptied one loaded gun, reached for the next.

The Texian artillery added to the deafening din of the battle. In the absence of standard-issue canister and grapeshot, Almeron Dickinson and his fellow artillerymen had packed their cannon barrels with metal fragments, such as nails, horseshoe pieces, and chain links; the more jagged the scrap, the better. Powered by superior American-made gunpowder, the hail of deadly debris added to the numbers of fallen men on the field, taking down officers as well as foot soldiers. One stunned Mexican colonel watched as "a single cannon volley did away with half [a] company" of his men.[3]

The officer who had surrendered San Antonio back in December, General Martín Perfecto de Cos, ignoring the promise he had made not to return and fight in Texas, led his three hundred infantrymen as they charged Travis's battery. Having lost once to the Texians, Cos needed to redeem his tarnished reputation in Santa Anna's eyes. Some four hundred men under Colonel Duque advanced on the other corner of the Alamo's north wall. Three hundred soldiers commanded by Colonel José María Romero attacked the strong east front, where Captain Dickinson's three twelve-pound cannons, mounted high on the rear wall of the ruins of the Alamo's chapel, appeared to its attackers to be "a sort of high fortress."[4] Colonel Juan Morales's one hundred men moved on the south wall, looking to capture the main entrance and penetrate the palisade guarded by Crockett and his company.

The "terrible shower" that burst from the Texian cannons opened gaps in the Mexican ranks on all fronts. Colonel Duque went down with a thigh wound, but the swarm of Mexicans kept coming. These were soldiers trained to "scorn life and welcome death," to seek "honor and glory."[5]

On approach, some light infantrymen had fanned out and, armed with accurate Baker rifles, they targeted the Alamo defenders on the roofs, exposed with no parapets to protect them. At closer range, the short-barreled guns the troops carried—the Texians dismissively called them "blunderbusses"—gained effectiveness yard by yard. The Texians' earlier advantage of preloaded guns ended; each rifleman had to resort to reloading, costing him precious time.

On reaching the foot of the wall, however, the attackers discovered that next to none of the scaling ladders had made it across the killing field. Inside the Alamo the thuds of Mexican axes could be heard on the thick wooden doors; some Mexicans wielded crowbars, struggling to pry open the boarded-up windows. But the attackers were suddenly stymied.

Acutely aware of their losses—according to one Mexican soldier, "it seemed every cannon ball or pistol shot of the enemy embedded itself in the breasts of our men,"[6] the north wall attackers wavered. With gunfire still raining down from above—one cannon now raked the attackers in the lee of the wall—Santa Anna's men fell back.

From a distance, a noncombatant, José Francisco Ruiz, mayor of San Antonio, called it as he saw it. The Mexican army's initial assault, he observed, was "repulsed by the deadly fire of Travis's artillery, which resembled a constant thunder."[7]

The Texians were holding strong.

HIS EXCELLENCY

For Santa Anna, no glory could be claimed without bloodshed. Watching the attack on the Alamo, he took grim pleasure in the dirge-like notes of the "Degüello," the rhythmic march that, on his orders, accompanied the assault. Sounded by his buglers, it signaled to his men that no quarter would be given.* To their enemy, it was "the music of merciless murder."[8]

Standing with the reserve troops just fifteen minutes into the battle, Santa Anna looked on as dozens and dozens of his own men lay slaughtered after the first assault. His officers, aware that a full attack would result in a "great sacrifice" of men, had wondered at the timing of the attack: *Why not wait? The siege was working. More big guns were due any day.* But such niceties were wasted on Santa Anna, who remained firm. The generals and colonels had no choice but to obey His Excellency's orders, "[choosing] silence, knowing that he would not tolerate opposition, his sole pleasure being in hearing what met with his wishes."[9]

Dressed as usual for a campaign—he wore a green frock coat—Santa Anna got his bloody battle. To prevent any Texians from escaping the Alamo, he had taken the precaution of positioning a squadron near the Gonzales road and ordered a veteran cavalry unit to run down any rebels who tried to flee. He wanted to obliterate the defiant Texians, no matter what the cost.

But the fight wasn't going as he had hoped. He studied the Alamo, where, in the morning's first glimmer of daylight, he could still see the bright blasts of flame from the mouths of the Texian cannons. Two of his columns had slowed in the face of the artillery fire; another veered off its course; and the fourth, attacking the main gate, had been forced to take shelter behind a few remaining huts near the Alamo's southwest corner.

The initial attack failed to penetrate the Alamo's defenses.

His reserves were among the best men in Santa Anna's army, consisting of four hundred men. Now, he decided, was the time to order them into battle. This second wave would penetrate the wall, he hoped, ending Texian resistance once and for all.

---

* Derived from the Spanish *degollar*, "Degüello" literally means throat-cutting.

THE SECOND WAVE

Inside the Alamo, Travis lay dead. His second in command, Jim Bowie, could not take his place. Weak with disease, sweating feverishly, he lay in his bed, only dimly aware of the firefight. But the Texians kept fighting.

At the southwest corner of the Alamo enclosure, the biggest of the Alamo's guns pounded the Mexicans. On the platform at the rear of the church, three smaller cannons looked east. But nowhere were there enough Texians to man all the guns properly. Instead of a usual crew of a half dozen per gun, the Texians depended on skeleton crews half that size.

The gunners along the north wall aimed at the army of attackers as they regrouped. Despite the losses sustained on the first attack, this force grew larger as the Texians watched. Along with Santa Anna's reserves, the third column, deflected by the big guns in the chapel, now joined in a full-frontal assault along the length of the northern exposure. This time, on reaching the base of the wall, they took a determined new approach.

Green Jameson and his men had worked to stiffen the northern defenses, facing a once-crumbling stone and adobe wall with a layer of timber and stone. Though as high as twelve feet in places, the earthworks were not yet finished—and the exposed beams and stacked stones made the wall vulnerable. General Juan Amador grasped the opportunity: He began to climb and ordered his men, their guns slung over their shoulders, to follow. They found footholds and handholds, with one soldier helping the next, despite the continued Texian fire from above. Before long they had breached the Alamo's walls.

Some of the agile ones who cleared the wall first met with the bayonets and rifle butts of Texian fighters who stabbed and bludgeoned them. At other places along the expanse of the wall, the appearance of a Mexican head was greeted with lead fired by nearby Texians or riflemen on top of a central building within the Alamo, the Long Barracks. Despite the falling dead and wounded, one Mexican officer reported, "the courage of our soldiers was not diminished . . . and they hurried to occupy their places, . . . climbing over their bleeding bodies."[10]

This time, despite the casualties, there would be no Mexican retreat. "We could hear the Mexican officers shouting to the men to jump over," the Tejano boy, Enrique Esparza, later remembered.[11] That moment—it was a shift in the tide of battle—would stay with him forever. The fall of the Alamo became inevitable when the first uniformed men of Mexico climbed over the wall. The few were followed by the many, as a surge of attackers cleared the parapet and, one by one, dropped to the plaza below.

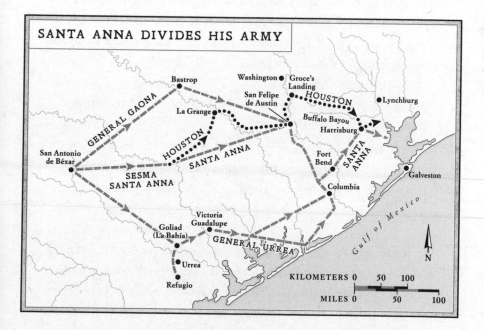

SANTA ANNA DIVIDES HIS ARMY

This time the Texians were the ones to retreat, withdrawing the soldiers who were at the perimeter wall to the Long Barracks in hopes of one final holdout.

CAPTAIN ALMERON DICKINSON manned the chapel's big guns. Bunked down in the church, he and his gun crew had slept close to their post, and in the early moments of the battle, one of his cannons had been the first to fire. The intimidating cannon had done its work, raking the left flank of the oncoming Mexican third column, causing Colonel Romero's command to veer away from the church and head northward, seeking a new point of attack unprotected by cannons.

As the battle continued, however, the artillery captain read the changing situation. With the Mexicans entering the Alamo compound, he knew the Alamo defenders lost ground they couldn't afford to lose. With the tumult still raging hottest along the north wall, Dickinson left his post, stealing a few moments for words he had to say.

He managed to find his wife, Susanna, and their daughter, in the family quarters in the sacristy adjacent to the chapel.

"My dear wife," Almeron began. "They are coming over the wall." But that didn't say it all, and she deserved to know the harsh truth.

"We are all lost," he told her.

More remained to be said, but he needed to return to his post on the scaffold. He made just one parting request of Susanna Dickinson.

"If they spare you, love our child." He kissed her in farewell.[12]

WITH THE NORTH WALL BREACHED, the Alamo gunners manning the southwest cannon turned their gun inward to fire on the enemy soldiers flooding the Alamo plaza. But the cannon fire would not halt the swarm of attackers; Santa Anna's men opened the northern gate, permitting many more Mexican soldiers to rush in. From the west, the Mexicans pried and hacked open the boarded-up openings and climbed through.

Now members of the fourth column, until then pinned down by the Texians' southern cannon, charged the south wall. Within moments, they overran the artillery position, killing the gunners and capturing their weapons. With possession of the largest gun, the Mexicans set about turning it on the Texians.

At the palisade, the riflemen, led by David Crockett, watched the battle turn. They saw no alternative: Crockett and his Tennessee boys withdrew, taking cover in the church.

Barely a half hour into the battle, the fight had been redefined, the perimeter walls lost and Texian territory reduced to two buildings. The Texians, deprived of most of their cannons, were effectively caged inside the adobe walls of the Long Barracks and the Alamo church.

THE END

Many of the Texians, now truly trapped, had no means of escape from the two-story, brick-and-adobe Long Barracks. For the moment they remained safe inside its solid walls and behind the heavy wooden doors. From windows and loopholes, the Texian sharpshooters could pick off Mexican soldiers in the plaza with impunity, forcing the attackers to take cover where they could. But the Mexicans soon pivoted the captured cannons and sent their cannonballs crashing through the adobe walls.

Once the guns turned, it was only minutes before the first of the Long Barracks doors had been blasted open. Firing as they surged through, the Mexicans met with a hail of gunfire from the Texians. "The tumult was great, the disorder frightful," according to a Mexican officer. "Different groups of soldiers were firing in all directions, on their comrades and on their officers, so that one was as likely to die by a friend's hand as by an enemy's."[13] The fight became room-by-room as the Mexicans broke down doors. "The struggle," one Mexican sergeant remembered, "was made up of a number of separate and desperate combats, often hand to hand."[14]

Even the inmates of the so-called hospital—men still recovering from wounds sustained in December or from illness—fought valiantly. Despite being confined to their beds, they shot at the attackers from where they lay. According to one Mexican sergeant, he and his soldiers rolled a small cannon into the hospital doorway and fired canister shot into the room, killing fifteen sick men.

Although, according to one Mexican sergeant, "the Texians fought like devils," in just a few more minutes, no Texians were left alive in the barracks.

Meanwhile, along the south wall, the Mexicans burst into one of the small dwellings. At first, in the near darkness, the Mexicans saw no one. Then they spied something, someone, a human form that lay motionless on a makeshift bed, mostly obscured beneath a blanket. In the heat of the bloody battle, they assumed that, out of terror, the man hid himself beneath the covers "like a woman."[15]

Then he moved. Awakening to a nightmare, Jim Bowie struggled to reach a seated position. But the attackers moved quickly toward him. Though he reached for his notorious knife, for the first time Jim Bowie's instinct for self-preservation fell short and, before he could defend himself, he was "butchered in bed."[16]

Whether his killers knew the identity of their famous victim isn't clear, but, later, one of the Mexican generals acknowledged that the troops had skewered "the perverse and boastful James Bowie" with their bayonets.[17] The end of his life had been a brutal one: Dying or perhaps already dead, his body had been raised on enemy bayonets and tossed about until his killers' uniforms were soaked with his blood.

Another fifty or sixty Texians, looking to retreat but unable to reach either the church or the barracks, had gone over the mission wall to make a run for freedom. Taking cover in a drainage trench, they ran for the Gonzales road. But Santa Anna's cavalry stood ready, stationed, as instructed, "to scout the country, to prevent the possibility of escape."[18] The skilled horsemen made short work of running down the fleeing men, and none of the defenders survived the slaughter.

Now only the church remained in Texian hands. The Mexicans once again pivoted the Alamo's biggest cannon, directing its fire upon the church, barely a hundred yards away. The piles of sandbags that protected the church facade were blasted into a cloud of sand, and Santa Anna's men shouldered through the entrance doors.

In those minutes of desperate chaos, Almeron Dickinson fell. Only Crockett and the diminished ranks of his men remained to fight on, but they no longer defended the Alamo; theirs was a matter of survival. As the enemy flooded every space in the Alamo, these last remaining defenders no longer had time to reload their muzzle-loading rifles, and there weren't enough bowie knives or bayonets to defeat Santa Anna's hundreds.

The Mexicans had their orders—none but women and children were to be spared—but the last men standing surrendered to General Castrillón. The Mexican officer respected their honorable plea for mercy, and seven men, led by David Crockett, put down their weapons, trusting the Mexican general would treat them honorably as prisoners of war.

By 6:30 A.M., a strange half silence fell as the sun rose over the horizon. The firing had ended, permitting the "groans of the wounded and the last breaths of the dying" to be heard.[19]

NINE

Bring Out the Dead

The gallantry of the few Texans who defended the Alamo was really wondered at by the Mexican army. Even the generals were astonished at their vigorous resistance, and how dearly victory was bought.

—José Francisco Ruiz

With the fight over, Santa Anna made his way across the field of battle. At a distance of a hundred yards, he saw a few scattered bodies of his soldiers. By the time he reached the Alamo's main gate, the number of dead Mexicans lying on the ground was shocking.

Inside the old mission walls, the bloodletting had been even worse. Intermingled on its central plaza were dead Mexicans in blue uniforms and Texians dressed in stained deerskin and filthy homespun.

Santa Anna, a veteran of many bloody battles, expressed no regrets. "These are the chickens," he remarked to one of his captains, dismissing the dead. "Much blood has been shed; but the battle is over. It was but a small affair."[1]

His lack of compassion extended to survivors in his own army. No hospital tents or field surgery had been readied, and the lack of adequate medical corps and supplies would, in the days and weeks to come, cost many a wounded Mexican his life.

Hearing no more than an occasional stray gunshot outside the mission—the dragoons still hunted down the last of the escapees, who hid in gullies and underbrush—Santa Anna wanted only to be able to report with finality his great victory. Before writing to his minister of war, he ordered the dead bodies of Travis, Bowie, and Crockett identified. The first two were easily found: Travis's remains rested just where he had fallen, on the northwest battery, and Bowie's body, crudely torn by bayonets, lay in a bloody heap in what had been his sickroom.

Despite his orders that no quarter be given any Texian fighter, Santa Anna discovered that David Crockett wasn't dead. When brought before him, Crockett stood tall, unwilling to grovel.

The man who'd captured him, General Castrillón, counseled generosity toward *"Coket,"* whom he described as a "venerable old man."[2] But Santa Anna scolded Castrillón for sparing the Texians. "What right have you to disobey my orders? I want no prisoners."[3]

Personally affronted by Crockett's survival, the indignant Santa Anna chose mercilessness. True to his word, he ordered the immediate execution of Crockett and the handful of survivors.

After a moment of shocked hesitation—the officers engaged in the previous hour's action thought such a step dishonorable—Santa Anna's own staff officers, men who had remained out of the fight, "thrust themselves forward, in order to flatter their commander, and with swords in hand fell upon these unfortunate defenseless men just as a tiger leaps upon his prey."

Not killed in battle, but murdered, Crockett was thus among the last to die at the Alamo. At least one of the Mexicans, appalled at the dishonorable mutilation of defenseless men, turned away so as not to witness the final annihilation of the Texians.[4]

. . .

SANTA ANNA DICTATED his report, addressed to His Excellency the Secretary of War and Navy.

"Most Excellent Sir—Victory belongs to the army, which, at this very moment, 8 o'clock A.M., achieved a complete and glorious triumph that will render its memory imperishable."

Not content to claim victory, Santa Anna went on to improve upon the facts. He exaggerated the strength of the Texians, more than tripling their numbers, to make his success sound all the greater.

"Among the corpses are those of Bowie and Travis, who styled themselves colonels, and also that of Crockett," his report said. That much was true, but when he cited Mexican losses—"70 men killed and 309 wounded"—he told less than the truth.[5] The Texians had actually killed or wounded 521 Mexicans, wiping out more than a third of Santa Anna's finest fighters.

Santa Anna's claim that the victory was glorious may have fooled his superiors, but his men knew better. As one of his officers remarked, "With another victory such as this, we'll go to the devil."[6]

MRS. DICKINSON, WITNESS

Captured and watched over by an armed Mexican guard, the women and children of the Alamo huddled in a corner of the chapel. Susanna Dickinson held her terrified daughter, Angelina, to her breast. When a Mexican officer came looking for the lone Anglo woman in the Alamo, he spoke to her in English.

"Are you Mrs. Dickinson?"

Though in shock from the carnage of the preceding hour and mourning her husband, she managed to acknowledge that she was.

"If you wish to save your life," the officer commanded, "follow me."

She limped along behind him, her leg bleeding from a wound sustained when a bullet fragment ricocheted and struck her calf.

She would remember that walk the rest of her life. "As we passed through the enclosed ground in front of the church," she told an interviewer many decades later, "I saw heaps of dead and dying." One had been her friend, a man "frequently an inmate" in her home.[7] That was the great Crockett—and here he was, beside her path, mutilated but recognizable, his "peculiar cap" on the ground beside him. She had enjoyed his fiddling, and just days before, contemplating the coming battle, he had confided in the pretty, black-haired lady. As a man of the great wide open, Crockett never expected his life to end penned up like cattle. "I don't like being hemmed up," he told her.[8]

The guard escorted her to Santa Anna himself.

Despite being afraid for her life, she unexpectedly met with something like kindness. The general ordered the woman's wound dressed while the two spoke through an interpreter. As he asked her mother questions, the fifteen-month-old daughter, blithely unaware of who the dark-eyed man in the uniform was, engaged the hard-hearted general.

Utterly charmed by the pretty child who climbed onto his lap, Santa Anna decided she should be taken back to Mexico. She would be educated properly, he told her mother. He promised to provide generously for the child; she would be raised like the heir of a nobleman.

Yet even the shock of all that had happened wasn't enough to persuade Susanna Dickinson to hand over the care of all she had left in the world to the man responsible for the death of her husband. Though barely into her twenties, having lived the hard life of a frontier settler, she held her head high. She found the courage to refuse and waited to hear how Santa Anna would respond.

To her surprise, he did not react with the cruelty she'd expected. To the other women, Santa Anna gave a blanket and two silver dollars each before dismissing them.⁹ But Mrs. Dickinson, who had outright rejected his larger gesture of charity, got different treatment, not violence, but a kind of psychological punishment. Summoning a servant, he ordered him to accompany Susanna Dickinson, taking Angelina with her, to carry a message to her fellow Texians.

The letter—though addressed to "the inhabitants of Texas," the true addressee should have been Sam Houston—would justify what his army had done to the "parcel of audacious adventurers" at the Alamo.¹⁰ But the messenger herself would underscore his message. Santa Anna forced the widow of a man he had killed to do his bidding, to carry a message justifying his actions.

BURYING THE DEAD

That afternoon, Santa Anna dealt with the dead. His men collected the remains of the Mexicans killed in the battle. They would be buried in the Catholic burial ground.

For the Texians, Santa Anna had in mind only desecration.

He ordered his cavalrymen to drag the corpses of the defeated defenders away from the Alamo. Taken to the east of the town, they were piled with the remains of the Texian fighters who had attempted to make their escape on the Gonzales road.

The mayor of San Antonio led a company of dragoons to collect firewood and dry branches from nearby stands of trees. When they returned, the first of the Anglo dead had been dragged into a heap; the freshly collected mesquite and cottonwood was piled on top. Another layer of the dead came next and, on the return of the dragoons with a second load of wood, the pile grew higher as more fuel was added. By the time the job was done, there were three large bonfires containing layers of wood and some sixty bodies each.

At five o'clock that evening the Mexicans lit the funeral pyres. By Mayor Ruiz's count, "the men burnt numbered one hundred and eighty-two. I was an eyewitness."[11]

As fire blazed that evening, a small company of cavalrymen escorted Susanna and Angelina, along with the servant, out of San Antonio. From her seat on a mule, Mrs. Dickinson left the ruin of the Alamo behind. The little party passed the pyres and the unmistakable smell of burning flesh. In the wan light of the setting sun, vultures circled overhead.

TEN

Houston Hears the News

The capture of the Alamo . . . gave us a prodigious moral prestige. . . . The attainment of our goal [is] now almost certain.

—General Antonio López de Santa Anna

I n the year 1836, news traveled across Texas only as quickly as an express rider could carry it. That meant Colonel Travis's appeal for help, written on Thursday, March 3, arrived in Washington-on-the-Brazos three days later. The courier interrupted breakfast in the newly designated capital on the same Sunday morning that the Alamo had awakened to an overwhelming assault.

Though the new government of Texas had adjourned until Monday, a special session was immediately called to order to hear what the chair called "a communication of the most important character ever received by any assembly of men."[1]

Travis's letter was read aloud. "At least two hundred shells have fallen inside of our works. . . . The spirits of my men are still high. . . . We have contended for ten days against an enemy whose numbers are variously estimated from fifteen hundred to six thousand men. . . . I look to the colonies alone for aid . . . unless it arrives soon, I shall have to fight the enemy on its own terms. . . . Our supply of ammunition is limited."[2]

No one in the room knew these lines had been written by a man now dead. But his closing words—*"God and Texas—Victory or Death"*—inspired delegate Robert Potter to get to his feet. Another second-chance man—a North Carolinian by birth and former U.S. congressman (he had fled west after castrating two men he suspected of consorting with his wife)—Potter made a motion that "the Convention do immediately adjourn, arm, and march to the relief of the Alamo."[3]

The new nation's commander in chief of the Armies of the Republic, Sam Houston, rose to disagree. Houston's instincts told him that this moment meant everything: "The next movement made in the Convention," he believed, "would be likely to decide the fate of Texas."

Major General Houston had the floor and, with all eyes on him, he denounced the idea as "madness, worse than treason." Having just declared Texas independent, he argued, if the convention went to war before setting up a structure for the new country, they would set themselves up for disaster. "There must be a government, and it must have organic form," he argued; "without it, they would be nothing but outlaws, and could hope neither for the sympathy nor respect of mankind."

At his eloquent best, Houston spoke for an hour—and made the men around him a promise. The delegates should "feel no alarm," he advised. He pledged that he himself would head to Gonzales to rally the militia, that he would defend Texas, and that the enemy would have to march over his "dead body."[4] If Santa Anna wanted to destroy rebel Texas, Houston saw his job as ensuring it survived.

One hour later, dressed in a Cherokee coat, he mounted his horse, a saber hanging at one side, a flintlock pistol jammed into his belt on the other. Together with his aide-de-camp and three volunteers, Houston headed out on the open prairie. Though he was a general without an army, the fight had just become Sam Houston's.

WHEN GENERAL HOUSTON arrived in Gonzales, at four o'clock on the afternoon of March 11, he found 374 men, many without guns or ammunition; two usable cannons; and rations for just two days. Before dark the news got worse: Two Mexicans appeared telling a terrible tale, reporting the Alamo captured, its defenders all dead.

Wanting to avoid panic in the town, Houston publicly dismissed the report and took the two men into custody. But the word had already spread and, on hearing of the slaughter, twenty volunteers deserted. To quell the alarm, Houston ordered his officers to mix with the volunteers and pass the word that the two Mexicans were spies.

Privately he believed the story to be true. The day before, drawing on his Cherokee training, he had paused to put his ear to the ground on the way to Gonzales. He expected to hear the reverberation of guns, which for days had been "a dull rumbling rumor . . . booming over the prairie like distant thunder." When he rose from the ground, Houston had heard "not the faintest murmur" from the hard-packed prairie soil.[5]

He wrote immediately to Colonel Fannin; if the Alamo was gone, then the only other organized military force of any size was Fannin's Goliad garrison. Informing Fannin of the reported fate of the Alamo, Houston admitted he worried the "melancholy [report]" was true. He ordered Fannin to retreat, to move his force to the town of Victoria.[6]

Houston, on the morning of March 13, dispatched the reliable Deaf Smith, who knew the territory well, to "proceed within sight" of San Antonio. He wanted the facts of what had happened at the Alamo, and Smith, along with Henry Karnes, promised Houston they could make it to San Antonio and back in three days.[7]

· · ·

ONLY HOURS WERE REQUIRED. Returning at twilight, the entourage led by Deaf Smith made a strange sight emerging from the darkness. He rode in with a child in his arms, a woman riding alongside.

Just twenty miles west of Gonzales, Smith had met up with Mrs. Dickinson; she was, in Houston's words, a "stricken and bereaved messenger." Taken to his private tent, where Houston took her hand, she recounted "her fearful narrative of the butchering and burning." The earlier reports about the "dark tragedy" at the Alamo were true.[8] Houston himself "wept like a child" as he listened to Mrs. Dickinson's narrative.[9]

To the people of Gonzales, the news hit very close to home. Two weeks before, thirty-two village men and boys had gone to the Alamo's aid; this report of their loss left twenty widows keening and many children fatherless. As one of Smith's fellow scouts reported, "Here the public and private grief was alike heavy; it sunk deep into the heart of the rudest soldier."[10]

Santa Anna had succeeded in striking fear in the hearts of those who opposed him. But he had also provoked rage. Not just Texians, but Americans in the states were appalled at the way Mexico had treated not just men fighting for liberty, but also women and children. Many of the dead had been imperfect, yet by dying they became heroes. And people who loved freedom wanted their deaths avenged.

Santa Anna had overplayed his hand. His brutality at the Alamo hadn't left Texians shaking in their boots; instead of intimidating the population of Tejas, the news brought to a boil anger and outrage even in Texians reluctant to declare for revolution. He had provided a cause that would unite the undisciplined troops, and had even caused more Americans to flow to the aid of the Texians.

He hadn't put out a fire: He had lit one.

But the fire was going to take some time to reach him, and in the meantime there was more bad news for more than the people of Gonzales. Mrs. Dickinson reported that five thousand men marched toward them. According to very recent "disagreeable intelligence," Goliad was a primary target of the large Mexican force crossing the Rio Grande. Santa Anna aimed to live up to his sworn promise "to *Take Texas or lose Mexico.*"[11]

With the Alamo no longer an obstacle in Santa Anna's path, Houston believed the Army of Texas had no choice: They would not march forward to engage the enemy but would retreat, staying alive to fight another day. Fannin's men at Goliad would have to fend for themselves.

ELEVEN

Fort Defiance

[Fannin] is an ill-fated man.

—SAM HOUSTON TO THOMAS J. RUSK, MARCH 23, 1836

On Saturday, March 12, James Fannin, commander of Goliad, received General Sam Houston's order to withdraw. The young colonel had a mixed past, having come to Texas to escape debts and the shame of flunking out of West Point. But he wanted to redeem himself, and after his success with Bowie at Concepción, he had worked hard to get what he called this "post of danger."[1] To Fannin, this reversal of plans came as a surprise.

Only a month before, he'd been instructed to fortify Goliad against the Mexicans and, at first, all had gone well. He and his men shored up the defenses of the old Spanish fort, built on the highest hill in the vicinity. Three-foot-thick stone walls, standing eight to ten feet in height, enclosed some three and a half acres that held a church, a barracks, and a handful of other buildings. They rebuilt the fort's gate and secured its water supply. The Mexicans had called it La Bahía, but the Texians renamed it Fort Defiance, and here Fannin martialed the men who had marched from all over the United States to fight for Texas, happy to consider himself the main obstacle to the Mexicans.

But things had gone wrong, too. First, there had been the indecision at helping the men trapped in the Alamo. When Travis had called for help ("In this extremity, we hope you will send us all the men you can spare promptly"), Fannin's immediate instinct had been to go to the rescue of his brothers-in-arms.[2] Then the march to San Antonio had ended prematurely, just one day in, with wagon failures and a vote by

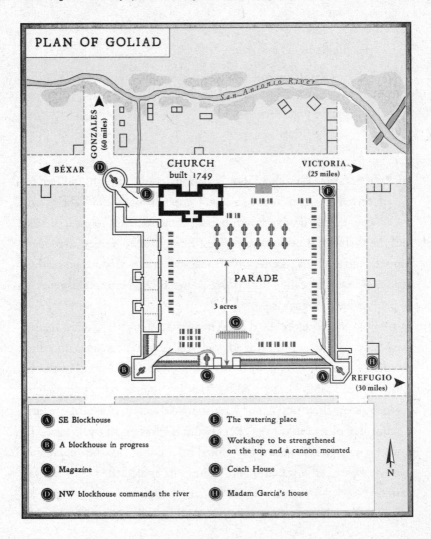

PLAN OF GOLIAD

San Antonio River

GONZALES (60 miles)

◄ BÉXAR   Ⓓ

CHURCH
built 1749

VICTORIA (25 miles) ►

Ⓔ

Ⓕ

PARADE

3 acres

Ⓖ

Ⓑ

Ⓒ

Ⓐ

Ⓗ

REFUGIO (30 miles) ►

Ⓐ SE Blockhouse

Ⓑ A blockhouse in progress

Ⓒ Magazine

Ⓓ NW blockhouse commands the river

Ⓔ The watering place

Ⓕ Workshop to be strengthened on the top and a cannon mounted

Ⓖ Coach House

Ⓗ Madam García's house

N

Fannin's officers to abandon the mission. They had returned to Fort Defiance in the freezing rain, leaving Travis and his men to prepare to fight their own battle.

Soon after, Fannin began to run out of supplies. He spent many hours writing long letters to the new government. Like Travis, he begged for promised supplies. He reported his men were hungry and ill clothed, but got little response. He had difficulties disciplining his men—some refused to obey him. But he put the best face on things when he wrote to his sometime business partner, on the last day of February, immediately after the aborted rescue trip to the Alamo. "I will never give up the ship," he wrote. "If I am whipped, it will be *well done*—and you may never expect to see me. . . . I am too mad . . . to do—any thing but fight."[3]

Now, as Fannin read Houston's orders—and as Mexican general Urrea and his army approached—he harbored doubts. Humbled and now hesitant, Fannin wondered if perhaps his strengths "[do] not constitute me a commander."[4] The man who had sworn never to leave his post was now ready to retreat, but there was a practical obstacle.

RETREAT

Houston expected him to move, but the previous day, Fannin had sent a small force of two dozen men, along with most of Fort Defiance's wagons, to Refugio, a village thirty miles away, to help evacuate settlers before the Mexicans arrived. Concerned for his men and settlers, Fannin decided the soldiers at Goliad would have to wait for the party's return.

Then two more couriers arrived from Gonzales. Exhausted from their thirty-hour ride, they handed over another letter from Sam Houston, informing Fannin that the Alamo had fallen.

Reading that "the bodies of the Americans were burned after the massacre" was a body blow.[5] He had failed to help Travis, Crockett, Bowie, and the rest. He had done nothing and now some of Texas's greatest fighters were dead.

Just after midnight on Sunday morning, March 13, still another messenger interrupted the quiet night, this one from Refugio. He brought more bad news: The wagons full of retreating settlers had run into Urrea's advance cavalry. Though they'd managed to escape capture and take shelter in an old church, they were trapped and desperately needed reinforcements. Before daylight, at Fannin's order, reinforcements galloped south to help.

They did their job well, driving off the outnumbered Mexicans by three o'clock that afternoon. But Fannin, back at Fort Defiance, could only watch the horizon, seeing no messenger with news of his troops' fate. And a second travel day was lost, one that might have been spent obeying Houston's orders to move what had become a key part of his army out of harm's way.

On Monday, Fannin sent a scout to Refugio to learn the fate of the men he'd sent. What he couldn't know was that, defying Fannin's order to return, one of his officers had chosen to attack a nearby encampment of Spanish settlers rumored to be spies. All Fannin knew was that his courier did not return and, with the setting sun, three days had passed since the order to retreat.

Tuesday brought no news so, on Wednesday, now four days after receiving Houston's order, Fannin sent one last messenger, this one a Captain Frazer, who pledged that, given "a good horse . . . if alive, [I will] return in twenty-four hours, with intelligence." True to his word, Captain Frazer reappeared at four o'clock the following day—with the worst news possible. Their powder soaked by an attempt to cross the river, a contingent of Fannin's men had surrendered. The Mexicans, ignoring the rules of war, did as they had at the Alamo, massacring the captives on the open prairie.

In the absence of commanding general Houston, Fannin held a council with his officers. They had no clear sense of their enemy—were they facing two hundred or four hundred or a thousand men? Now that their pointless wait for the return of the others was over, they decided the best course was to evacuate Fort Defiance the next day, an action, in looking back, he probably should have taken in the first place.

But, as they prepared to head out the next morning, Fannin delayed yet again. After spotting a Mexican cavalry patrol, a cat-and-mouse fight unfolded with Texians and Mexicans playing a deadly and time-consuming game of pursuit-and-retreat. The result was another day lost.

Finally, at nine o'clock on Saturday, March 19, after a full week's delay in following orders, a line of three hundred troops marched out of Fort Defiance. Oxen pulled heavily loaded wagons and carts carrying baggage and the sick, as well as a half dozen cannons, a brass howitzer, and hundreds of spare muskets. As a parting gesture, the Texians put the torch to the town, leaving "the half-destroyed buildings of the fort, still overhung with dark clouds of smoke from the smouldering flames."[6]

RETREAT FROM GOLIAD

The San Antonio River presented the first obstacle to the fleeing Texians. The horsemen and infantry crossed the shallow water easily. But some of the draft animals balked at climbing the muddy east bank, and one of the largest of the cannons tumbled into the river.

The Alabama Red Rovers in the vanguard turned back. Putting down their guns, they waded into the water; putting their shoulders to the wheels, they helped push the rest of the cannons up the steep and slippery slope. But forward progress slowed to a halt and the men's determination flagged—just as had happened on the aborted mission to the Alamo weeks earlier.

Despite the delay, advance scouts reported that the due-east escape route was still clear. General Urrea apparently remained unaware of the Texian evacuation. On clearing the river, the Texians trudged on. But men and officers alike recognized that the large quantities of goods they carried held them back and began to jettison their supplies. "Before we had gone half a mile," reported one of the New Orleans Greys, "our track was marked by objects of various kinds scattered about the road, and several carts had broken down or been left behind."[7]

Six miles on, Colonel Fannin decided to rest the oxen, which showed signs of becoming "wild and contrary."[8] While the animals grazed on a patch of green grass, the men rested—and the officers argued.

Several took exception to Fannin's order to halt the line of march in the middle of open prairie. Coleto Creek lay less than five miles away, its banks lined with trees, which offered a defensive situation quite like that at Concepción. *Better there than here,* some thought. *We should press on.* One Alabama captain, Jack Shackelford, argued vehemently for "the necessity of getting under the *protection of timber*" as soon as possible.[9] But Fannin rejected Shackelford's pleas. Having prevailed once in a fight with the Mexicans, he clung to the desperate belief that he could beat them again. Shackelford was overruled, and an hour elapsed before the march resumed at one o'clock.

Fannin's little army crossed another stream, the Manahuilla Creek, and three miles further on, with the tree line at Coleto Creek now in plain view, several soldiers in the rear guard noticed "something that resembled a man on horseback."

When the silhouette remained motionless, the scouts decided the object "must be a tree or some other inanimate object."[10]

Some minutes later, they squinted hard at a barely distinguishable thin black line along the horizon. Again the lookouts decided there was nothing to fear, maybe just a herd of cattle. But soon a black mass, growing larger by the moment, took on the unmistakable shape of men on horseback. It was Urrea's cavalry.

Fannin reacted immediately, ordering artillerymen with a six-pound cannon to move to the rear of the column and fire on what the Texians could now see were two companies of Mexican cavalry and one of infantry. The cannon fire fell short, and Fannin, convinced the Mexicans planned only to skirmish and plunder the Texian supplies, ordered his men to keep marching toward the cover offered by the wooded riverbank, now less than two miles ahead. As ordered, the Texians "marched onward, cool and deliberately," so as not to spook the oxen.[11]

Once again, however—this time for the last time—an equipment failure brought Fannin's column to a standstill. An ammunition cart broke down, and with no time for repairs, Fannin saw no alternative. The fight would have to happen here.

He tried to make the best of a bad situation, and he ordered his men to establish a perimeter. Unable to move to higher ground, the Texians occupied a small depression, several feet lower in altitude than the surrounding prairie. Stands of trees were within sight but unreachable.

The Texian defense took the shape of a hollow square. Needing cover, they arranged piles of cargo and the wagons around its perimeter, then shot some of the oxen, using the carcasses to fill some of the gaps in an improvised breastwork. Fannin had cannons positioned in the corners of the square, manned by four artillery companies. They finished setting up their improvised defense not a moment too soon; by this time a second Mexican force was in sight to the north, maneuvering into a position to prevent the Texians from reaching the creek.

Left outside the defenses were several hospital wagons full of wounded. Frightened by the oncoming army, Mexican wagon drivers, who had been working for the Texians, had abandoned their carts and headed for the Mexican line, leaving the frightened steers to run where they would. Now the wagons were stranded, about fifty yards outside the defensive square, vulnerable to the approaching Mexicans.

There was no time to bring them back, but one of the orderlies assigned to caring for the wounded, Abel Morgan, refused to abandon them. He got himself a musket from a munitions wagon inside the defensive square and sprinted back to his wagon, along with four other volunteers. They positioned themselves to defend the wounded in the fight that, everyone knew, was only minutes away.

In the moments before the battle began, the Texians gazed out on an intimidating array of the enemy, which now virtually surrounded their improvised defensive position. The rules of engagement had changed in one major way: With many of their oxen now dead, the Texians were going nowhere. They had no choice but to make their stand.

THE BATTLE OF THE PRAIRIE

As the Mexican army approached, Colonel Fannin ordered his troops to hold their fire. He didn't want to hear the report of a Texian rifle until the enemy was in point-blank range—there was no ammunition to spare.

The first of General Urrea's men moved on what had been the front of the advancing Texian column. Mexican cavalrymen, now dismounted, marched forward and, from a distance of some two hundred yards, unleashed their first volley. No men fell, but the Mexicans continued to advance. When their second volley went "whizzing over our heads," Captain Shackelford ordered his men to sit down for cover. The third volley drew blood, with several Texians hit by musket balls.

Fannin issued "orders . . . in a calm and decided manner," despite

Serving under General Andrew Jackson at the Battle at Horseshoe Bend in 1814, Sam Houston famously ordered another officer to pull a Creek arrow from his thigh. Jackson's army won the battle, but hundreds of lives were lost—and Houston paid a high price for his drive to win.

General Andrew Jackson was a mentor and father figure to young Houston. Even after Jackson's victory at New Orleans ended America's years-long war with Britain, he remained a mentor to Houston, encouraging him in his quest for Texas.

When President Thomas Jefferson made the Louisiana Purchase in 1803, he thought Texas was part of the deal. He later predicted, "The province of Te[x]as will be the richest state of our Union."

John Quincy Adams was the man who, in Andrew Jackson's judgment, gave away Texas.

Sam Houston spent some of his childhood years with the Cherokee nation, and he found refuge with them again as an adult when he fell from grace in Washington. To his Indian friends, he was known by the name Co-lon-neh ("the Raven"), and he is shown here wearing a turban after the Cherokee custom.

When Houston first arrived in Texas in the hopes of winning it for America, he knew he had to meet Stephen F. Austin, the "Father of Texas." In this mural, which is now unfortunately destroyed, Austin is shown distributing land deeds to new, ambitious Texas settlers from the United States.

William Howard painted Stephen F. Austin, in 1833, as a settler, Empresario, hunter, and statesman. The open book at Austin's feet is a copy of the Law of Mexico.

Mexican general Antonio Lópes de Santa Anna liked
to be thought of as the "Napoleon of the West,"
and his attempt to consolidate his power once he
rose to prominence in Mexico was partially
responsible for the Texians' rebellion.

General Martín Perfecto de Cos, as pictured in this contemporary woodcut, was one of the first of Santa Anna's commanders to attempt to suppress the Texian rebels. After hearing that Santa Anna had dispatched Cos and his army of 500 to march along the San Antonio River to preempt Texian resistance, Stephen Austin declared "war in full."

The Texas Revolution's "Lexington and Concord" moment took place at Gonzales, as pictured here in a modern reimagining. During this first battle of the Texas Revolution, the Texian army collected the few guns they had and hung a six-foot flag large enough to be seen from enemy lines that read, "COME AND TAKE IT." Even though outnumbered and outgunned, the Texians won their first victory over the Mexicans at Gonzales.

A major landholder and a man with nearly the status of Stephen Austin, brave Ben Milam had a long history in Texas. When he heard that the Texian rebellion had finally begun, "his heart was full" at the thought of a band of volunteers working together to fight off the Mexicans. His life ended prematurely at the Siege of San Antonio.

Like Houston, James Bowie was a "second chance man" who came to Texas searching for a new life. Known for his knife-fighting and alligator-riding abilities, Bowie led his men to victory at Concepción, but perished at the Battle of the Alamo.

William Barrett Travis, commander of the Alamo, pictured here as sketched by fellow soldier Wiley Martin in December 1835, also perished at the Battle of the Alamo—after pledging to fight until the very end.

Known as "Deaf," Erastus Smith was a resident of San Antonio before proving invaluable to Sam Houston as a spy and messenger. After he became president of Texas, Houston acknowledged Smith's contribution, commissioning T. Jefferson Wright to paint this portrait.

For Colonel James W. Fannin, a West Point dropout, Texas held the promise of a new life—one where he could pay off his debts and renew his reputation. As commander at Goliad, he displayed his bravery and conviction for the cause of Texian independence—but also a lack of decisiveness that would have a deadly cost. Here, Fannin poses for a portrait that was likely painted during his days at West Point.

Like Houston, Bowie, and Fannin, David Crockett came to Texas looking for a second chance. The former Congressman, known for his back-country character and for his tall tales, was among those killed at the Alamo.

Despite Houston's wishes, a small crew of Texians attempted to defend San Antonio from Santa Anna's army of 3,500. The odds were against them, but they agreed to fight to the death—a fight that later would be memorialized by many artists.

Perhaps the best of the Mexican generals—unlike Santa Anna and Cos, he lost none of his battles in Tejas—José de Urrea was the victor at the Battle of Coleto, the fight that led to the execution of the hundreds captured at Goliad.

Even though they were far outnumbered by Santa Anna's army, the Texians were not intimidated. When they saw the Mexicans approaching, they immediately fired their biggest cannon, an eighteen-pounder, with a great, resounding boom. This image of the fight at the Alamo suggests something of the furor of the battle.

During the massacre, Santa Anna employed Napoleon's tactics. While his army overwhelmed the Texians in manpower and artillery and surrounded the Alamo, Santa Anna remained an observer. Even with Colonel Travis dead and Bowie weak with disease trapped inside the mission, the Texians fought until the end. The mythologizing of the Alamo has resulted in many later images like this one, which pictures the Alamo in flames. The artist in this case took many liberties, among them a burning building that little resembles the Alamo as it looked in 1836.

Susanna, the young wife—and widow—of Almeron Dickinson was among the few Texian survivors of the Alamo Massacre. Wounded during the battle, she refused Santa Anna's offer to take her and her daughter back to Mexico and instead was tasked with carrying a message from Santa Anna to the Texians. Here, she's pictured late in life.

Not long after the massacre at the Alamo, General Urrea's army perpetrated another massacre of Texians at Goliad. After promising their safety, Urrea's men marched the unsuspecting Texian prisoners from Goliad to their execution.

THE GOLIAD MASSACRE.

Not long after the slaughter of his men, Goliad commander James Fannin faced a Mexican firing squad.

In the weeks leading up to the final battle of America's fight for Texas, Houston employed a strategy of retreat—nearly losing the trust of his army. The strategy kept the Texian army safe until they attacked Santa Anna's army in the Battle of San Jacinto.

Houston delivered the most rousing speech of his lifetime before the Battle of San Jacinto, declaring: "We will meet the enemy. Some of us may be killed and must be killed; but soldiers, remember the Alamo, *the Alamo, the Alamo*!"

During the battle, Houston twice had his horse shot out from under him, as depicted in this detail from McArdle's *Battle of San Jacinto*. The second time, Houston himself was also shot, taking a musket ball to his ankle.

After the defeat of the Mexicans in just eighteen minutes
and their subsequent capture, Houston, shown here nursing
his wounded leg, negotiated terms of surrender in the
shade of a tree hung with Spanish moss.

A late-in-life photograph of Santa Anna,
who survived his defeat at San Jacinto
to take power again (and again) in
Mexican politics. He lived to age eighty.

A Mathew Brady photograph of the sixty-eight-year-old Houston. By 1861, he had once again become a national figure, having served in the U.S. Senate after his short-lived nation became the state of Texas. A city had been named for him, too. He died in Huntsville, Texas, in 1863.

Few men remained in the ranks of the Old Texian Veterans when, in 1906, they gathered at Goliad to commemorate the seventieth anniversary of the battle. Just six survivors attended what would be the last reunion.

the tension.[12] As he stood just behind the front line, reminding his men to hold their fire, he narrowly missed death. A musket ball blasted away the hammer of his rifle, disabling the gun but leaving him unhurt.

At a distance of a hundred yards, the enemy halted to reload their guns. Fannin saw his moment: At last, he ordered his men to open fire.

Despite a hail of bullets, balls, and cannonballs, the Mexicans, some of whom had fought at the Alamo, charged. With their officers prodding and directing, they advanced in the face of the musketry and the crack of the Texian rifles. Many Mexicans fell, dead and wounded, but to the Texians, uncertain of how many attackers there were—some thought five hundred, others a thousand or more—the tide of Mexicans never seemed to stop.

The firing took a toll on the Texian defenders, too. A ball struck Fannin in the thigh; though it missed the bone, it opened a serious flesh wound. But he remained standing, issuing orders.

To the rear, a second front opened when an even larger body of Mexican infantry swarmed forward to fire their first volley. Once the smoke cleared, the Texians defending the rear fired back with both rifles and cannons, "mowing [the enemy] down with tremendous slaughter."[13] The Mexican infantrymen left standing went down on their bellies, rising only to shoot at—and be shot at by—the defender's marksmen.

The orderly Abel Morgan found himself in the middle of the intense fight "where balls were whizzing about like bees swarming." Of the four men who'd joined him at the hospital wagons, one took a musket to the skull; it opened a hole in the man's head but didn't kill him on the spot; he handed his rifle to Morgan. Another rifleman went down, a bone in his upper leg smashed by a musket ball. One of the doctors, Joseph Barnard, came from inside Fannin's square to help defend the hospital wagons, and with his help the men held off the Mexicans.

A cavalry charge to the Texians' rear came next. More than two hundred strong, the Mexicans raced forward, lances gleaming, issuing war cries as they came. At a distance of sixty yards, they met with a barrage of rifle fire. Two loads of canister fire ripped into their ranks, and the survivors who could retreated. It would be the last cavalry charge of the day. "Many were the Mexicans I saw leave their horses that day," remembered one Texian, "who never were to mount them again."[14]

But the Texians couldn't maintain their fire. Mexican sharpshooters had targeted the artillerymen, and many lay dead or wounded. The cannons grew overheated; with no source of water to cool and swab them, their touchholes clogged. The artillery gradually went silent, leaving the Texians to rely on muskets and rifles alone.

The Mexicans made repeated charges; in the face of Texian gunfire, still doing damage without the cannons, they retreated each time. Only when darkness began to fall, more than two hours into the fighting, did the firing cease. The Mexicans withdrew, making camp in the trees at Coleto Creek a mile away.

Men and horses, wounded and dead, lay on a battlefield littered with abandoned guns and other weapons. The outmanned Texians, even without natural cover, had made the Mexicans pay dearly.

SURRENDER

With the quieting of the guns, the terrible aftersounds of battle grew audible, with the groans of the dying accompanying the cries of the wounded calling for water. There was no water to be had in the middle of the prairie, and, as one doctor reported of the injured, their "misery was greatly aggravated" by the lack of water.[15] Then the word went around there was no food. In the rush to render Goliad unusable, the food supplies had accidentally been burned in Fort Defiance.

The wounded Fannin, barely able to stand, took the counsel of his officers. There were nine Texians dead and more than fifty wounded.

Many of the oxen had wandered off and others shot by Texians and Mexicans. There were simply too few teams to transport the wounded disabled by their injuries. That made a full retreat impossible.

One option called for abandoning the wounded, spiking the guns, and taking the fight directly to the Mexican line, hoping to break through, find cover in the woods beyond, and eventually gain the road to Victoria. "Better to sacrifice a part than the whole," the argument went, better to avoid "plac[ing] ourselves at the mercy of a foe in whose honour and humanity no trust could be reposed."[16] The massacre at the Alamo taught them that.

But Fannin and most of his officers rejected the desperate plan. They refused to leave the wounded, men whose lives might be saved; if left behind, he was certain, they would face only death by bayonet. Instead, they decided, the Texians would dig in and fight on.

Fannin ordered his men to make a trench around the perimeter, and for hours men wielding shovels worked to dig a two-foot-deep ditch around the one-acre Texian camp. The carts and more animal carcasses were rearranged to provide better cover. And then the men attempted to sleep, though the night was cold, the blankets few.

The long and starless night also offered the Mexicans cover, and they could be heard retrieving the dead and wounded; their casualties far exceeded Texian losses. But the Mexicans also busied themselves in other ways. They peppered the Texian camp with occasional sniper shot from what seemed like every direction. Buglers accompanying patrols played Mexican battle songs to disrupt the sleep—and the nerves—of the Texians. General Urrea wanted to rattle his enemy.

At daylight, the Mexicans presented a new and impressive military front. Reinforcements had arrived, bringing with them two four-pound cannons and a howitzer. The artillery now stood poised, ready to fire, two hundred yards away between the Texians and the timberline, fronting a long line of Mexican troops. Fannin and his men had known they were greatly outnumbered, but this display led some to estimate the disparity was seven to one, or more, now that the Texians' effective force had been reduced to some two hundred men.

At seven o'clock the Mexican cannons roared, sending cannonballs arcing toward the Texian camp. But the firing stopped as suddenly as it had begun and, during the quiet that followed, the Mexicans did not charge. Instead, they raised a white flag, indicating not surrender, but a request for parley.

The Texians responded with a white flag of their own.

Despite his painful leg wound, Fannin limped to a midpoint on the empty prairie, accompanied by two officers. Met by three of Urrea's officers, the Texian colonel listened to their terms of surrender. The Mexicans promised the lives of the Texians would be spared, and that those who surrendered would be treated in all respects as prisoners of war consistent with the practice of civilized nations. The victors further promised to return the wounded to Goliad, where they would be properly tended, and the healthy prisoners would, in eight days, be permitted to sail from a nearby port back to the United States. In return, the Texians must lay down their guns and promise not to raise arms against Mexico in future.[17]

Houston was too far away to consult, but Fannin, his officers, and his men saw little alternative: They accepted Urrea's terms. In the face of annihilation, they opted for what they understood would be survival.

RETREAT UNDER GUARD

At first, the Mexicans remained true to their word. That afternoon—the date was March 20—they marched the Texian prisoners who were well enough to walk back to Goliad, where they arrived shortly after sunset.

At Fort Defiance, the Texian force was confined to the church.

There wasn't enough room in the small space for the hundreds of men, many of them wounded, to lie down. They huddled together, with armed Mexican guards occupying the center of the church that had become a prison.

The next day, carts ferried more wounded, including Colonel Fannin, from the field of battle back to Goliad. Meanwhile, the men shut up in the church received no food or water.

On Wednesday, the prisoners were permitted to leave their cramped quarters to sleep outdoors, and the Mexicans moved their own wounded men into the shelter of the church. The men breathed a sigh of relief in the open air and were cheered to hear that Colonel Fannin had been sent to the port of Copano to charter a schooner, the *William and Francis*, for their return.

While Fannin was gone, the Mexicans marched in more prisoners. Some of those who had gone to Refugio had been captured after their attempt to aid the settlers. The prisoner head count now exceeded four hundred men.

When he returned on Saturday, Fannin's good spirits cheered the men. He expressed confidence in their imminent release. Although the *William and Francis* had sailed, he expected another ship would soon be found to carry them to New Orleans.

On the Mexican side, however, a different end of the drama at Goliad was being discussed. General Urrea respected Fannin. He recognized that the Texians had surrendered because they trusted him; "under any other circumstances they would have sold their lives dearly, fighting to the last." Despite being under orders to take no prisoners, he had done so, and now had written to Santa Anna, seeking to use "my influence with the general-in-chief to save them if possible, from being butchered, particularly Fannin."[18]

It seems Santa Anna was not persuaded. On the morning of March 27, the eighth day of captivity, a Mexican officer summoned two of the

Texian doctors to his tent, pleasantly located in a peach orchard several hundred yards from the fort. "He was very serious and grave in countenance," one of the doctors later wrote, "but we took little notice of it at that time."[19] His purpose unclear, the officer left the doctors to wait, though they wished to get back to their patients in the fortress.

While the doctors waited in puzzlement, the Mexican soldiers, acting under orders from Santa Anna, divided the prisoners into three companies and marched them out of the fort in different directions. Reassured by rumors that a ship awaited them and they were being evacuated for the coast, some of the men departed Fort Defiance singing "Home Sweet Home," assuming they were going to freedom.

Flanked on both sides by armed soldiers, the unsuspecting Texians marched perhaps a half mile before being ordered to halt. The Mexicans then formed a line across from them, revealing themselves to be a long and efficient firing squad.

Before the Texians could react, the soldiers raised their rifles and muskets and shot their prisoners at short range. Mexican lancers and infantrymen armed with bayonets pursued any Texians who managed to survive the gunfire to turn and run.

Back at the fort, Colonel Fannin was imprisoned in a small room inside the church. He heard the executioners' volleys and was told that he, too, would be shot. His captors took him into the church courtyard, assisting him in this final walk, as the wound in his right thigh left him lame. Knowing he would soon die, he handed over his watch to the officer in charge, asking that, in return, his body might be buried. He gave the officer all the money he had and asked that the executioners not "place their muskets so near as to scorch his face with powder." The officer, in broken English, promised that Fannin's remains would be interred "with all necessary formalities."

Seated on a chair because of his leg wound, his own handkerchief covering his eyes, Fannin unbuttoned his shirt, accepting his fate. Yet, once again, the Mexicans broke their word. The firing squad shot him from a distance of two feet, and Fannin's remains were unceremoniously added to a funeral pyre with other Texians.[20]

Two dozen Texians lived, among them orderlies and doctors the Mexicans needed to care for their wounded and a few carpenters and other artisans. Some survived thanks to the intervention of a Mexican woman, Francita Alavez. The wife of a cavalry captain, she used her influence—and the unspoken approval of some Mexican officers disgusted at the needless slaughter of the Texian prisoners—to save some of the soldiers. Having secured their release the previous night, she kept them hidden.[21] Alavez would be remembered as the Angel of Goliad: As one survivor put it, "Her name deserves to be recorded in letters of gold."[22] But more than four hundred men had been murdered in cold blood.

The fortress that was Goliad now belonged to Santa Anna's army. Another atrocity had been committed in the name of El Presidente. And the ranks of Sam Houston's already small army had just become significantly smaller.

TWELVE

The Texian Exodus

There was not a man in the Alamo but what, in his death, honored the proud name of an American.

Let the men of Texas avenge their deaths.

—SAM HOUSTON TO JAMES COLLINSWORTH, MARCH 17, 1836

After he had issued his orders to Fannin, Sam Houston, then in Gonzales some sixty miles north, worried and wondered. "I am fearful Goliad is besieged by the enemy," he confided to a fellow officer.[1] It would be weeks before he learned of Fannin's fate, and in the meantime, more immediate worries occupied his mind.

In mid-March, with the Alamo gone and the status of Fannin and his men uncertain, Houston understood that the survival of the republic depended on the few men he still had at his command. When Mrs. Dickinson told him of the fall of the Alamo, she warned that as many as *five thousand* Mexican troops were on the march; with a force of less than a tenth that size, there was no way the Texians, at least for the moment, could afford to face down the enemy. In short, Houston and his troops needed to get out of the reach of Santa Anna's army. For the moment, at least, there was only one wise strategy: Retreat.

No time could be wasted. The army would travel light, he decreed, telling his troops to take only what they could carry on their persons. He had the men sink two unwieldy cannons—his only artillery—in the Guadalupe River. Extra clothing and supplies were ordered left behind.

Left without army protection, the civilians had no choice but to retreat, too. Knowing the Mexicans could not be trusted not to punish civilians, Houston ordered that most of the army's baggage wagons and oxen be given to the citizens of the town to aid in their escape.

The caravan of troops and tagalong civilians, including women and children, was on the march by midnight on Wednesday, March 16. They kept moving through the night; not until near morning did Houston order a halt for an hour's rest. As his men ate breakfast, they heard explosions from the direction of Gonzales.

Deaf Smith, along with red-headed Captain Henry Karnes and a handful of other men, had been instructed by Houston that "not a roof large enough to shelter a Mexican's head was to be left, [along] with everything else that could be of any service to the enemy." Staying behind, Smith and his men had placed canisters of gunpowder in the houses before lighting the town on fire.

All of Texas was at stake and Houston didn't want to leave *anything* that would be of use to Santa Anna.

MARCHING TOWARD THE COLORADO RIVER, which he wanted to put between his army and the Mexicans, General Houston worked hard to keep morale up. He made sure the men saw him, riding slowly from the front to the rear of the column, wagging his forefinger as he went, counting his troops. On the way to the rear of the column, he was heard to say, "We are the rise of eight hundred strong, and with a good position can whip ten to one of the enemy."[2]

By sundown on March 17, the caravan reached the Colorado, and the Army of Texas camped at Burnham Crossing. As the moon rose,

Houston sat before a flickering fire. He held a knife in one hand, an oak stick in the other, nervously whittling and talking quietly with an aide, George Washington Hockley, a friend from Tennessee days.

When he had let his head count be overheard, Houston had exaggerated; his numbers and his confident words, he hoped, would keep spirits up. In fact, his army numbered more like six hundred men, including a hundred-odd new volunteers who'd joined the march that day.

Houston had also exaggerated when he had said that his Texians were ten times the fighters the Mexicans were. Most of his men were raw recruits. "It would have been madness to have hazarded a contest," Houston believed. "The first principles of the drill had not been taught the men."[3] He also needed to rein in the overeager men who were outraged at the retreat, those who wanted to fight the enemy at the first opportunity. They wanted revenge for the Alamo; he wanted to win the war. Fighting too soon could risk everything.

To shape a disciplined fighting force, he needed, above all, time. He needed to establish discipline, to practice formations, to teach his troops how to attack and withdraw. He must rely on speed and mobility—and surprise—and that required practiced coordination. "Our forces must not be shut in forts," Houston believed.[4] Even before Travis and his men had met their end at the Alamo, Houston had learned that lesson at Horseshoe Bend fighting with Andrew Jackson. Even a good fortification is not impregnable.

In the morning, the river crossing began in a heavy rain; with Mexicans in pursuit, the Texians couldn't afford to wait for the sky to clear. Families first, Houston ordered, and the fleeing citizens, numbering more than a thousand, carrying what little they could, took turns going aboard the flat-topped vessel to be poled to the Colorado's east bank. Next Texian troops crowded onto the ferry's broad deck, which shuttled back and forth all day.

The rain swelled what was already a wide, deep, and fast-moving watercourse; no Mexican army could get troops and supplies across by crossing the Colorado under these conditions. And Houston, his entourage safely on the river's left bank, made sure. He ordered the ferry set afire. With its useless remains on the bottom of the Colorado River, he had just bought his army some time.

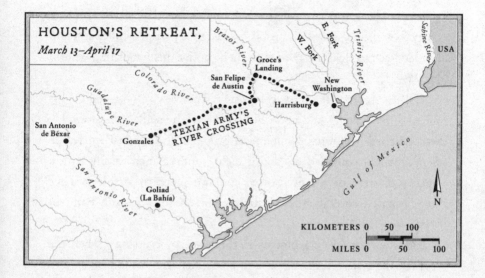

THE ENEMY ACROSS THE WATER

Two days after Houston's army established camp on the other side of the river, Deaf Smith caught up with Houston. Dressed in his battered hat, ragged shoes, and oversized pantaloons he could hardly have looked less military. But he had done his job and more: While the army's officers marched and drilled the army, Houston's little spy company, led by Smith and Henry Karnes, had been on the move, constantly on the lookout for the enemy. When they observed fresh horse tracks in the saturated sandy soil a few miles from the camp, they guessed a band of enemy scouts had passed within the hour.

After checking their guns, they set off in pursuit. The Mexicans tried to flee, but in an exchange of fire, one enemy rider was killed, a horse was lamed by a pistol shot—and the Texians got themselves a prisoner. The rest of the Mexicans got away, but the Texian scouting party took the dead lancer's pistols, picked up a pair of saddlebags, and headed back to Beason's Ford with their captive, his hands tied behind his back.

Karnes escorted the man to Houston. The Mexican begged for his life and, after being told he would be spared, he spilled his story. He was attached to a force commanded by General Joaquín Ramírez de Sesma, which consisted of "six or eight hundred men" along with a cavalry of sixty or seventy horses and two pieces of artillery. They were camped several miles upstream but on the opposite bank of the Colorado.

Houston posted detachments at three nearby crossings; when the level of the river fell in the days to come, his army would be able to cross it. Meanwhile, the usual hot-blooded officers were keen to take the offensive. Some men who had eagerly awaited a strong leader to take charge of the army began to doubt whether Houston was the right man after all, and a few quiet voices questioned his bravery, asking aloud whether Houston wasn't a coward for not immediately engaging Sesma's force. But cooler heads understood, as one captain put it, that "there are times when it requires more courage to retreat than to stand and fight."[5] A few soldiers deserted in frustration, but, since Houston held the reins, for the next several days his army made no major moves.

Couriers came and went, bringing disheartening news. To Houston's shock, he learned that the government of the Texas republic had also retreated. When word of the Alamo debacle reached Washington-on-the-Brazos, some delegates immediately saddled their horses and rode out of town. Others got blind drunk. The good men who stayed got down to business, convening a session of the convention that lasted until 4:00 A.M. the next morning. David G. Burnet, a transplanted New Yorker, emerged as president. Thomas Jefferson Rusk, a veteran of the Come-and-Take-It fight at Gonzales, became secretary of war. Once elected, however, the new officeholders' first order of business had been to organize a removal eastward to Harrisburg.

Houston took the government's decision as a personal insult. "It was a poor compliment to me," he wrote to Rusk, a sometime legal client of Houston's back in Nacogdoches, "to suppose I would not advise the convention" when the need arose to move.[6] If the nation's leading officers ran in panic, then wouldn't every settler do the same? Houston had seen the hardships of the Gonzales families in his party, and now he feared the panic would spread quickly.

The scenes of civilian retreat varied little, as one witness reported. "The road was filled with carts and wagons loaded with women and children, while other women, for whom there was no room in the wagons, were seen walking, some of them barefoot, some carrying their smaller children in their arms or on their backs, their other children following barefooted; and other women were again seen with but one shoe, having lost the other in the mud; some of the wagons were broken down and others again were bogged in the deep mud. Taken all in all, the sight was the most painful by far, that I ever witnessed."[7]

A Gonzales man brought more ill tidings: Fannin had surrendered. Though the ultimate fate of Goliad's defenders remained unknown to Houston, he was certain Fannin and his four hundred men could no longer be counted on to fight for Texas, imprisoned as they were in Fort Defiance. That meant not only had his army lost one wing at the Alamo but the other had been captured. Appointed commander in chief of the Armies of the Republic, Houston now had just his own command, some hundreds of men living in the cold without tents, drilling along the Colorado. It had become Texas's last best hope.

THIRTEEN

An Army Assembles

It were perhaps hyperbolical to say "the eyes of the world are upon him," but assuredly the people of Texas . . . regard his present conduct as decisive of the fate of their country.

—PRESIDENT OF TEXAS DAVID BURNET ON SAM HOUSTON

You know I am not easily depressed," Sam Houston admitted in a letter to Secretary of War Rusk, but "I have found the darkest hours of my life! . . . For forty-eight hours, I have not eaten an ounce, nor have I slept."[1]

The widespread fear that swept across Texas did produce one positive result: Houston's army began to grow rapidly. His considered strategy of retreat was beginning to win converts, as men from the more populated region of East Texas saw the risks expanding toward them; they flocked to save their homes, to fight for their families, and to stand up for the fragile new republic. The Army of Texas camped at Beason's Ford grew to eleven hundred, then twelve hundred, and the ranks continued to swell. "Men are flocking to camp," reported Houston. "In a few days my force will be highly respectable."[2]

If his wasn't yet a true fighting machine, these green volunteers, with a smattering of former American soldiers, did show signs of learning how to obey orders. One night Houston discovered for himself that the training had begun to take.

After an inspection of the camp perimeter, Houston returned well after dark. An armed sentry spied him in the gloom and demanded, "Who comes there?"

"I am General Houston," he replied. "Let me pass on."

The guard would have none of it. His orders forbade him to permit any stranger to enter the camp.

"I don't know you to be General Houston," he said, raising his gun. "Don't you move or I'll shoot."

Houston swallowed his surprise—and he couldn't help but be pleased.

"Well, my friend," Houston allowed, "if such were your orders, you are right." Houston took a seat on a nearby stump and waited patiently. Only after the officer of the day was summoned and the visitor's identity confirmed was Major General Houston permitted to reenter the camp.[3]

With boys like this one—many of Houston's soldiers were teenagers, very few aged thirty or more—he might yet lead a fine fighting force into battle with Santa Anna. Still, just as new men were coming, others were going, impatient and tired, returning to their homes. Somehow Sam Houston had to hold this army together. He had to keep his volunteers with him—and avoid confronting his larger and more experienced enemy.

THE ENEMY

Santa Anna expressed no regrets. "The capture of the Alamo," as he saw it, "gave us a prodigious moral prestige. Our name terrified the enemy, and . . . they fled disconcerted."[4]

The victory also made the Mexican want to go home, believing he had accomplished his goal of suppressing the uprising. But after consulting with his generals—some of whom argued the fight had only begun—His Excellency accepted that he had business to finish in Texas. And a tricky business it was.

On the one hand, he wanted to avoid provoking a fight with Andrew Jackson and the United States. That the American president coveted Texas was hardly a secret, and the longer Santa Anna stayed and the closer he got to the Louisiana border, the greater was the risk of escalating what, in his opinion, was a matter for the Mexican nation. Although he hoped that many of his troops would settle in Texas after the war, he would bring the fight to a rapid and, if necessary, brutal close.

Santa Anna wasn't wrong to worry about President Jackson: Sam Houston's mentor still shared his interests in Texas's independence. In not-so-far-away Washington, as news of the fighting in Texas reached him, Jackson considered his country's western boundaries, looking down his hawk-like nose at the map of the country he wanted to expand. If Texan refugees—most of them American—began to pour into the United States, he might well have the excuse to engage Mexico and wrest control of Texas on the battlefield. And maybe more than Texas? Jackson's generals—one of whom was poised very near that border— kept him in the picture and, though his on-the-record instructions were measured, General Jackson and his former aide-de-camp Sam Houston understood one another as only old friends can.

Santa Anna had spent weeks at San Antonio after the fight at the Alamo. It was a civilized place, where he found a young woman for company and he contented himself with shaping a plan. Three divisions of his army would march on the enemy. In order to drive the rebels out of Tejas, he aimed at the more populous East Texas. One force would take a northern route. The second, led by General Urrea, would veer south to capture Goliad before continuing toward the coast to take control of the port towns and shut off Texian sources of supply. The third and largest expeditionary force, led by Santa Anna himself, would be the tip of the arrow. Then the separate forces would reunite along the Brazos River and pursue the rebel army to its end.

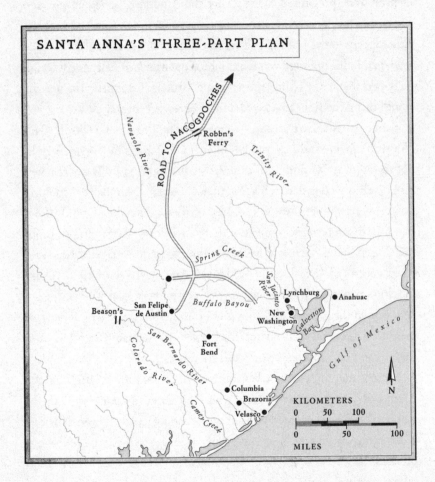

SANTA ANNA'S THREE-PART PLAN

A MISERY OF MUD

Fearing the Mexicans now knew his whereabouts and might destroy his army before they were ready, Houston and his army stole into the night on March 26. To mislead any Mexican scouts keeping watch at a distance, the Texians lit blazing campfires before they slipped into the shadows. A few infantry sentinels remained behind as the rest of the army began the trek toward San Felipe de Austin. Five miles later the troops rested, waiting while the pickets caught up, then resumed the march.

But the tide of soldiers had turned again in recent days. The ranks of the army now shrank, with more men drifting away than arriving. Fannin's capture hadn't helped, and a growing number of men wondered at the prospects of the campaign in the face of Santa Anna's army; some reported the enemy force numbered in the tens of thousands. Worse yet, Houston was still falling back, meaning more families would be left exposed as the battle line shifted east. Many of the departing soldiers left to return to their homes to help loved ones. Noah Smithwick, veteran of the Battle of Gonzales, described the abandoned homesteads he saw. "Houses were standing open, the beds unmade, the breakfast things still on the tables, pans of milk moulding in dairies."[5] Countless settlers up and ran for their lives.

For the families, the journey posed immense dangers and hardships. Just ten at the time, one girl later recalled her father piling the family into a wagon. She and her three sisters, including a three-month-old baby, left almost everything behind, including the ten-year-old's treasured books. On the journey they witnessed death and illness, experienced dangerous river crossings and all-night travels, and ended up with nothing but "what clothes we were wearing." Fear was a constant; in the midst of the trip, they learned of the terrible events at Goliad. One night her father, a veteran of the War of 1812, recognized the boom of cannon fire not so far in the distance. By early April, she later wrote, "we were as wretched as we could be; for we had been five weeks from home, and there was not much prospect of our ever returning."[6]

For families and soldiers alike, the retreat wasn't easy. No true roads existed in Texas, only paths through undeveloped lands made by travelers on foot, horseback, and cart. The name by which many such routes were commonly known—"trace"—was accurate. A journey of any distance was a slog, since the traces were frequently interrupted by rivers, creeks, and bayous, few of which were spanned by bridges.

Despite the difficulties, Houston persisted in drawing the men back. Perhaps he considered the Alamo proof that his strategy of waiting until he was strong enough to fight was correct. Perhaps he remembered his own youthful insistence on fighting while wounded—a fight that had hurt more than helped the cause. Whatever his reasons, one thing was clear: no matter how eager his men were to face their enemy, Houston's strategy was to play keep-away for now.

When he reached the Brazos River, Houston faced a new challenge to his authority: Some of his men now threatened to defy his orders. One of the mutinous voices belonged to Captain Moseley Baker, another second-chance man. He had left large debts behind in Alabama (and an accusation of defrauding a bank). More recently, having established himself in Texas as a lawyer, he was quick to join the rebel cause. He had fought at Gonzales, and when he gathered a group of volunteers together in his adopted town of San Felipe de Austin, he took a hard line. "Let us all, with one accord, raise our hands to heaven and swear," he insisted. "The Texas flag shall wave triumphant, or we shall sleep in death."[7]

Baker took it personally that Houston was leading the army away from central Texas. As a married man with a daughter, he understood the hardships of the settlers as they left their homes and marched to who-knows-where; as a fighter, he accused Houston of avoiding a battle. "You had before you the example of Fannin, of Burleson and Milam

[but] . . . you determined that your first military act should be a retreat." Instead of attacking, as Baker saw it, Houston was "content to hear yourself spoke of as the Patrick Henry of revolution."[8]

In order to deflect the rumblings in the ranks, Houston ordered Baker and Major Wyly Martin—the latter was a veteran of Horseshoe Bend who, like Baker, also wished to take an immediate stand—to defend the Brazos River. The two men could hardly say no when asked to prepare for the action they said they wanted. Baker and his men took up a position on the east bank, ready to slow the advance of any enemy force near San Felipe de Austin, while Martin and company were to defend the Fort Bend crossing a short distance downstream. Houston thus defused the ire of the unhappy fighters and also managed to avoid a premature confrontation with the Mexican troops on his trail.

Secretary of War Rusk had become Houston's main confidant within the government. Like so many others, Rusk came to Texas as a seeker; in his case, he was in pursuit of men who had embezzled a small fortune from the Georgia mining company that had been his business. The son of an Irish immigrant stonemason, the broad-shouldered Rusk had stayed and made a place for himself. Though just thirty-two, he had a native authority about him, and believing fervently in a free Texas, he had organized a company of volunteers in Nacogdoches to join the fight.

Houston explained his actions concerning Baker and Martin in a letter to Rusk. "Had I consulted the wishes of all, I should have been like the ass between two stacks of hay. Many wished me to go [downstream], others above. I consulted none—I held no councils of war. If I err, the blame is mine."[9] Houston's thinking put him at odds with his men, but he saw no alternative. He would have to square his shoulders and tough it out. Texas's survival depended on him, and he was not going to let a desire for revenge lead to a premature fight and defeat.

The army's retreat resumed. Leaving Martin and Baker behind, Houston and his troops headed upstream along the west bank of the

Brazos River. Houston was continuing to play his cards close to his vest: The only certainty was that the army needed to stay ahead of the Mexicans—until the time (and no one knew when that would be) that Houston chose to turn and fight.

BORROWED TIME AT BERNARDO PLANTATION

Was this trek across Texas an act of cowardice? More and more of Houston's young detractors had begun to think so. But people old enough to recall the American Revolution discerned a method where others saw madness.

The elders could remember that General George Washington, fearful of losing his army, retreated out of enemy range more often than not. Washington wished to fight battles he could win, to wait for the days when the odds favored him. Might General Houston be thinking the same way?

Some wise men also recalled that Baron Von Steuben, Washington's Prussian-trained inspector general, introduced a rebel rabble to the essentials of order and discipline, to drills and tactics. Perhaps at their April encampment, just across the Brazos River from a place called Groce's Landing, Houston could finally shape this haggard, rain-soaked, underfed, and undisciplined bunch of stragglers into a fighting force.

The man who welcomed Houston and his army, Jared Groce, was among the richest settlers in Stephen Austin's district. He grew cotton and owned Texas's first cotton gin, as well as a sawmill and land as far as you could see. From the columned porch that ran the length of his rambling plantation home, called Bernardo, he took in a panoramic view of the Brazos River. But his plantation amounted to much more than a homestead. When the army pitched its camp, twenty miles north of San Felipe, on April 1, Groce had the fields, flocks, fodder, and livestock to provide for a hungry army.

The weather refused to cooperate, and with nearly constant rain, the "camp became extremely muddy and disagreeable."[10] But the sickest soldiers recuperated in the Bernardo mansion house, which became a hospital. After weeks of exposure and tainted water, many men suffered from colds, whooping cough, or persistent diarrhea. This period of rest at Groce's permitted a reorganization of the medical staff, too, consisting of a half dozen physicians, and the installation of the medicine chest into a designated cart for transport in the battles to come.

As the Texians settled in, however, Santa Anna's army was never far from Sam Houston's mind.

SANTA ANNA ON THE MOVE

On the last day of March, Santa Anna had begun to march his force eastward, leaving San Antonio for the first time since the fall of the Alamo. He reached Gonzales on April 2. His troops crossed the prairie, passing small wooded areas—"a vast garden," according to one of his officers, "beautifully interrupted by woods."[11] They saw lilies and poppies coming into spring bloom, a stark contrast to towns burned beyond habitation. Many fields and pastures had been torched by departing citizens or Houston's army, in keeping with the American commander's wish that nothing be left behind that might be of use to the enemy army on his trail.

Rains slowed the march, but by Easter Sunday, April 3, Santa Anna led an advance force consisting of five hundred infantry, fifty cavalry, and scouts. The rest of his army would follow after a barge got the heavy loads of baggage and ammunition and the pair of eight-pound cannons safely across the Guadalupe River.

On April 5, His Excellency's force crossed the Colorado, a few miles downstream from the Texians' recently abandoned camp at Beason's Ford. Houston's trail was far from cold—he was still at Groce's Landing—but when the main Mexican column reached San Felipe on April 7, Santa Anna found that "the town . . . no longer existed, because the enemy had burned it and sent the inhabitants into the interior." Baker's company had burned the place and, by coincidence, three of his men had returned to inspect the ruins the day the Mexicans arrived. Caught by surprise, two of them got away—but the third got caught. When interrogated, the captive revealed he knew Houston's whereabouts (a few miles upstream at Groce's crossing) and the size of his force (he said eight hundred men), and "that [Houston's] intention was to retire to the Trinity river, in case the Mexicans cross the Brazos."[12]

Santa Anna was gaining on the Texians. But first he had to cross the Brazos and that, he found, would take some time. He confronted two problems. One, Houston had ordered every vessel in the vicinity destroyed; and two, Captain Moseley Baker and his skilled riflemen awaited across the water, ready to pepper anyone who tried to come ashore at the landing with deadly rifle shot.

LITTLE MORE THAN a dozen miles north, Houston's officers drilled the healthy troops almost nonstop. He reorganized the regimental command structure. The infantry learned military basics, including line tactics, in which two or more ranks of soldiers march in close alignment toward the enemy, then fire in unison for maximum effect.

Houston spent much time in his tent, studying maps and tending to his correspondence. He dispatched letter after letter to East Texas and to the government, seeking supplies and more manpower. He addressed one "to the Citizens of Texas," assuring them that "the enemy . . . are treading the soil on which they are to be conquered."[13] He issued orders to Baker and debriefed his scouts, who were constantly coming and going, doing their best to keep him apprised of enemy movements. "Mr. E. Smith is out, and, if living, I will hear the truth and all important news," Houston told Rusk.[14]

Bad news arrived: Three survivors of Goliad, "wounded, barefoot, and ragged," staggered in with the first word of the slaughter.[15] Houston learned the details of a demise he had feared, when the Texians who surrendered as POWs had been divided into groups, marched out of town, and shot like dogs. To an army preparing to fight, the news was a terrible shock; the manpower would be missed. According to the rolls, Houston's army now numbered nearly a thousand men. But that included substantial detachments that remained under the command of Baker and Martin; by Houston's calculation, the Army of Texas at Groce's land barely exceeded five hundred effectives.

The politicians felt the reverberations, too. Commander in Chief Houston got a desperate letter from the Texas president, David Burnet. "Sir: the Enemy are laughing you to scorn. You must fight them. You must retreat no farther. The country expects you to fight. The Salvation of the country depends on your doing so."[16] Secretary of War Rusk arrived in person, looking to encourage Houston to take on the enemy but also adding his gravitas and support to Houston's leadership. Eighty volunteers arrived from East Texas, regulars from the U.S. Army, some of them still wearing their uniforms. Then cannon fire in the distance, on April 7, announced the presence of Mexican troops in San Felipe de Austin, though Houston did not know whether or not Santa Anna was in command.

DIG THE GRAVES

Discontent remained common in the ranks. Many an impatient soldier was heard grumbling that "it was time to be doing something besides lying in idleness and getting sick." No longer ignoring the rising volume of complaints, Houston ordered two graves dug and issued a notice, which appeared on trees around the camp. The first man who called for volunteers to strike out on their own would be court-martialed and shot. The threat—together with a rumor that the army would break camp in a matter of days—defused the situation.[17] Houston was walking a delicate line, weighing matters of discipline even as he worried about his soldiers' devotion to the cause. They needed to be together to right the wrongs perpetrated by Santa Anna.

The appearance of a gift from the people of Cincinnati lifted plummeting morale. On hearing of the uprising in Texas the previous fall, citizens of the Ohio city commissioned the manufacture of two cannons. Shipped via New Orleans, the cannons arrived at Groce's on April 11. Colonel James Neill took charge of a new artillery battery, with nine volunteers manning each of the cast-iron guns, which were christened the "Twin Sisters." Blacksmiths set to work cutting up horseshoes and other available iron scrap for use as canister shot.

The blacksmiths shared Groce's shop with gunsmiths. Both groups kept busy. Groce had donated his plantation's plumbing pipes—they were made of lead, an expensive import in frontier Texas—and the smiths melted the lead to cast as bullets.

It was with the blacksmiths—for barely a moment and for the first time in a month—that Houston relaxed enough to allow his lighter side to show.

When a new volunteer arrived carrying an old flintlock rifle in need of repair, some wag in the ranks pointed. "The blacksmith is there," the recruit was told; looking up, he saw a man dressed in a well-worn leather jacket, watching the other smiths at work.

The new recruit approached. "I want you to fix my gun," he began, speaking to Houston, whom he did not recognize. "The lock is out of order, it won't stand cocked."

The general played along. "Very well," he said. "Set her down there, and call in one hour and she will be ready."

When the owner learned—to his horror—Houston's identity, he returned. Afraid he might be punished for insubordination, he approached the commander, hat in hand, asking for forgiveness.

The general just laughed. "My friend," he reassured the soldier, "they told you right, I am a very good blacksmith." He handed over the gun, which he had dismantled and cleaned. "She is in good order now, and I hope you are going to do some good fighting."[18]

Houston had learned much from his mentor. Jackson was a master at winning his men's allegiance on the march; part of that was to maintain his authority and yet become one of them.

THOMPSON'S FERRY

Santa Anna looked across the Brazos River from San Felipe de Austin. His first attempt to get his army to the opposite shore had failed when a flatboat, manned by a squad of his men, had returned, rebuffed by a hail of bullets from Moseley Baker's riflemen. Baker got his wish: He got to mix it up with the enemy, and he and his men acquitted themselves honorably. The Mexican general had ordered his artillerymen to return fire, but two days of bombardment—booms were heard at Groce's—hadn't cleared the nest of snipers.

Santa Anna decided to leave General Sesma to continue the fight, while he headed downstream to find another crossing.

At Thompson's Ferry, on April 12, he tested his luck again, only this time he resorted to trickery. Before being observed by anyone on the opposite bank, the general and his men concealed themselves in the bushes. Then Colonel Juan Almonte, who spoke fluent English, showed himself on the shore.

He hailed a boatman standing across the Brazos.

Thinking the lone figure calling to him was a Texian looking to join the exodus, the ferryman poled over. The Mexicans quickly overpowered the unsuspecting boatman (by one account, Santa Anna himself wrestled him to the ground), and his vessel soon began shuttling Santa Anna's force—seven hundred infantry, fifty cavalry, and a cannon—to the opposite bank.

Santa Anna wondered about Sam Houston. He held the Texian army in contempt after the Alamo and Goliad and saw no reason to think his present opponent any more dangerous than Travis or Fannin. His campaign, he believed, had become little more than "a military parade," in the face of an opponent who "was not undertaking a retreat but was in full flight."[19]

A new piece of intelligence inspired a new plan. From a Mexican colonist, Santa Anna learned that the "so-called government of Texas" was within striking distance at Harrisburg. He saw a clear way to end this fight: If he could capture the leaders of the revolution, he would strike "a single blow . . . mortal to their cause." His first objective wouldn't be to snare Houston but, rather, to capture the entire rebel government. If he moved quickly, Houston couldn't—or wouldn't—interfere, since the Texians were camped well to the north, out of Santa Anna's direct line of attack, and reportedly heading east.[20]

Santa Anna measured the odds. Tradition was not with him—most military planners regarded keeping an army together of paramount importance—but he was certain he saw the opening he wanted, an easy and major win in an immediate strike. And on April 14, Santa Anna led his contingent of dragoons, grenadiers, and riflemen toward Harrisburg, planning to end this rebellion once and forever.

FIGHT OR FLIGHT

Two days before, plumes of thick black smoke from the twin stacks had signaled departure time for Houston's army. Fired by green wood, the steam engine of the *Yellow Stone* began the work, at ten o'clock on the morning of April 12, of carrying the Army of Texas across the Brazos. The retreat east resumed.

On seeing the steamboat docked at Groce's wharf ten days before, Houston had impressed the side-wheeler into service "for the benefit of the Republic."[21] Having the ship meant that the high waters of the rising river no longer posed an obstacle.

Captain John Ross and his crew ferried the men across. With the 120-foot-long deck stacked with bales of cotton to protect her boilers and pilothouse from enemy rifles, the *Yellow Stone* required seven trips to carry the seven hundred soldiers (including more than a hundred sick and wounded), two hundred horses, and ten ox-drawn wagons loaded with ammunition and baggage to the left bank.

Houston went across with the first load of men and cargo; Rusk came last after supervising the loading. Secretary of War Rusk had emerged as an invaluable Houston ally, rebutting criticisms from the government and soldiers alike.

On April 13, Houston and his army marched along Cypress Creek—but away from Santa Anna's forces. Again the dissention in the ranks grew louder—*Did Houston intend to retreat all the way to Louisiana, to seek the direct military aid of Jackson and the United States?*[22] It didn't help that Moseley Baker and Wyly Martin, together with more than three hundred men, had retreated from the Brazos and rejoined Houston's force. Their voices only added to the discontent.

By April 16, the Texians marched through Cypress City; a few miles later they reached a fork in the road. There a local landmark, the Which-Way Tree, stood like a scarecrow with its arms raised. One craggy limb indicated the road to Nacogdoches; to tread that path meant further retreat, perhaps to the Sabine River and beyond. Another gnarled branch pointed due south, toward Harrisburg and—very likely—the long-awaited fight. The tree remained silent, but, according to Dr. Nicholas Labadie, a physician riding with the advance guard, a local man named Roberts did the talking.

He stood near the gate to his farm. Just as Houston rode up, Roberts was asked, *Which way to Harrisburg?*

"The right hand road will carry you," he replied, "just as straight as a compass."

Before Houston could say a word, a shout came from the ranks. "To the right, boys, to the right." The cry was repeated by others—"loud and joyous shouts followed in succession." The army's band made the turn, too, following the right arm of the Which-Way Tree.

Houston had kept his plan to himself, issuing no standing orders regarding which way to turn. Would Houston rather have had the army head straight for the Sabine—the cowardly way out, his skeptics thought—or turn south and fight? Suddenly, though, Houston's preference no longer mattered. As one soldier remembered, "the head of the column . . . took the right-hand without being either bid or forbid."[23]

The soldiers may have been pleased, but not everyone liked the southward turn.

Mrs. Pamelia Mann, for one, was miffed. An inn operator fleeing Washington-on-the-Brazos, she had recognized there was safety in numbers and had reached an understanding with the Texian army when the army left Groce's landing. "If you are going on the Nacogdoches road," she had said, "you can have my oxen." Yoked to the Cincinnati cannons, the sturdy animals pulled the heavy equipment along the muddy route and Pamelia Mann had joined the caravan.

Now the deal had changed. When she realized the destination had shifted with the turn toward Harrisburg, Mrs. Mann, well-known for her hot temper, galloped to the head of the column. She was said to have "fought everyone except Indians,"[24] and now she confronted the commander in chief.

"General, you told me a damn lie," spat out the angry woman. "Sir, I want my oxen."

"Well, Mrs. Mann, we can't spare them," Houston replied as reasonably as he could. "We can't get our cannon along without them."

"I don't care a damn for your cannon," she replied, brandishing a pistol. She soon headed north, away from the army, trailed by the oxen she had unharnessed herself, cutting the rawhide tug with her knife as the men looked on wordlessly.

Captain Rohrer, one of the wagon masters charged with delivering the cannons, remonstrated with Houston. "We can't get along without them oxen, the cannon is bogged down."

Houston, caught in the middle, offered a noncommittal reply. "Well . . ."

Rohrer, determined to get the draft animals back, turned and rode off with another soldier in pursuit of Mrs. Mann. He was a hundred yards away when Houston, rising up in his saddle, hollered a warning. "Captain Rohrer, that woman will fight."

"Damn her fighting," was the reply.

Nothing more was heard on the matter until nine o'clock that evening, well after the army had made camp for the night. Rohrer returned, his shirt badly torn—without the oxen.

"Hey, captain, where is your oxen?" someone hollered.

To the amusement of many, Captain Rohrer's abashed reply was, "She would not let me have them."

Mrs. Mann had won her fight, and it seemed the soldiers had won theirs, too. Houston had kept them fighting battles they could not win—now he would find out if he had held them back long enough.[25]

FOURTEEN

The Battle at San Jacinto

We go to conquer. It is wisdom, growing out of necessity, to
meet the enemy now; every consideration enforces it. No previous occasion would justify it.

—SAM HOUSTON TO HENRY RAGUET, APRIL 19, 1836

The heavy spring rains meant misery to every soldier, Mexican
and Texian, as the confrontation between the mismatched
armies drew closer. Drenched clothing never seemed to dry,
and the mud on what passed for roads grew deeper by the day. Streams
swelled into rivers and rivers looked like lakes. The challenging conditions also revealed something about the characters of both generals.

General Sam Houston—seemingly now committed to confront
Santa Anna—won new respect from some of his troops when, in the
course of the demanding, two-and-a-half-day, fifty-five-mile march to
Harrisburg, he dismounted his horse to help the wagon drivers when
their carts bogged down in the mud. Despite his high rank and old
war wounds, again and again he leaned his good shoulder into wagon
wheels. His men took note.

On Santa Anna's trip to Harrisburg, he grew impatient at the progress of his column. When a fallen tree bridged one creek bed, its broad

trunk easing the passage for men on foot, Santa Anna stepped carefully across, and a dragoon swam his horse through the rushing waters. But rather than wait for his soldiers to help carry the baggage and commissary stores safely across, His Excellency ordered the fully loaded mule train to cross the swollen stream. Up to their withers in water, several mules lost their balance. There was a "terrible jamming of officers and dragoons, pack-mules and horses," one of his officers noted in his diary. Several animals drowned "in a scene of wild confusion."

Santa Anna's reaction to the dangerous situation? "His Excellency witnessed [it] with hearty laughter."[1] The lives of men, Mexican or Texian, meant little to His Excellency.

Santa Anna had a particular reason for hurrying to Harrisburg. He was keen to arrest the Texas government and especially its vice president. Previously a provincial governor and Mexico's ambassador to France, Lorenzo de Zavala had opposed Santa Anna's power grab in Mexico City and His Excellency's reversal of democratic reforms. Santa Anna regarded the exiled Zavala as a sworn enemy and a traitor to his country; he wanted to make Zavala his prisoner.

As far as Santa Anna was concerned, Houston's army could be dealt with later. His exact location wasn't clear, but scouts reported that the retreating Texian general aimed for Nacogdoches and the Sabine. "Since he is escorting families and supplies in ox-drawn wagons, his march is slow," Santa Anna noted. He believed that if he could promptly capture the government, he would still have time to subdue Houston. "The Trinity River, moreover, should detain him many days."[2]

On April 15, the morning after the hazardous crossing, Santa Anna headed for Harrisburg. Despite marching at double-time pace, per Santa Anna's orders, the Mexicans remained far from the town at sunset. But their commander, accompanied by an officer and fifteen dragoons, rode on. The midnight hour approached before they finally reached their destination.

Harrisburg's streets were desolate. The only sign of life the Mexicans managed to find was in a printshop, the new offices of the *Telegraph and Texas Register*. At gunpoint, three ink-spattered men told Santa Anna he had arrived too late. The government had departed hours before, boarding the steamboat *Cayuga*, along with most of the inhabitants of Harrisburg. The vessel had steamed for New Washington, a town some twenty miles southeast on a river known as Buffalo Bayou.

Angry that his prey had eluded him, Santa Anna ordered the printing equipment destroyed, the ruined press parts and type cases thrown into the river. Only weeks earlier this same press had inked the first impression of the Texas Declaration of Independence.

HARRISBURG

Three days later, when General Houston looked across Buffalo Bayou, Santa Anna's army had come and gone, leaving the river town unrecognizable. "We arrived at Harrisburg about noon," one Texian private reported, "[and] the smoke at the town told us too plainly . . . that the enemy had been there before us, and set fire to its buildings."[3]

Exhausted after the long march, the Texians made camp. Deaf Smith and his team departed on another mission. Houston wanted to know the exact whereabouts of the enemy that had burned Harrisburg. Tired as they were, the Texians felt ready to engage. "They were of one mind," one colonel remembered, "to march down and fight the enemy."[4]

Smith, Henry Karnes, and their scouting party swam their horses across the wide, slow-moving Buffalo Bayou. A dozen miles downstream, they met—and promptly took as their prisoners—three men. One was a Mexican captain; his companions were a guard and a Tejano guide. A search of their belongings revealed that the captain was a government courier, and his saddlebags contained for-his-eyes-only dispatches addressed to Santa Anna.

On the little party's return to Houston's camp at eight o'clock that evening, the captives' arms were bound behind their backs. The general summoned Sergeant Moses Austin Bryan, nephew of Stephen Austin and fluent Spanish speaker, to help question the prisoners.

The guide claimed he had been detained by the Mexicans in San Antonio while on a furlough from the Texian army. His commanding officer was summoned and confirmed both the man's identity and his commitment to the rebel cause.

How many men had been in the force that burned Harrisburg? Houston wanted to know.

The Tejano wasn't certain, but he had "heard some of the officers say . . . that there were 500 infantry and 100 cavalry and one twelve pound cannon."[5]

The numbers reassured Houston and Secretary of War Rusk. At least for the moment, the Mexican force in the vicinity was smaller than the Army of Texas, which now hovered around a thousand men.

Major Lorenzo de Zavala Jr., son of the republic's vice president, and a team of Tejanos speedily translated the documents the courier carried. They found some were letters home, addressed to loved ones back in Mexico, and of no strategic value. But others offered invaluable intelligence.

One revealed that General Cos and 650 soldiers would soon arrive to reinforce the men who had burned Harrisburg. It also became clear that the Mexicans didn't know where Houston's army was or that it was following in their footsteps. Still another fact emerged, one that galvanized Houston's interest: "I learned," he noted, "that General Santa Anna, with one division of his choice troops, had marched in the direction of Lynch's Ferry, on the San Jacinto."[6]

The man who had ordered the slaughter at both the Alamo and

Goliad was in striking distance, just downstream on the Buffalo Bayou. As they reviewed the documents together, Houston and Rusk reacted as one.

"We need not talk," said Houston, turning to Rusk. "You think we ought to fight, and I think so too."[7]

FROM HUNTER TO HUNTED

The capture of the courier changed everything. The roles that Houston and Santa Anna played suddenly reversed: Houston became the hunter, His Excellency the hunted. Thanks to Deaf Smith's brilliant intelligence gathering, Houston, now armed with the who, what, where, and when, could plan a surprise attack. Here was his chance to steal the initiative from Santa Anna; the enemy commander, by making his impulsive move to capture the government, had given Houston an opening. Santa Anna had isolated himself with a fraction of his forces at hand.

At the same time, Houston's army showed signs of finally coalescing. The time at Groce's had helped. By retreating across Texas, Houston had bought time for these men to grow together, to gain experience, to learn military tactics. He had identified who among his officers were to be trusted in battle. Now Houston saw an army that showed its readiness to act in unison: He'd seen that when, spontaneously, the rank and file had chosen to move toward the fight at the Which-Way Tree crossroad.

But time was suddenly of the essence. If the Texians could move quickly—that is, if Houston could strike before the larger Mexican army reassembled—he might be the one doing the capturing. This war was about revolution, about freedom, but it was also about avenging the annihilation at the Alamo. And at Goliad. For the first time since Houston had taken command of the Army of Texas, a big battle loomed in his immediate future, suddenly inevitable, perhaps only a day or two away. After a long reluctance to engage until the right moment, Houston now foresaw a battle he was ready to fight.

Houston and his men may have needed no further motivation to carry this fight to the Mexicans, but, on close inspection, another grim reminder emerged of the savagery of their enemy. Only weeks before, the saddlebags containing the Mexican documents had been the property of a fellow Texian. There, on the underside, the name *W. B. Travis* had been inscribed. Travis's bags had become a battlefield souvenir, scavenged by the murderous victors at the Alamo.

A NARROW ESCAPE

Santa Anna's impulsive pursuit of the Texas government wasn't accomplishing what he'd hoped it would. On Sunday, April 17, he again missed a chance to roll up the rebel officials.

His advance guard galloped into New Washington just in time to watch a rowboat, with President David Burnet and his party aboard, make for the schooner *Flash*. Though the retreating Texians remained in rifle range, the chivalrous colonel Juan Almonte, commander of the Mexican cavalrymen on the shore, spotted a woman in the boat—she was Mrs. Burnet—and ordered his men to hold their fire. The Mexican horsemen watched helplessly as the Texians boarded the *Flash*, a riverboat outfitted as a privateer in service to the newly founded Texas navy. Riding the tide, the little vessel sailed downstream toward Galveston Island.

When he got the news of Burnet's escape, Santa Anna chose not to countermarch; he would not rejoin the rest of his army but instead pushed on to New Washington. When they reached the town the next day, most of his men enjoyed the considerable stores in its warehouses, including flour, soap, tobacco, and other goods. Santa Anna would make the Texians pay once more—he planned to burn this town on departing—but first he dispatched a squad of scouts to locate Houston.

In his mind's eye, His Excellency saw a new main objective, Houston's army. If it was within striking distance, he would, he decided, "intercept Houston's march and . . . destroy with one stroke the armed forces and the hopes of the revolutionists."[8] That goal seemed suddenly close at hand when his scouts returned, bringing word that Houston was less than a day's march away. With opportunity near, a plan was made.

Thus, both armies aimed for a point of convergence. Their common destination was a place called Lynchburg, yet another river town. This one overlooked the watery intersection where the Buffalo Bayou joined the San Jacinto River.

Believing Houston to be in full retreat, Santa Anna expected the Texian commander to make for Lynch's Ferry, where ferry service connected the open prairie on the west bank of the San Jacinto with Lynchburg and the rest of East Texas; this was Houston's best and probably only escape route. Santa Anna planned to surprise the Texian army before it crossed and, at last, finish the job of crushing the rebellion.

Meanwhile, Sam Houston was doing everything in his power to get there first. He, too, hoped for the element of surprise, when his men, now more than ever ready to fight for their freedom, turned and made their stand.

Just two roads led to Lynch's landing. With the Texians coming from the west and the Mexicans from the south, the armies were on a collision course. Their now inevitable meeting would decide the future of Texas.

A CHANCE TO SAVE TEXAS

General Houston's orders worked their way down the line. Leave the baggage behind, the men were told; pack just three days' worth of rations for a quick march. A small contingent of some seventy-five healthy men would be staying in Harrisburg to safeguard the two hundred or so sick and wounded. If attacked, these guards were to shoot the two Mexican prisoners and blow up the ammunition wagon. For everyone else, as one soldier put it, "The long cherished wish of our men to meet the enemy seemed likely to be speedily gratified."[9]

Whatever the skepticism of a few officers and soldiers who still held deep reservations concerning Houston's leadership, more of his men had warmed to him—and to the *cause*. On the eve of the battle, they fell into line, ready to face up to the cold cruelty of Santa Anna.

Before the army broke camp, Houston, seated in the saddle on his tall white horse, addressed his army, which surrounded him in an open square formation. After weeks of revealing little of his strategy, in the speech of a lifetime he told his soldiers that the time to fight now approached. Houston spoke of glory, of a great victory. But as he reached the conclusion of his address, he minced no words.

"We will meet the enemy. Some of us may be killed and must be killed; but, soldiers, remember the Alamo, *the Alamo! The Alamo!*"[10]

The men heard his passion—and they shared it. "The watchword had no sooner fallen from his mouth, then it was caught up by every man in the army, and one simultaneous shout broke up into the sky— *Remember the Alamo.*"[11] They were ready to fight in memory of their brother Texians, fallen for their cause. As one colonel observed, "After such a speech, but damned few will be taking prisoners—that I know."[12]

A private in Captain Moseley Baker's company spoke for many, if not all, the soldiers when he remarked, "Had General Houston called upon me to jump into the whirlpool of the Niagara as the only means of saving Texas, I would have made the leap."[13] With a battle imminent, the disgruntled rumblings diminished with the rise of the primal urge to avenge the deaths of Travis's and Fannin's forces.

Privately, Houston was philosophical. As he wrote in a letter to his friend Henry Raguet in Nacogdoches, "This morning we are in preparation to meet Santa Anna. It is the only chance to save Texas. . . . We will only have about seven hundred to march with [and] . . . the odds are greatly against us. I leave the result in the hands of a wise God."[14]

At least his men would proceed with full stomachs. After many meals of half-cooked meat from beeves slaughtered along the route, the men ate corn bread. A flatboat loaded with supplies for the enemy—confiscated from a Tory Texian—provided cornmeal, out of which the men improvised crude dough cakes on sticks, cooked over their open fires. And then they marched.

Two miles downstream from Harrisburg, they met their first obstacle, but the scouts and the cavalry led the way, swimming their horses across Buffalo Bayou, twenty feet deep and flooding its banks. The infantry followed aboard a leaky ferryboat. Houston went across first and helped rig a makeshift cable of rope "fastened to both sides of the stream, which enabled the boat to make more rapid trips, and kept it from floating down the stream."[15]

Lookouts maintained a vigilant watch: General Cos and the Mexican reinforcements, coming from the rear, could be expected to be following the same route. A delay for repairs to the boat using the floorboards from a nearby house meant the process took much of the day. The men already across took cover in bushes beside the road, but no enemy sightings occurred before Rusk stepped back onto solid ground with the last of the soldiers. He had stood ankle deep in water as the ferry rode lower and lower, but the men, along with the two heavy cannons, the Twin Sisters, were now safely across.

Reunited on the same side of the Buffalo Bayou, the army resumed its advance, following along the right bank. Only after midnight did Houston call a halt, "for a short time, and without refreshments."[16] The

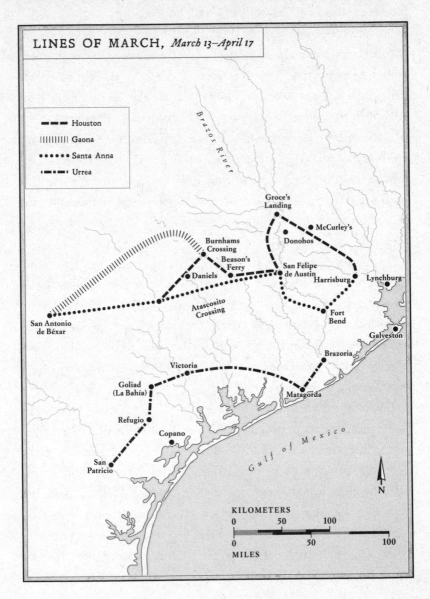

LINES OF MARCH, *March 13–April 17*

- – – Houston
- ||||||||| Gaona
- • • • • • Santa Anna
- – ∙ – ∙ – Urrea

army passed a tense night, sleeping on the cold and soggy ground, rifles within reach.

AS THE TEXIANS moved along the Buffalo Bayou, the Mexicans, barely a dozen miles away, set fire to New Washington, torching "a fine warehouse on the wharf, and all the houses in town." Even as the smoke filled the sky, a messenger arrived in a rush: Houston and his force had been sighted.

When the news reached Santa Anna, still in the town, he leapt onto his horse. He spurred the animal toward the front of the column. "The enemy are coming!" he yelled. "The enemy are coming."[17]

A column of attack was soon formed, and Santa Anna's army headed north. The fight for Texas loomed closer yet, now mere hours away.

A SMALL SKIRMISH

On April 20, the Texians moved out at daybreak. After crossing a timber bridge over another watercourse, Vince's Bayou, they filed past the remnants of campfires. The rain-soaked ash was a reminder that Santa Anna's army recently walked this route, before veering south toward New Washington.

After two hours of trudging through mud, Houston ordered a halt for breakfast. But before the food could come off the fires, a scouting party brought news that the Mexicans were also within striking distance of Lynch's Ferry.

General Houston knew one thing above all: His Texians had to get there first, and following a flurry of orders, the hungry men, bolting half-cooked meat, hustled on. The morning became a race for strategic

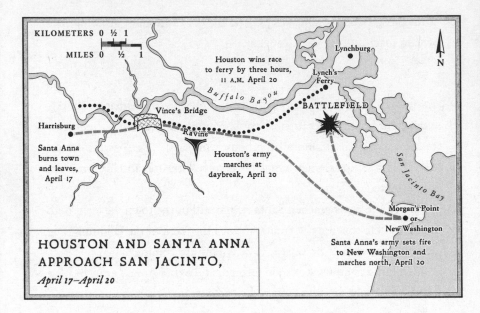

KILOMETERS 0 ½ 1

MILES 0 ½ 1

Lynchburg

Houston wins race
to ferry by three hours,
11 A.M. April 20

Lynch's
Ferry

Buffalo Bayou

Vince's Bridge

BATTLEFIELD

Harrisburg

Ravine

Santa Anna
burns town
and leaves,
April 17

Houston's army
marches at
daybreak, April 20

San Jacinto Bay

Morgan's Point
or
New Washington

Santa Anna's army sets fire
to New Washington and
marches north, April 20

N

**HOUSTON AND SANTA ANNA
APPROACH SAN JACINTO,**
April 17–April 20

ground, and by midmorning, the Army of Texas reached their destination. To the relief of all, no Mexicans were within sight.

Looking to establish his line of defense, Houston and his officers surveyed the likely battlefield. It consisted of open prairie, two miles wide east to west. Thickets of trees dotted the perimeter, and the field was bounded on three sides by water. The Buffalo Bayou formed the north boundary, the San Jacinto River the east, with the ferry crossing at their joining. A small body of water, Peggy Lake, occupied the southeast corner of the field. After one of the wettest springs in Texas memory, all the shorelines had broadened into swamps.

Houston selected a grove of live oaks for his army. The immense trees, their branches curtained with low-hanging Spanish moss, would provide ideal cover for his riflemen. Before them lay the broad prairie, covered with tall grasses. Houston posted his cavalry on his right flank, half-hidden by a copse of trees. At the center, the Twin Sisters would anchor the Texian line.

The men were well fed and their guns stacked when, shortly after midday, the first of Santa Anna's force came into view. Mexican cavalrymen appeared atop the low rise that divided the prairie, a line of infantrymen in their wake.

From his vantage a mile away, Santa Anna could see little of Houston's force, obscured as it was in the shadows of the trees. His scouts advised him that the enemy had two cannons, but that did not deter him. The Mexican leader ordered a company of troops to advance on the rebels while he moved closer and took cover in a stand of trees. He hoped to lure these backwoodsmen from their lair; in the open field, the trained Mexican horsemen would have the enemy at their mercy.

On the Texian side, the music of blaring trumpets grew audible as a company of Mexican cavalry approached. "Houston showed himself restless and uneasy," remembered one Texian, "casting his eyes towards the cannon and toward the advancing enemy."

The general ordered most of the men to lie flat on the grass; the less Santa Anna knew about the size and arrangement of the Texian force, the better. Then he issued the order all had been waiting for. "Clear the guns and Fire!"[18]

His artillerymen had no practice firing the Twin Sisters—they had neither powder nor cannonballs to spare—so the great booms at that moment were the first heard from the Cincinnati cannons. The shots wounded no Mexicans—the angle of fire was too high—but the dragoons halted, then wheeled, reversing their course back to Santa Anna's ranks.

Next His Excellency ordered his own cannon brought forward. Once it had been hauled under the cover of a dense wood within range of the Texian camp, the Mexican twelve-pounder opened fire. The first round fired by the brass cannon known as the Golden Standard ripped through the treetops, soaring into the Buffalo Bayou beyond. Only a few branches fell harmlessly among the Texians.

In response, Houston ordered the Twin Sisters advanced to the edge of the prairie. When the Texian six-pounders resumed firing, their loads of iron balls and scrap drew the first blood of the afternoon. A Mexican captain was badly wounded, his horse and two mules killed. As the exchange of fire continued, the Texians, too, sustained a casualty when a copper ball struck their artillery commander, Lieutenant Colonel Neill, smashing his hip.

The action slowed, but some of Houston's officers urged a major attack, arguing they might gain the upper hand if they could seize the single Mexican cannon. The general had his doubts, but at about four o'clock Colonel Sidney Sherman rode up and proposed a mission to capture the Mexicans' gun. Houston at first resisted. But Sherman, a Kentucky volunteer who had sold his cotton business to come to Texas to join the fight, persisted. He wasn't alone and, in the face of many men eager to carry the battle to the enemy, Houston agreed to permit one foray onto enemy ground.

Though Houston authorized only a reconnaissance mission, almost seventy Texian cavalrymen rode out. Deaf Smith and Henry Karnes were among those who joined Sherman's ranks, as was Mirabeau Lamar, a Georgian who rode a borrowed horse. But in midexecution, the mission changed: Upon seeing the Mexican cannon being withdrawn from its advance position, the Texians charged into a nest of Mexican horsemen.

A brutal fight ensued. It nearly ended in disaster, since the improvised Texas cavalry—they were merely riflemen on horseback—needed to dismount after discharging their unwieldly long rifles if they wished to reload. But Mexican cavalry, armed with sabers and lances, just kept coming.

It was a near thing. Secretary of War Rusk had joined in—and he was lucky to survive the episode. Surrounded by enemy lancers, Rusk made it back to the Texian camp only after Private Mirabeau Buonaparte Lamar (a future president of Texas) came to his rescue, driving his stallion into a circle of Mexican dragoons about to capture Rusk, creating an opening for both men to escape. The Texians scampered back to their defensive line, having lost several horses and sustained two casualties. With the Twin Sisters firing on them, the Mexicans also retreated.

Houston wasn't happy: Even on the eve of what he thought might be the biggest battle of the war, his overeager men only half listened to his orders. Tomorrow, he thought, they would have to do better.

Like two Texas bull elks circling one another before locking horns, Houston and Santa Anna were each getting the measure of the other, assessing and gauging. They had traded cavalry charges and artillery fire; both sides suffered a few casualties. As darkness fell, neither army occupied an enviable position, with the Texians boxed in by a bayou behind and a bottleneck at the Lynchburg crossing. They had no line of easy retreat. Santa Anna's camp was no better, situated on a small rise with the San Jacinto River on one flank and Peggy Lake to the rear.

Yet the terms of battle had been established, as two armies and two commanders regarded each other, separated by fewer than a thousand yards of prairie grass that swayed peacefully in the evening breeze.

FIFTEEN

"Remember the Alamo!"

We are nerved for the contest, and must conquer or perish.

—SAM HOUSTON, APRIL 19, 1836

S am Houston slept late on April 21. For the first time in days, he lay until full daylight, eyes closed, his head on a coil of rope. As he remembered later, he rested "calmly and profoundly," newly confident that his "soldiers had eaten the last meal they were to eat till they had won their independence."[1] In a report penned the night before to President Burnet, he dubbed their bivouac "Camp Safety."

Around the sleeping general, however, "a restless and anxious spirit pervad[ed] the camp."[2] Some men rose at 4:00 A.M., still believing an all-in encounter the day before would have won the day for Houston's army. That air of discontent heightened when, at eight o'clock, a Texian scout spotted a column of men approaching from the direction of Harrisburg. Karnes and Smith investigated and reported—as the intercepted dispatches had warned them might happen—that Mexican reinforcements had arrived. General Martín Perfecto de Cos, accompanied by some four hundred men and two hundred supply mules, had marched into Santa Anna's camp to drumrolls and shouts of joy.

At that moment, Deaf Smith, always a man of few words, spoke for many. "The enemy is increasing," he said simply. "Today we *must* fight, or never."[3] The head count of Houston's Texian force numbered roughly eight hundred.

As for the enemy across the field, the Texian scouts reported that Santa Anna's force had not only grown in number but had spent much of the night constructing a breastwork. Their defensive line, set back from the midfield ridge, now had a five-foot-high mass of luggage, crates, barrels of grain, sacks of corn, and hastily cut brush protecting

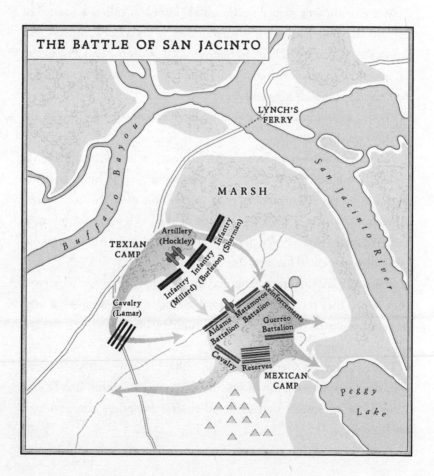

its left side. The breastwork was flanked by cannons and infantrymen on the river side and cavalry on the other.

As the sun rose toward its zenith, so did the frustrations of the Texian volunteers. By some accounts, every man was ready to fight and impatient of further delay. But Houston was biding his time one last time. He dispatched Deaf Smith to estimate the size of the enemy force. Ignoring the bullets that whistled past, Smith held his glass to his eyes, counting. The numbers were not encouraging: By this latest count, Houston's army consisted of 783 men, the enemy's more like fifteen hundred.[4]

Aware of the impatience in the ranks, Houston called a council of war. He sat beneath an oak tree surrounded by his six field officers. For almost two hours, he listened to their views, but, in the end, one essential question occupied everyone's attention: *Shall we attack the enemy in their position, or shall we await his attack?*

Finally, Houston called for a vote. By a margin of two to one, the decision was to wait.

Next Houston sent for Deaf Smith. Houston wanted the bridge over Vince's Bayou destroyed. This region was unfamiliar to him, relying as he did upon his scouts and a crude map now covered with smudged pencil annotations. But the destruction of the bridge that both armies had used might slow or even prevent the arrival of more Mexican troops and it also prevented his men from retreating.

Smith and six volunteers mounted up and rode out of camp carrying axes. When they returned—the bridge was eight miles away—the master scout reported that cutting a few timbers "made [Vince's Bridge] fall into the bayou."[5]

In the meantime, General Houston walked among the men, looking to measure their mood just as his mentor General Jackson liked to do. Many of the volunteers were gathered around campfires, some taking a late lunch.

"[He] asked us if we wanted to fight," remembered Private James Winters. "We replied with a shout that we were most anxious to do so."

Houston's response was unambiguous. "Very well," he told them, "get your dinners and I will lead you into the fight, and if you whip them every one of you shall be a captain."[6]

At 3:30 P.M. the order finally came down the line. "PARADE AND PREPARE FOR ACTION!"

REST FOR THE WEARY?

On the other side of the line, Santa Anna was taking a siesta.

That morning he had risen early. He watched the approach of Cos and his men; their arrival gave the Mexican commander added confidence, but, since they had marched all night, he permitted the exhausted soldiers to stack their arms and bed down in a nearby grove of trees. He personally made a foray into the field to appraise the Texian line through his spyglass. But by midafternoon, with no sign of action from the Texian side, Santa Anna relaxed his guard and permitted the rest of his men to stand down and stack their guns. The Texians showed no signs of attacking and, with their backs to the bayou, Houston's army certainly wasn't going to slip away.

Santa Anna decided upon a rest and, like him, many officers and soldiers lay down. Others in his army ate, took their horses to the water, or wandered into the woods to harvest tree branches for shelter. The officer in charge, General Fernández Castrillón, took the opportunity to shave, wash, and change uniforms. He paid little or no attention to the sentries who remained on duty.[7]

THE PLAN

The rise between the armies, as well as the trees overhead, helped mask Houston's battle array. Unseen by the Mexicans, he positioned his infantry divisions in two lines, with his men divided in half on either side of the cannons, which were now commanded, with Neill wounded, by his aide Colonel Hockley. The cavalry, led by Mirabeau Lamar, newly promoted by Houston to the rank of colonel, waited on his extreme right, largely hidden by a stand of trees.

His battle plan could hardly have been simpler. First, the sixty-one men on horseback would move on the Mexicans' left, "for the purpose," said Houston, "of attracting their notice." Thus distracted, the enemy might remain unaware of the infantry—shoulders hunched, half-hidden by the topography and the grasses—trotting across the prairie that separated the armies. At the same time, the Twin Sisters would be wheeled to a station within two hundred yards of the enemy's breastwork.[8]

From the treetops, lookouts reported that no Mexicans seemed to be standing sentinel.

While the uniformed Mexicans the previous day had, according to one Texian captain, looked "exceedingly grand in the[ir] picturesque costume," no two of the Texians waiting to fight looked alike.[9] They could lay no claim to being a proudly uniformed army; they remained, in looks and origin, a diverse blending of men. Frontiersmen in buckskin lined up with merchants wearing waistcoats and cravats; Stephen Austin's nephew Moses Austin Bryan wore a claw-hammer-tailed frock coat. On their heads they wore top hats, sombreros, fur caps, or round hats of wool or velvet. A few wore remnants of military uniforms, but, mud stained and tattered, none met West Point standards. The troops looked unkempt and unwashed, with matted hair and beards. There were Tejanos and Yankees, Georgians and Kentuckians, Alabamians and Virginians, Americans of all sorts with a smattering of immigrants from Europe. Houston's army shared little but a deep desire to avenge the needless slaying at the Alamo and Goliad—and to defend a free and sovereign Texas.

Houston, riding a gray stallion named Saracen, moved along the lines, which extended some twenty-five hundred feet end to end. He spoke to all the captains. He conferred with Secretary Rusk. And at four o'clock, he raised his sword.

"Trail arms!" he ordered. "Forward!"

As instructed, the men began to move through the grass carrying their guns butt down, with muzzles inclined upward. The cannoneers pulled the pair of guns forward, their low-angled barrels almost invisible in the tall grass. As the army advanced, Houston patrolled the line. "Hold your fire, men," he ordered, "hold your fire."[10]

One of the older soldiers on the field, fifty-seven-year-old Jimmy Curtis—known as "Uncle Jimmy"—carried two guns. When Secretary Rusk asked why, the settler (he had been among Stephen Austin's original Three Hundred) replied, "Damn the Mexicans; they killed my son and son-in-law in the Alamo, and I intend to kill two of them for it, or be killed myself."[11]

The men on the far left, who remained partly hidden by the thicket of trees that lined the San Jacinto River, moved quickly. They were the first to fire.

"THE ENEMY! THEY COME!"

"The enemy!" the call rang out. *"They come! They come!"*

When, shortly after four o'clock, a single Mexican bugler sounded the alarm, an officer climbed atop a stack of ammunition boxes. He saw a long line of determined men approaching.

"We marched upon the enemy," one Texian private noted, "with the stillness of death."[12]

The bloodletting had begun moments before with gunfire in the woods, followed by cannon fire from the Twin Sisters. For most of the Mexicans, the ominous booms had been a complete surprise. Hunks of deadly, high-flying horseshoe scrap and grapeshot suddenly fell from the sky into their camp.

Soon a few muzzle flashes could be seen from along the Mexican line, but the disorganized defense managed only an erratic counterfire before the Texian cavalry charged the Mexicans' left flank. And the main army kept coming.

Moments later, Houston, atop his horse some twenty yards in front of his infantry battle line, brought Saracen to a stop. He ordered the army to halt. On his command, the men, now melded into one line, knelt on one knee, raised their guns, and, as one, fired their first musket and rifle volley at a distance of sixty yards.

Through the blue haze of gun smoke, Houston ordered the men to reload, but Secretary Rusk overruled his commander in chief. "If we stop," he yelled, "we are cut to pieces. Don't stop—go ahead—give them hell."[13]

Behind the Mexican lines, chaos and confusion reigned. Men awakened from their siestas were racing for their guns. Officers screamed contradictory orders.

Suddenly the earth seemed to rise up to meet General Houston. His big stallion collapsed beneath him, the animal's hide pierced by five balls. Houston kept his feet as Saracen sank to the ground, and a soldier corralled a riderless horse for the commander. Swinging his leg over the shorter horse, Houston found his feet dangled well below the stirrups.

The Texian infantry surged forward and, as the attackers came within earshot, the Mexicans heard another terrifying sound rend the air: Houston's men unleashed bloodcurdling war cries: *"Remember the*

Alamo! Remember La Bahía! Remember Fannin!" The chorus of angry men, bent on revenge, now came at such speed that few of the surprised Mexicans had time to man their proper positions.

The infantry on their right flank surprised a division of Mexican soldiers in the trees. After an exchange of fire, Santa Anna's men retreated quickly, and the Texians moved relentlessly on.

With shocking suddenness—few of the men had stopped to reload—Houston's army was vaulting the Mexican barricade.

One regiment of attackers made the artillerists manning the Golden Standard a particular target. The Mexican gun had fired on the Texian cavalry but had turned in the direction of the Texian infantry when a rifle shot took down the man who, match in hand, was about to fire the next volley. Most of the members of the gun crew soon fell to well-aimed bullets or to charging Texians clambering over the breastwork; the surviving gunners, outmanned and overwhelmed, abandoned their station, "commenc[ing] an immediate and disorderly flight." Their commander, General Castrillón, who had stood resolutely behind the gun, urging his men to fight on, "folded up his arms, stood and looked on sullenly" before walking off. With the posture of a proud military man, Castrillón made an excellent target and soon fell, mortally wounded, his body riddled by rifle balls.[14]

The battle had barely begun when Houston, a highly visible target as he patrolled the battlefield, had another horse shot from beneath him. But this time, as the horse went down, the general himself felt a sudden pain in his left ankle. A musket ball, fired from a Mexican gun, smashed into his ankle, fracturing his leg. Houston staggered as he came off the dead horse but, leaning on a soldier who came to his aid, remained upright. Another Texian gave up his mount, and the men helped General Houston into the saddle.

Once behind the Mexican line, the attackers used their rifles as clubs; few had bayonets. Some long guns fractured, and the fighters resorted to using "heavy hunting knives as cleavers [and] their guns as clubs to knock out the brains of the Mexicans."[15] Early in the battle, Deaf Smith, thrown from his horse in the melee at the breastwork, found himself amid the enemy. "Having dropped his sword in the fall, he jumped up, drew one of his belt pistols, presented it at the head of a Mexican who was attempting to bayonet him, and the percussion-cap exploded without the pistol's going off. Upon which, Smith threw the pistol at the head of the Mexican, staggered him back, seized his gun . . . and defended himself with it."[16] Smith lived to tell the tale.

"A BEWILDERED AND PANIC STRICKEN HERD"[17]

Many, many Mexicans soon lay dead or wounded, but some Texians fell, too. One company of nineteen men sustained four casualties in the charge as the rest fought on. Another wounded man who kept fighting, despite a boot filling with blood, was General Sam Houston.

Terrified Mexican soldiers made for the trees, looking for shelter. Santa Anna himself proved unable to rally the men; he was observed "running about in the most excited manner, wringing his hands and unable to give an order."[18] Just one battalion had managed to confront the oncoming Texians when a desperate recognition struck one of Santa Anna's generals as he attempted to organize a counterattack. "In a few minutes [the Texians] won the victory that could not even be imagined."[19]

"In ten minutes after the firing of the first gun," Secretary Rusk reported the next day, "we were charging through the camp, and driving them before us."[20] In eighteen minutes, they had won.

The fight deteriorated into a one-sided rout. The Texians' blood was up as they avenged the loss of so many at the Alamo and Goliad. Some

Mexicans asked for quarter, kneeling and pleading for mercy. *"Mi no Alamo! Mi no La Bahía,"* claiming to have fought at neither the Alamo nor at Goliad.[21] The Texians were beyond hearing the enemy's denials or even the orders of Houston and his officers for the men to fall back, "to take prisoners, not to kill anyone." One lieutenant interpreted such directives for his men: "Boys, take prisoners. You know how to take prisoners: take them with the butt of your guns."[22]

Many retreating Mexicans, on reaching the shore of Peggy Lake, abandoned their guns and dove in, hoping to swim to safety. The Texian riflemen in pursuit raised their guns and commenced a deadly target practice, picking off the fleeing soldiers "as fast as they could load and shoot." The waters of the lake turned blood red.[23]

When an officer ordered them to stop, one soldier turned on him. "If Jesus Christ would come down from Heaven and order me to quit shooting yellow bellies I wouldn't do it, Sir!"

The officer reached for his sword. The soldier countered by cocking his rifle, and the officer "very discreetly . . . turned his horse and left."[24]

Some of the Mexican cavalry took to the prairie, making for Vince's Bridge, only to find it collapsed into the river and impassable. Men and horses alike drowned attempting to cross; still more men died when the Texians in pursuit caught up and "pour[ed] down upon them a deadly fire, which cut off all escape."[25]

With victory assured, Houston rode slowly back to the stand of live oaks, blood dripping from the bullet hole in his boot. On reaching the tree beneath which he'd slept the night before, he collapsed; his friend and chief of staff, Colonel Hockley, caught the half-unconscious general as he slid off his horse.

A surgeon was summoned. Once he cut the boot off Houston's badly swollen leg, bones could be seen protruding from the flesh. Dr. Alexander Ewing cleaned and dressed the wound.

Only twilight brought an end to the slaughter, and Secretary of War

Rusk accepted the surrender of Mexican colonel Juan Almonte and some two hundred men. As the shooting slowly stopped, the wounded were cared for. Guns, ammunition, horses, mules, and sabers were collected by the hundreds, and a lockbox of some $12,000 worth of silver pesos was uncovered in the Mexican camp.

The Texians had fewer than a dozen men dead or dying, another thirty or so wounded. But virtually all of the men under Santa Anna's immediate command were either dead, wounded, captive, or soon-to-be-captured. Under the watchful eyes of more than two dozen guards, the prisoners huddled around campfires they themselves built although, at first, when ordered to cut wood to build the fires, more than one Mexican worried that "we were to be burnt alive in retaliation for those who had been burnt in the Alamo."[26] Though casualty estimates varied widely, almost certainly some 630 Mexicans died in the battle, with more than two hundred wounded. The total prisoners would in the coming days exceed seven hundred.

The Texians had outperformed everybody's expectations. As Houston put it, "Every officer and man proved himself worthy of the cause in which he battled."[27] To many, the overwhelming victory brought to mind the stunning success of Andrew Jackson's army at New Orleans two decades earlier.

But as night fell, one large question remained unanswered: Where was His Excellency, Santa Anna? Additional Mexican troops were not all that far away, and if he reached them he might return for revenge.

SIXTEEN

Old San Jacinto

The 22nd day of April was the first *free* day in Texas. Before then, her people had declared their independence, but now they had won it in a noble contest. The victory was physically and morally complete [and] . . . the Texans had their revenge.

—H. YOAKUM, *History of Texas*

The morning after the big battle, a detachment of Kentucky volunteers swept the prairie looking for Mexicans on the run. Near the bridge that Deaf Smith downed, Captain James Sylvester rode alone when a movement in the ravine caught his eye. He turned to call out to his squad, scouting for game in nearby woods. By the time Sylvester looked back, the figure seemed to have vanished.

The Texian captain rode closer. At first, he saw only a Mexican blanket on the ground, almost obscured by the vegetation. Then he noticed that the blanket, worn as a serape, covered a man lying motionless.

Sylvester ordered him to stand, and the stranger—certainly a Mexican—rose reluctantly. The Kentuckians surrounded him. "He was tolerably dark skinned," noted one of them, "weighed about a hundred and forty-five pounds, and wore side whiskers." Dressed in a plain cotton jacket and an old hide cap, he appeared to carry no weapons.

Despite the language barrier, they managed to learn he was a soldier and that, no, he didn't know where Santa Anna was. But Sylvester's sharp eye saw something amiss. Beneath his plain outer garments, the Mexican wore a fine shirt with studs that glimmered like precious stones.[1]

Accused of being a liar—no mere soldier would possess such a garment—the man then admitted he was an aide to Santa Anna. To prove it, he showed them a letter in his possession from one of the Mexican generals. Sylvester and his men decided Houston might wish to interrogate this man.

Once they returned with their prisoner to their battlefield camp, however, the Mexican prisoners they passed did something unexpected. On seeing the man in the humble serape, they leapt to their feet and saluted or lifted their caps. Some clapped and cheered.

"El Presidente!" they called out to him. *"General Santa Anna!"*

Captain Sylvester and his men had captured not an aide to Santa Anna but His Excellency himself.

GENERAL MEETS GENERAL

After a night deprived of sleep due to the pain, Houston lay dozing on the ground at midday. He stirred with the approach of the company and their captive. Colonel Hockley escorted Santa Anna to Houston, where the enemy commander, his plain clothing spattered with mud, stepped forward, "advancing with an air of one born to command."[2]

He announced, in Spanish, "I am General Antonio López de Santa Anna, President of Mexico, Commander-in-Chief of the Army of Operations. I place myself at the disposal of the brave General Houston."

The surprised Houston, according to one account, replied, "Ah! Ah! indeed, General Santa Anna. Happy to see you, General." He gestured toward a nearby toolbox. "Take a seat, take a seat." General Almonte, who spoke English, was summoned into the circle.

Half sitting, Houston listened. With his officer translating, Santa Anna began with flattery. "That man may consider himself born to no common destiny, who has conquered the Napoleon of the west."

Then he added, "And it now remains for [you] to be generous to the vanquished."

Houston stared at the man, then shot back, "You should have remembered that at the Alamo."

A crowd had begun to gather as word spread around the camp of the prisoner's identity.

Houston waited, but Santa Anna offered his justification.

"I had summoned a surrender and they had refused," he explained. "The place was taken by storm, and the usages of war justified the slaughter of the vanquished."

Though Sam Houston's anger was rising, his response was measured.

"That was the case once but it is now obsolete. Such usages among civilized nations have yielded to the influences of Humanity."

As the generals' exchange grew more heated, a growing undertone of voices became audible. Among the men outside the circle of officers there were "demands for the captive's blood."[3] Some called for "the butcher of the Alamo" to be shot; others wanted to hang the man.

Santa Anna, now entirely surrounded by hostile faces, asked that his medicine box be brought to him. From it he withdrew a wad of a tincture of opium, which he swallowed, to calm his nerves. For a man accustomed to complete deference from any and everyone he met, these jarring calls for his head, even if only half understood, intimidated His Excellency.

Houston pressed him on Goliad. "If you feel excused for your conduct at San Antonio, you have not the same excuse for the massacre of Colonel Fannin's command." As if twisting the sword, he went on. "They had capitulated on terms proffered by your General. And, yet, after the capitulation, they were all perfidiously massacred."

Again, Santa Anna deflected, refusing responsibility. "I was not apprised of the fact that they had capitulated," he claimed, then he blamed General Urrea. "And if the day ever comes that I can get Urrea into my hands, I will execute him for his duplicity in not giving me information of the facts."

Aware of his men and their angry murmurs, Houston realized that pursuing these questions would only fire their fury. They already wished to exact retribution. Another thought surfaced: He must keep His Excellency alive. As a matter of honor, he could not execute this man. Furthermore, his corpse would be of little value, but alive, Santa Anna carried authority with his troops. He could be an instrument, useful in negotiating a formal armistice and in securing the surrender of the other Mexican forces in Texas.

With that, Houston veered the conversation away from confrontation.

He ordered Santa Anna's tent be set up nearby, that his trunks be brought to him. The time had come for negotiation, and Secretary of War Rusk entered the conversation; the exchange that day would last nearly two hours. Rusk would ask His Excellency to order his other generals "to evacuate the country." Santa Anna, according to one of Houston's aides, "displayed great diplomatic skill in the negotiation." He refused at first, but eventually he agreed to do as asked.[4]

The agreed-upon terms would bring a complete stop to the fighting. Santa Anna would order his generals to retreat the way they had come. In time, a treaty would be negotiated and signed (neither Houston nor Rusk could speak for the Texas government), but an armistice had been reached between these men. Provided with his own writing desk, Santa Anna wrote out orders.

Once the letters were done, Deaf Smith stowed them in his saddle-bags. He would gallop that night toward the banks of the Brazos River, where Santa Anna's orders would be delivered into the hands of General Filisola.

"I am a prisoner," His Excellency wrote to his generals, "in the hands of the enemy." More important, he informed them, "I have agreed with General Houston for an armistice." Then he issued a command: The other Mexican regiments in Texas were to countermarch to San Antonio. All prisoners were to be freed. No inhabitants of Texas were to be interfered with. "Negotiations are under way to bring the war to an end for ever."[5]

The fight for Texas's freedom had been won.

SEVENTEEN

President Sam Houston

My venerated friend, you will perceive that Texas is presented
to the United States as a bride adorned for her espousal.

—SAM HOUSTON TO ANDREW JACKSON

Two weeks after the battle, infection threatened Houston's leg.
He rested on a cot, a mile or so from the battlefield but within
range of the stench of unburied and rotting Mexican corpses.
Without proper medicines and treatment, Dr. Ewing warned, lockjaw
might kill him. Houston agreed to travel to New Orleans to seek the
medical care he needed after handing off his duties to Secretary of War
Rusk.

Several days earlier, the *Yellow Stone* had returned to Lynch's Ferry.
The riverboat's passengers included President Burnet and the cabinet,
who arrived to take charge of the peace. Never an admirer of Houston
and jealous at his success, Burnet was angered that a preliminary treaty
had been signed without his consultation; he had few good words for
the victorious general. He held Houston in low regard, despite the
events of April 21, blaming him for the long campaign, for the plight of
the fleeing settlers—the "Runaway Scrape," as it would be known—

and even the failure of the Texian army to capture the entire Mexican force.

On May 5, the feverish Houston bade his soldiers farewell. Unlike Burnet, the troops now revered their general, and he returned their esteem. "Your valor and heroism have proved you unrivalled," Houston told them. "You have patiently endured privations, hardships, and difficulties." He promised them that, one day, they would be justly famous and would proudly say, "I was a member of the army of San Jacinto."[1]

When Rusk and his brother brought Houston, still prone on a cot, to the dock, President Burnet refused Houston passage on the *Yellow Stone*. The ship was to carry the president and his cabinet, along with Santa Anna, back to Galveston, where they planned to complete the peace negotiations. According to Burnet, Houston, having resigned his commission, was no longer welcome aboard the vessel.

The ship's captain disagreed. "This ship is not sailing," he said firmly, "unless General Houston is on it."[2]

Captain John Ross knew and admired Houston; Ross's ship had played a crucial role earlier in the fight, ferrying Houston's army across the Brazos River at Groce's Landing. In the face of Ross's insistence, Burnet had no choice but to watch Major General Rusk and his brother, David, carry the ailing Houston aboard.

When the *Yellow Stone* reached Galveston, the parties went in separate directions. Burnet and his cabinet, together with their prisoner, Santa Anna, proceeded to Velasco, where they negotiated what would become known as the Treaty of Velasco. The terms were much as Houston and Rusk had suggested in the articles of understanding they prepared: Santa Anna pledged not to attack Texas and, on his return to Mexico, to use his influence on his government to agree to the peace. Santa Anna also signed a second, secret document in which he agreed to try to persuade his fellow Mexicans to recognize the Republic of

Texas as an independent state and to accept the Rio Grande as the international boundary.

As for Houston, he found passage aboard the schooner *Flora*, and lay semiconscious on the narrow deck. The ship's captain believed his famous passenger, his leg loosely wrapped in a bloodstained shirt, to be a dying man. But word of Houston's imminent arrival preceded him, and on May 22, when the *Flora* arrived in New Orleans, a cheering throng lined the levee. Some of the crowd surged aboard the little merchant vessel, nearly swamping the two-masted merchantman. All had come to see the general.

With a great effort, Houston rose to his feet to greet them. The man that many Texans now thought of as "Old San Jacinto" had become a hero, but the crowd fell silent when, after briefly bracing himself against the gunwale to greet them, he collapsed onto a litter. As she would recall years later, the sight of the great man so perilously ill caused a seventeen-year-old named Margaret Lea to burst into tears.

THE SAME SURGEON WHO, twenty-one years before, treated the wounds Houston sustained at the Battle of Horseshoe Bend removed twenty shards of bone from Houston's ankle. The patient improved slowly, recuperating in the home of a friend, a fellow soldier with whom he had marched into battle during the War of 1812. A week passed before he felt able to sit up for more than a few sips of water.

Although still weak, he began the trip back to Texas in mid-June. He regarded Nacogdoches as his home, but the ambitious Houston, a veteran of more than a few political battles, understood he now possessed real clout in Texas—and in these formative weeks in Texas's quickly evolving history, he couldn't afford to be out of sight and out of mind. He made it to Nacogdoches on June 26. Exhausted by the journey, he had no choice but to rest a few days before moving on to San Augustine, arriving there on July 5.

He corresponded constantly with friends, worrying about the state of the army and the continuing Mexican threat. General Rusk kept him apprised of political events and, in particular, of interim president Burnet's proclamation, issued July 23, calling for a general election so Texians could choose the newly independent state's president and vice president and the first Congress. The ballot also contained two crucial referenda: One sought approval of the new constitution; the other was a vote on whether the republic's citizens desired annexation by the United States. Six weeks later the people would cast their ballots.

Given his fame, he seemed a logical candidate for president, but Houston played hard to get. He insisted he could not run against the two announced candidates, his respected colleagues Stephen Austin and former governor Henry Smith. Only after repeated popular outcries—among them a mass meeting in San Augustine and a petition with six hundred signatures from Columbia—did Houston agree to run. "You will learn that I have yielded to the wishes of my friends in allowing my name to be run for President," he announced in a letter published in the *Telegraph and Texas Register.* "The crisis requires it or I would not have yielded."[3]

A week later, on September 5, Texians spoke with one voice. The voters approved the proposed state constitution by an overwhelming margin. Virtually every voter favored annexation. And Sam Houston won in a landslide, elected the republic's president by a margin of almost nine to one (5,119 for Houston, 743 for Smith, and 587 for Austin). Gracious in victory, he named Austin secretary of state and Smith secretary of the treasury. Mirabeau Buonaparte Lamar, the man Houston promoted to colonel on the San Jacinto battlefield, was seated as vice president.

After his swearing in, on October 22, Houston faced many challenges, but one of the most immediate was the matter of His Excellency. Despite having been promised his freedom after the Treaty of Velasco, Santa Anna remained a prisoner of the Republic of Texas.

SANTA ANNA MEETS ANDREW JACKSON

His Excellency lived in limbo. On May 14, he had signed the two treaties with the Republic of Texas. The documents stipulated that he was free to return home, and on June 1, he boarded the armed schooner *Invincible*, ordered to carry him to the Mexican city of Vera Cruz. Suddenly, however, the rules changed and Santa Anna embarked instead on a bizarre, nine-month odyssey.

Before the *Invincible* could put to sea, a mob of Texian volunteers interceded. Against his will, His Excellency was escorted back to shore, where, "in accordance with the overwhelming public will of the citizens of the country, he should . . . await the public will to determine his fate."⁴ In spite of what their government had agreed, many citizens wanted this man to face court-martial for war crimes. In one widely distributed pamphlet published that summer, the Mexican general's fall from grace was put in mythological terms: "Don Antonio, Icarus, in attempting to soar too high, was precipitated into the abyss below." The pamphlet condemned him as a "monster."⁵ There were rumors of a plan to take him to Goliad for execution.

In July, Stephen Austin attempted to resolve the dispute. Having recently returned from the United States, Austin visited the Mexican general, whom he knew from his own time of incarceration in Mexico City two years before. Austin suggested that perhaps the American government might mediate. Impatient and nervous at his fate, Santa Anna promptly wrote directly to Andrew Jackson, complaining of his "close confinement."[6] The recuperating Sam Houston added his voice to the conversation, writing on Santa Anna's behalf to President Jackson.

Jackson took no action; he had carefully maintained his country's neutrality throughout the conflict. But he did register his opinion with his friend Sam Houston. A trial and execution of the foreign leader would be contrary to the rules of civilized warfare. "Nothing could tarnish the character of Texas more," Jackson argued. "Let not his blood be shed . . . both wisdom and humanity enjoin this course."[7]

Santa Anna had spent six weeks with a ball and chain on his leg after a suspected escape plot. Little changed until Houston was sworn in as the first duly elected president of Texas, when he took immediate charge of the matter. First, he visited the prisoner and came away persuaded that Santa Anna was the best advocate for the new nation's quest for formal recognition by Mexico. Santa Anna had already signed a treaty in which he acknowledged "in his official character as the chief of the Mexican nations . . . the full, entire, and perfect Independence of the republic of Texas."[8]

Santa Anna agreed to undertake a mission to Washington, D.C. "Convinced as I am that Texas will never be reunited with Mexico," he promised to negotiate for peace and a final resolution of boundaries.[9] After another hot debate with the Texas government about Santa Anna's fate—the Texas Congress passed a resolution to further detain Santa Anna—Houston, claiming executive privilege, authorized the departure of his old nemesis. Santa Anna quietly headed for the American capital via an overland route, accompanied by his aides and a military escort led by Colonel Hockley.

Unlikely as it seemed, the defeated dictator had become an emissary for Sam Houston and the Republic of Texas. The United States had yet to recognize Texas and thus would not meet officially with its representatives. But in an oddity of diplomatic formalities, Santa Anna could sit down with Old Hickory—a man whose interest in Texas had never waned—and speak on Texas's behalf.

THE ROUTE TOOK His Excellency to the Sabine River, then across Louisiana. "We traveled in the *Tennessee* up the Mississippi for twenty days, then continued up the Ohio river, landing close to Louisville."[10] On the stage journey that followed, Santa Anna fell ill and spent a few days with a severe cold. But he managed to charm many of the Americans he met, impressing them as a man "pleasant of countenance and speech . . . very polite, and using stately compliments."[11] Finally, on January 17, 1837, Santa Anna's entourage arrived in Washington.

President Jackson had closely followed the progress of the Texas war; during Houston's retreat, one visitor to the president's house had found him tracing the movements of both armies on a map spread before him. And he knew the score in Mexico, since the Mexican ambassador had told him officially that, as a prisoner, Santa Anna no longer spoke for his country. Nevertheless, Jackson treated him like a head of state.

"General Jackson greeted me warmly," Santa Anna reported, "and honored me at a dinner attended by notables of all countries."[12] The formal dinner with the cabinet and foreign diplomats wasn't the end of it; over the coming days, the two leaders talked privately at least twice.

At the first private meeting, Santa Anna spoke freely in favor of Texan independence. Jackson listened, dressed casually in an old calico robe and smoking a long-stemmed pipe. The Mexican reminded Jackson that, not so many years earlier, the American ambassador had offered to purchase Texas. The circumstances were different now, he admitted, but perhaps $3.5 million might be a reasonable amount. Both men knew the Texians would oppose any such deal—wasn't Texas already independent?—and the conversation carried on.

Santa Anna managed to ingratiate himself with Jackson, who commissioned his "court painter," Ralph E. W. Earl, to take the Mexican's portrait. Santa Anna went daily to the president's house to sit for Earl, who, as an intimate friend of Jackson, maintained his studio there. After six days, Jackson authorized a U.S. Navy vessel, the *Pioneer*, to carry Santa Anna to Vera Cruz, the very destination designated many months before in the Velasco treaty. His Excellency sailed from Norfolk, Virginia, on January 26.

Their conversations left President Jackson with much to think about. Perhaps Santa Anna would persuade the new Mexican administration to recognize the treaties of Velasco or the independence of Texas; maybe he wouldn't. But Jackson did know the voters of Texas wanted to join the United States, a desire shared for many years by Houston and Jackson, who now served as presidents of their respective countries. Yet, for the moment, at least, the political realities in Washington made that impossible.

The nation was grappling with a growing and angry debate about slavery. Powerful people in the North—among them Jackson's old nemesis John Quincy Adams, now an outspoken congressman— zealously guarded a delicate balance in Congress, and the admission of Texas as a slaveholding state would topple that house of cards. Jackson couldn't simply order annexation; the powers of the president did not extend that far. But he did have a hand he could play.

In the waning days of his second term, he reached out to his allies in Congress and a resolution passed; it wasn't annexation but the next best thing: recognition of the Republic of Texas as an independent nation. In Jackson's last official act before leaving office, he named a chargé d'affaires to Texas. When the appointment was confirmed by Congress near midnight on Friday, March 4, Jackson invited two Texas officials to join him in a glass of wine. They toasted: *To Texas!*[13] Officially, in the view of the United States of America, the Republic of Texas became an independent country.

The Founding and the Founders of Texas

Our success in the action is conclusive proof of such daring intrepidity and courage; every officer and man proved himself worthy of the cause in which he battled, while the triumph received a lustre from the humanity which characterized their conduct after victory.

—SAM HOUSTON, APRIL 25, 1836

The men who fought for Texas in 1835–36 would fill the ranks of its first generation of leaders. Some held important political offices; others continued to serve in its army. They became a permanent part of Texas history.

Not a few of those who fought—and some who died in the cause—became half-remembered names that appear on the map of today's Texas. There are counties named for Bowie, Fannin, Karnes, Milam, Burnet, and Deaf Smith, along with uncounted cities and towns whose names commemorate soldiers and officers in the Texian army. These names—and a shared commitment by the state and its educators—help keep the Texas Revolution alive in the minds of the state's citizens.

When STEPHEN F. AUSTIN died on December 27, 1836, President Houston proclaimed, "The Father of Texas is no more! The first pioneer of the wilderness has departed." He ordered a twenty-three-gun salute (one for each county in the republic), to be fired at all posts, garrisons, and detachments "as soon as information is received of this melancholy event."[1] The empresario was destined to be remembered as the William Bradford of Texas; his "Three Hundred" as the Texas pilgrims. When the Texas capital was relocated to a place called Waterloo on the Colorado River, the name was changed to Austin in his honor.

ERASTUS (DEAF) SMITH played an incalculably large role in the Texas Revolution. His intelligence gathering looms large in the narrative that led to the Battle of San Jacinto. His destruction of the bridge at Vince's Bayou meant a great deal after the battle; its destruction prevented Santa Anna's escape on the afternoon of April 21. If he had gotten away, His Excellency might have rejoined the rest of his army and engaged in further fights with the Texians. In the long list of historical what-ifs, one can only wonder.

After the war, Deaf Smith returned to San Antonio and his Tejana wife, Guadalupe. He remained in the army of the Texas republic, and after Sam Houston became president, the new chief executive commissioned a portrait of Smith from the same artist, T. Jefferson Wright, who would paint two of Houston. But Smith would die, at age fifty, just nine months after the Battle of San Jacinto. The cause of death was a lung ailment, quite likely consumption (tuberculosis), a condition no doubt worsened by his months of service to the Texian cause.

MIRABEAU BUONAPARTE LAMAR succeeded Houston, becoming the second president of Texas and Houston's chief political rival; DAVID G. BURNET served as Lamar's vice president. JAMES SYLVESTER returned to his first career and found work as a printer at the *New Orleans Picayune*. MOSELEY BAKER became a Methodist minister. JAMES COLLINSWORTH served as the republic's first chief justice (in 1836) before committing suicide (in 1838).

Although JIM BOWIE and DAVID CROCKETT died at the Alamo, both men gained the status of legend in Texas and beyond. Disputed mythologies emerged, with contradictory accounts of their actions and where and how each man died. Whatever the actual facts of their deaths, they did the opposite of slide into obscurity. Crockett became the ultimate symbol of the plain-speaking frontiersman—a man-versus-nature character uniquely equipped to confront the unknown, a man willing to fight for what he believed regardless of personal cost. Bowie stands as the ultimate fighter, a man as tough as he was resourceful, his fame only enhanced by the weapon that bore his name.

In military annals, the heroic lines of wordsmith WILLIAM BARRET TRAVIS—*"I am determined to sustain myself as long as possible & die like a soldier who never forgets what is due to his own honor & that of his country"*—still ring as raw and powerful as any prayer.

Many survivors of the Texas War of Independence went on to record their recollections in books, essays, and interviews. To name just a few . . . after his adventures with the New Orleans Greys—which involved escaping alive from Goliad—HERMAN EHRENBERG returned to his native Germany and wrote a book, *Texas und seine Revolution* (1843). It didn't appear in an English translation until 1935, when it was released bearing the title *With Milam and Fannin: Adventures of a German Boy in Texas' Revolution*. NOAH SMITHWICK, by then old and blind, dictated his memoirs to his daughter; though he died in 1899, she oversaw publication the following year. Drs. Barnard and Labadie wrote invaluable narratives of what happened at Goliad and San Jacinto, respectively. Perhaps the last of the survivors to die was Enrique Esparza, just twelve years old when the Alamo fell. As an old man, the Tejano was still telling the story into the early years of the twentieth century.

On the Mexican side, a number of officers also recorded their version of events, including Vicente Filisola, Pedro Delgado, and José Enrique de la Peña.

SUSANNA DICKINSON's life grew no less complicated. She would marry a total of five times; one soon-to-be ex-husband accused her of taking up residence in a "house of ill fame." But she lived until 1883, having spent the last quarter century married to a prosperous businessman and undertaker. Almeron and Susanna's daughter, Angelina, died less happily, of a hemorrhaging uterus, at age thirty-four, after a checkered life involving three abandoned children, three marriages, and years of working as a prostitute during the Civil War.

THE ALAMO itself assumed a place in the history and the mythology of Texas. The narrative is irresistible: Brave men fighting for freedom and democracy are crushed by a brutal autocrat and then avenged. It is a tale of good and evil, with the democratic future taking on a dictatorial regime that had robbed the people of their rights. The men at the Alamo lost both the battle and their lives, but they gained immortality in the epic of Texas.

On his return to Mexico, in February 1837, ANTONIO LÓPEZ DE SANTA ANNA, his reputation tarnished by the defeat at San Jacinto, went into retirement. A year later, however, he resumed military service and helped repel a French assault on Vera Cruz. After losing a leg in the engagement, his reputation rose to nearly its previous heights—the leg was given a state funeral—and, for a time in the early 1840s, he resumed power as president. He served as Mexico's provisional president during the war with the United States (1846–48), during which his army was defeated twice on the field of battle by American troops. He lived a long life, in and out of power, exiled for periods to Jamaica, Venezuela, Cuba, and even, in 1867, the United States. He completed his memoirs in 1874 and died two years later, lame, bitter, and senile, in Mexico City, aged eighty.

Santa Anna's role in the Texas Revolution would be debated over the decades. Even some of his own officers judged him a butcher, and within months of the events of early 1836, a Mexican officer wrote a memoir describing the "infamies that have occurred in this campaign, infamies that must have horrified the civility world." But his superiors suppressed the book; it would not be published until late in the twentieth century.[2] Military historians on all sides agree that the great Texian victory at San Jacinto was made possible in part by Santa Anna's tactical errors: He permitted too great a distance to separate him from reinforcements and his sources of supply and, even more important, he made his San Jacinto camp in a vulnerable location, with bodies of water on three sides and nearby piney woods and oak groves that provided cover for Houston and undercut the advantages of the Mexican cavalry.

THE STATE OF TEXAS

In 1838, forbidden by the Texas Constitution to serve consecutive terms, President SAM HOUSTON left office. He spent much of the following summer in Nashville, visiting Andrew Jackson at the Hermitage. In 1840, he remarried; his new wife, Margaret Lea, had first laid her violet eyes on him in New Orleans when the wounded General Houston could barely stand.

His wife was twenty-six years his junior but convinced the man once known as "the Big Drunk" to stop drinking. (Several years later at a public event he made a "Big Speech" before a barbecue that one in attendance described as "a cold water doins. The Old Chief did not touch or taste or handle the smallest drop of the ardent."[3]) Margaret would bear eight children, among them a son, Andrew Jackson Houston, who wrote a fine book about the Texas Revolution, published a century after the Battle of San Jacinto.

In 1841, Houston won reelection as president of a prosperous Texas (its population had more than doubled). As his three-year term grew to a close, he once again enlisted Andrew Jackson in a campaign to fulfill their shared wish for Texas, the immediate annexation into the Union.

By then the great Jackson suffered from many ailments; a hard life had taken a toll and he surely neared the end. But he immediately rose to Houston's challenge. The task proved sustaining for Jackson. He and his old Washington operatives made the case to congressional cohorts. It was Jackson's last great cause, and he fought for it against the determined opposition of two other great men of the time, John Quincy Adams and Henry Clay.

Houston and Jackson—and the Texans, as they soon became generally known—were rewarded with the passage of the annexation resolution. The great, unruly Texas would become the twenty-eighth American state, although Mexico, having never formally recognized the Republic of Texas, would not abandon its claims on Texas until after the Mexican-American War, with the signing of the Treaty of Guadalupe Hidalgo in 1848.

Although Jackson died within a few months, Sam Houston would, along with THOMAS JEFFERSON RUSK, represent Texas in the U.S. Senate. (Rusk would, however, take his own life in 1857, in his grief at the death of his wife.) Houston regularly found himself in the crossfire of controversy both during his two terms in the Senate and, after 1859, when, as Texas's aging elder statesman, he was reelected to yet another term as governor of Texas. His last public role ended prematurely when he was forced to resign, having taken an unpopular stance against secession. He would die on July 26, 1863, but among the last words Sam Houston spoke, according to his fifteen-year-old daughter Maggie, were *"Texas! Texas!"*[4]

The debates that seemed always to swirl around him did not end with his death. No two biographers or military historians agreed about

Houston's war, his politics, his character, or his life. In no instance is that more true than his role as Texas's commander in chief in early 1836.

As early as July 1837 a pamphlet appeared attacking his conduct of the war, asserting that the men in his command forced him to fight.[5] The debate endures to the present day concerning his willingness (or lack of willingness) to fight Santa Anna's army. The long retreat (the "Runaway Scrape"—the origins of the name remain obscure, but not its unflattering meaning); the turn south at the "Which-Way Tree"; and the final decision to attack on April 21 are all subject to disagreement. On the one hand, his detractors regarded him as a coward; among them were officers who had served him, including Moseley Baker, who in 1837 attempted to impeach Houston, who was then serving as president of Texas.

Houston defended himself, sometimes in the second person. Houston wasn't bashful about defending his "glorious victory" at San Jacinto. "Here was born, in the throes of revolution and amid the strike on contending legions, the infant of Texas independence!" he once said. "Here that latest scourge of mankind, the arrogantly self-styled 'Napoleon of the West,' met his fate."[6] Sam Houston, through some mix of luck, instinct, fortuitous timing, and the good counsel—and bravery—of the men around him, did something remarkable. He and his army of farmers and shopkeepers, men distracted by the plight of their families and friends, who had become homeless wanderers fleeing for their lives, faced off with a large professional army, one amply supplied with guns, artillery, and munitions. And won a stunning, one-sided victory.

In the days after that battle, he quickly emerged as a Texas icon, indispensable, the man most often credited with winning Texas her independence. And the flood of American citizens that poured into Texas thought of him as the founder.

Often he let other people speak to his character; for one, he gave Henderson King Yoakum, a lawyer friend, access to his closely held papers to write a history of early Texas, in which Houston was cast in favorable light (Yoakum's two-volume history of Texas's early days was published in 1846). Houston himself produced a remarkable memoir, *The Life of Sam Houston*, with the memorable subtitle *The Only Authentic Memoir of Him Ever Published*.

Sam Houston, a lover of books since childhood, recognized the power of the printed word.

IN THE END, this isn't a story of politics, local or geopolitical. The brief war of independence is a story of redemption: The slaughter at the Alamo was avenged with the stunning victory at San Jacinto. An unlikely hero emerged in the process and, schooled by Andrew Jackson, Sam Houston performed the role of Texas's George Washington.

In a larger context, the devastating losses and the remarkable outcome of the war helped shape the character of a new nation, one destined to flower only briefly before binding its destiny to that of the United States. Taken together, the events of spring 1836 were a defining moment in the formation of the larger American character.

In the American memory the Alamo defenders became martyrs to liberty. That's why we remember them and the place where they fell.

A wise man once observed, "Quarter hours decide the destinies of nations." The words have been credited to Napoléon, but whether he said them or not, he would undoubtedly have agreed that San Jacinto's eighteen minutes amounts to a textbook example. The fight at the Alamo remains the best-remembered event of the war, but in military and even political terms, the battle on April 21, 1836, at San Jacinto stands higher. Sam Houston's greatest day not only secured independence for what would be the Republic of Texas, but it also made possible the fulfillment of his and Jackon's dream. Thanks to Houston, Texas could now one day become part of the great American story. And thanks to Texas, America could one day spread from sea to shining sea.

Old Sam and Honest Abe

I am making my last effort to save Texas from the yawning
gulf of ruin.

—SAM HOUSTON TO ED BURLESON, NOVEMBER 9, 1860

During the winter of 1860–61, Sam Houston looked his age.
At sixty-seven, Governor Houston was a father figure to the
600,000 men, women, and children of Texas. Only it looked
like the Texans weren't going to listen to their elder this time.

Beyond Texas's borders, the nation was coming apart. In response to
Abraham Lincoln's election to the presidency, Southerners had called
for secession in November 1860. South Carolina had, in December,
withdrawn from the Union, followed the next month by Mississippi,
Florida, Alabama, Georgia, and Louisiana. Now there was talk that
Texas might follow them.

In 1859, Houston had run for the governorship on a pro-Union platform. At his inauguration in December he had preached unity, saying
that "When Texas united her destiny with that of the government of
the United States, she . . . entered into not the North, nor into the South,
but into the Union; her connection was not sectional but national."[1] He

wasn't about to let the state to which he had devoted his life leave the union without pushing back.

The odds were not in Houston's favor—no question, the fight for slavery and state rights was important to many, many Texans—but Houston was beloved by many Texans and used his influence. He wasn't afraid to pluck the heartstrings of those who revered him as a Texan founding father. "I cannot be long among you," he'd told a crowd the previous fall. "My sands of life are fast running out. As the glass becomes exhausted, if I can feel that I leave my country prosperous and united, I shall die content."[2]

As admired as he was, Houston's emotional appeal did not stop the secessionist tide, and Houston turned to his political wiles. First, he tried to outmaneuver the secessionists, refusing their demand that he call a special session of the Texas legislature. Then, when his opponents convened a special Texas Secession Convention anyway and promptly voted to secede, Houston declared a statewide ballot was required to make their vote legitimate. Finally, when the majority of the state voted to leave the Union, Houston insisted that Texas could withdraw from the Union only to return to independence. The reborn Republic of Texas, he argued, could not legitimately join the Confederacy.

The very last thing the old warrior wanted was for Texas to go to war—and he was sure that joining the Confederacy would make that inevitable. "I know what war is," he told a committee of Texas secessionists, opening his shirt to reveal to them fresh bandages on wounds he sustained in 1814 at the Battle of Horseshoe Bend, which had never fully healed. "War is no plaything and this war will be a bloody war. There will be thousands and thousands who march away from our homes never to come back."[3]

Houston's stratagems and arguments were ultimately in vain. On March 15, 1861, the delegates to the Texas Secession Convention swore a unanimous oath of allegiance to the Confederacy while he was not present. At eight o'clock that evening Houston heard a knock at the door of the governor's mansion. A convention delegate presented a demand, an order for Houston to appear at noon the following day to take the same vow.

With no way of pushing off the decision, the aged Houston now had to decide. Would he be loyal to Texas or the Union? Would he sign the oath presented by the representatives of the people? He had only hours to make up his mind.

After reading a Bible chapter aloud to his household, he bade his family good night. His gait uneven, he made his way upstairs to his bedroom, where he removed his coat, vest, and shoes. He then began to pace the length of the mansion's cavernous upper hall. As his eldest daughter Nancy described the long night, Houston "wrestl[ed] with his spirit as Jacob wrestled with the angel until the purple dawn of another day shone over the eastern hills."[4]

By morning, he had made a decision. His wife, who had listened to the nighttime creaking of the pine floorboards above, heard the news first when Old Sam descended.

"Margaret," he told her, "I will never do it."

As ordered, Houston did go to the capitol. In his office, he sat quietly in his chair, his eyes fixed on a small piece of wood, whittling as he so often did when deep in thought. He had prepared a speech, which read, in part, "In the name of the Constitution of Texas, which has been trampled upon, I refuse to take this oath." At noon he heard the summons.

"*Sam Houston! Sam Houston! Sam Houston*," rang out from the chamber above.

Houston heard the summons. He exited his office. But instead of heading upstairs and delivering his speech, he simply walked out the door.

He knew he was beaten, that to give another of his powerful speeches would only inflame things. The speech could be published later, he decided. For now, he would return to the governor's mansion and allow the conventioneers to conclude what they would.

When he failed to appear, the conventioneers promptly declared the office of governor vacant. Houston, once the hero of Texas, had been kicked out.

Back at the governor's mansion, he began to pack up his papers and his books. He and Margaret and their children would be moving, bound for political exile. At last, after devoting most of the previous half century to public service, his long history of leadership was coming to an end.

Or was it?

MR. LINCOLN'S LETTERS

That same week, a messenger arrived from Washington, D.C. Leaping from his exhausted horse, the rider handed Sam Houston a letter, its official wax seal intact. The letter had traveled more than fifteen hundred miles. The sender? Abraham Lincoln.

Houston's Union sympathies were well known in Washington. One of Lincoln's most trusted advisors, Francis P. Blair, Sr., described him as "a true union man." The rumor mill suggested he might even be Lincoln's choice for secretary of war.

In the letter, Lincoln made no such offer. Instead, he asked for Houston's help. Since his inauguration, Lincoln had focused his energy on retaining any southern states that had yet to secede. He thought it particularly important to keep Virginia, the state he could see from his upstairs office at the White House. He might well lose Tennessee and Arkansas, but could the Union hold the border states of Maryland, Kentucky, and Missouri? And then there was the vast territory of Texas: If the Union could retain Houston's state, could that be a bulwark?

Desperate to keep the largest state in the Union, Lincoln had a proposition for the man Texans most respected: he would provide federal support if Houston would help keep Texas in the Union.

With Lincoln's double request, Houston found himself in a quandary. On the one hand, the president wanted Houston to join the Union cause and promised him the support of the U.S. Army and Navy. On the other, the secessionists had already outflanked Houston, dismissing him from office; he was literally packing his bags, facing an unwanted retirement and unlikely to prevail through persuasion.

Should he accept the offer? He didn't fear being an outcast; he'd been one before. He had a chance to be back in military command: Lincoln had offered him the rank of major general and there were still federal troops in Texas that would be under his command. He could undoubtedly raise Texas volunteers, perhaps tens of thousands of men. But could such an army make a difference? Would Houston somehow turn the tide? Could he tip Texas back from the brink of the kind of bloodshed he so wanted to avoid? And did he want to take up arms against his beloved state?

Rarely a man to seek the counsel of others, Houston nonetheless summoned four valued friends in the wee hours after reading the letter. In a secret meeting in the upstairs library of the governor's mansion, he told the four of Lincoln's offer. He laid out the situation. He shared with them his dilemma.

Texas legislator Ben Epperson responded first. The youngest of the party, he spoke passionately in favor of accepting the offer, of taking up arms and fighting the secessionists. David Culberson, a transplanted Georgian, thought differently. He argued that Texas, given its great distance from the likely battlefields east of the Mississippi, would escape many of the war's horrors. If, however, they were to fight the secessionists, "the State would necessarily become the theatre of active and widespread hostilities, and the land be overrun and devastated with fire and sword."[5] The other two sided with Culberson, speaking against Lincoln's proposal.

After hearing his friends out, Houston sat silently, deep in thought. Then, moving abruptly to the mantel, he crumpled the correspondence from Lincoln and tossed it into the fire on the hearth. As the men watched, Lincoln's invitation burned to ashes, along with Houston's hopes for Texas.

He turned to his friends. "Gentlemen, I have asked your advice and will take it, but if I was twenty years younger I would not."[6] He knew he was too old to fight. His family was too young, with children ranging in age from seven months to seventeen years. The offer was too late. And Sam Houston could not bring himself to start a civil war between Texans.

TWO OLD SOLDIERS

On March 31, Houston would leave Austin, headed for his home near Galveston. But before he left, Noah Smithwick, one of his Alamo Avengers, came to call.

Secession, Smithwick said, filled him with "a feeling of inexpressible sadness." He had decided to leave Texas, to head for California, "fleeing the wrath to come." But before going, he wished to offer his services to Sam Houston one last time.

"General," he told Houston, "if you will again unfurl the Lone Star from the capitol, I will bring you a hundred men to help maintain it there."

Though honored by the man's willingness to fight for him, Houston remained firm. "My friend," he told Smithwick, "I have seen Texas pass through one long, bloody war. I do not wish to involve her in civil strife. I have done all I could to keep her from seceding, and now if she won't go with me I'll have to turn and go with her."[7]

Houston's biggest fear was the outcome of the imminent war, and, in April, he warned his fellow Texans they might well be the losers. "[T]he North is determined to preserve this Union. They are not a fiery, impulsive people as you are, for they live in colder climates. But when they begin to move in a given direction . . . they move with the steady momentum and perseverance of a mighty avalanche; and what I fear is, they will overwhelm the South."[8]

A few days later, after word of the bombardment at Fort Sumter reached Texas, he tried and failed to dissuade Sam Houston Jr. from enlisting in the Confederate Army. The teenaged Sam ignored his father's pleas; though wounded at Shiloh, he would survive the war, having gained a lieutenant's rank.

Sam Sr., however, would not live to see the end of the war, dying two years before Lincoln saw the country reunited in April 1865. Had he lived, he would have rejoiced to see the Union restored and mourned to see the death of Honest Abe. Unlikely brothers, their differences outnumbering their similarities, they shared a dread of civil war and a deep love for the Constitution. They were constitutionalists to the core who put their faith in the governing document, courageous men unafraid to take hard positions. They suffered for their country, and without them we would not have the great nation we've been privileged to inherit.

—Brian Kilmeade, May 2020

ACKNOWLEDGMENTS

This book would not have been possible without John Finley, who oversaw the launch of Fox Nation in 2018 and allowed me to host a series called "What Made America Great." Finley's passion and knowledge of history rivals anyone I have met, and his faith in me to pull off this series was truly gratifying. After American viewers received our first topic, the Alamo, enthusiastically, I knew it had to be the subject of my next book.

After I had decided to write about the Alamo, legendary documentarian Ken Burns prompted me to expand the story of the Alamo into a book about American victory, ending with the Battle of San Jacinto. I'm grateful to him for his guidance and inspiration.

Thanks for getting the book made goes to the team at Sentinel, led by its president and publisher, Adrian Zackheim. He once again spearheaded a tight-knit, visionary group, including first and foremost my editor, Bria Sandford, who guided me through the writing of this book fearlessly; her talent, intelligence, and expertise is indispensable on every project. Sentinel's publicity team, led by Tara Gilbride, is the best in the business, and publicist Marisol Salaman never leaves the smallest detail unaddressed. Thank you also to Madeline Montgomery and Helen Healey, who were crucial to the marketing and editorial efforts. Special thanks to Bob Barnett for making this relationship possible.

My producer, Alyson Mansfield, is the glue who brings all of these books and book tours together, along with lining up radio and TV; her leadership is formidable. Thank you to *Brian Kilmeade Radio Show* superstars Pete Catrina and Eric Albein, who offer each book tremendous support on our airwaves—from coming up with creative ways to spread the word to bringing on special guests to discuss the book. The special and on-air support would not be possible without the backing of John Sylvester and Doug Murphy.

The special media promotion was pioneered and produced by the husband-and-wife team of Paul and Amanda Guest, who might just be the best in the business.

Lauren Petterson, Gavin Hadden, and the entire *Fox and Friends* staff are without a doubt the engine behind this book. They make every book launch feel like a holiday, getting our audience excited about another great slice of American history is coming their way. Special thanks to anchors Ainsley Earhardt and Steve Doocy for their patriotism and support, along with weather machine Janis Dean and news anchor Jillian Mele.

I'd also like to thank UTA super-agents Adam Leibner, Jerry Silbowitz, Byrd Leavell, and powerhouse president Jay Sures for their vision and loyalty.

Extraordinary thanks goes to Rupert and Lachlan Murdoch, Suzanne Scott, and Jay Wallace. Through the turmoil of last few years, they have offered me tremendous support, while allowing me to grow the history side of my career. I know full well without Fox viewers and listeners I would not have my passionate, dedicated, patriotic readers.

Thank you to Bruce Winders, curator of the Alamo museum, for his impeccable research efforts. He was invaluable to us, as were Lisa Struthers of San Jacinto Library and Museum, historian Douglas Brinkley, and Scott McMahon, who helped bring the Battle of Goliad to life in my mind.

FOR FURTHER READING

Reconstructing history is always a difficult business. In the case of the Texas Revolution—and, in particular, the Battle of the Alamo—the uncertainties, paradoxes, and even outright contradictions are many among the primary sources.

Writing history is about judgments. Whose word do you take? We have testimony from Texians and Mexicans and, when their versions coincide, recounting the story is not difficult. But Santa Anna's version, for example, is self-serving and political and often at odds with not only Texian takes but even the recollections of his own officers. Historians largely discount some versions—Félix Nuñez's version of the fall of the Alamo, for example—but largely trust others, such as José Enrique de la Peña's. In truth, each version has its own imperfections; thus, my approach has been to examine all of them, to compare and contrast, and then make my best judgment as to what most likely happened.

This book could not exist were it not for many earlier students of this war who assembled the secondary sources I've also consulted. The literature of Texas independence is vast: The Alamo alone has been the subject of more than a hundred books; dozens more have examined the battles at San Jacinto and Goliad. Sam Houston himself has engaged many biographers.

All of which leads me to a few words of appreciation: One of the joys of writing a book like this is the opportunity to make the acquaintance of the many books and articles by authors living and dead who've tread this territory before. Again, though, there is the challenge of figuring out whose version is the closest to the truth—and, yes, as you would expect, the disagreements among the story-tellers are many, ranging from trivial to huge. Troop estimates always seem to vary; often dates and times do, too, along with the spelling of names (of people and places) and many other "facts." Some writers seem somehow to know what seems unknowable, which can make it difficult to distinguish between fresh but reasonable assumptions and out-there guesswork. One triangulates, makes considered judgments, consults experts where possible, and, in the end, as with any book that looks with care at the historic past, then refers back to the original documents.

Of those there are many. The papers of Sam Houston, Stephen F. Austin, and Andrew Jackson have been essential sources, along with the compendious *Papers of the Texas Revolution* (10 vols., 1973) and *Official Correspondence of the Texan Revolution* (2 vols., 1936).

In these pages you'll also find the words of many minor figures. Largely forgotten fighters like Noah Smithwick, W. C. Swearingen, Herman Ehrenberg, Abel Morgan, Pedro Delgado, Jack Shackelford, John Sowers Brooks, José Enrique de la Peña, Dr. John Sutherland, Charles Mason, Sergeant Francisco Becerra, David Macomb—and dozens of others—left us reports, letters, and memoirs. Not a few of those are found at the valuable online resource sonsofde wittcolony.org. Some of the recollections are more reliable than others, upon occasion contradicting one another and even taking sides to praise or to damn such commanders as James Fannin, William Travis, and, in particular, Sam Houston.

My thanks, then, to the writers, living and dead, and their books, listed below, for providing the facts and circumstances that enabled me to tell this tale.

Austin, Stephen F. *The Austin Papers: October 1834–January 1837.* Vol. 3. Eugene C. Barker, ed. Austin: University of Texas, 1924.

―――. "General Austin's Order Book for the Campaign of 1835." *Quarterly of the Texas State Historical Association.* Vol. 11, no. 1 (July 1907), pp. 1–55.

Austin, William T. "Siege and Battle of Bexar," 1844. https://sonsofdewittcol ony.org.

Barker, Eugene Campbell. "The San Jacinto Campaign." *Quarterly of the Texas State Historical Association.* Vol. 4 (April 1901), pp. 237–345.

———. "Stephen F. Austin and the Independence of Texas." *Quarterly of the Texas State Historical Association.* Vol. 1, no. 4 (April 1910), pp. 257–84.

Barnard, Joseph Henry. "Dr. J. H. Barnard's Journal." *The Goliad Advance.* June 1912.

Barr, Alwyn. *Texans in Revolt: The Battle for San Antonio, 1835.* Austin: University of Texas Press, 1990.

Becerra, Francisco. *A Mexican Sergeant's Recollections of the Alamo and San Jacinto.* Austin, TX: Jenkins, 1980.

Belohlavek, John M. *Let the Eagle Soar!* Lincoln: University of Nebraska Press, 1985.

Bennet, Miles A. "The Battle of Gonzales, the 'Lexington' of the Texas Revolution." *Quarterly of the Texas State Historical Association.* Vol. 2, no. 4 (April 1899), pp. 313–16.

Binkley, William C., ed. *Official Correspondence of the Texan Revolution, 1835–1836.* 2 vols. New York: D. Appleton-Century, 1936.

Bowie, John. "Early Life in the Southwest—The Bowies." *De Bow's Southern and Western Review,* October 1852, pp. 378–83.

Brack, Gene M. *Mexico Views Manifest Destiny.* Albuquerque: University of New Mexico Press, 1975.

Brands, H. W. *Lone Star Nation.* New York: Doubleday, 2004.

Brogan, Evelyn. *"James Bowie," A Hero of the Alamo.* San Antonio: T. Kunzman, 1922.

Brown, Gary. *Hesitant Martyr in the Texas Revolution: James Walker Fannin.* Plano, TX: Republic of Texas Press, 2000.

Brown, John Henry. *History of Texas, 1685 to 1892.* St. Louis: L. E. Daniell, 1892.

Bruce, Henry. *Life of General Houston, 1793–1863.* New York: Dodd, Mead, 1891.

Bryan, Moses Austin. "Reminiscences of M. A. Bryan." Typescript, Moses Austin Bryan Papers. Albert and Ethel Herzstein Library, San Jacinto Museum of History, n.d.

Buell, Augustus C. *History of Andrew Jackson: Pioneer, Patriot, Soldier, Politician, President.* 2 vols. New York: Charles Scribner's Sons, 1904.

Burleson, Rufus C. *The Life and Writings of Rufus C. Burleson.* [Waco, TX], 1901.

Calder, R. J. "Recollections of the Campaign of 1836." *The Texas Almanac, 1857–1873.* Waco, TX: Texian Press, 1967, pp. 444–56.

Callcott, Wilfrid Hardy. *Santa Anna.* Norman: University of Oklahoma Press, 1936.

Cantrell, Gregg. *Stephen F. Austin, Empresario of Texas.* New Haven, CT: Yale University Press, 1999.

Castañeda, Carlos, et al. *Mexican Side of the Texan Revolution, by the Mexican Participants.* Dallas: P. L. Turner, 1928.

Chariton, Wallace O. *100 Days in Texas: The Alamo Letters.* Plano, TX: Wordware, 1990.

Clarke, Mary Whatley. *Thomas J. Rusk: Soldier, Statesman, Jurist.* Austin: Jenkins, 1971.

Cole, Donald B. *The Presidency of Andrew Jackson.* Lawrence: University Press of Kansas, 1993.

Coleman, Robert Morris. *Houston Displayed, or Who Won the Battle of San Jacinto? By a Farmer in the Army.* Austin: Brick Row Book Shop, 1964.

Crimmins, M. L. "American Powder's Part in Winning Texas Independence." *Southwestern Historical Quarterly.* Vol. 52, no. 1 (July 1948), pp. 109–11.

Crisp, James E. *Sleuthing the Alamo: Davy Crockett's Last Stand and Other Mysteries of the Texas Revolution.* New York: Oxford University Press, 2005.

Crisp, James E., and Dan Kilgore. *How Did Davy Die? And Why Do We Care So Much?* College Station: Texas A&M University Press, 2010.

Crockett, Davy. *The Autobiography of David Crockett.* New York: Charles Scribner's Sons, 1923. (Note: This volume contains several Crockett works, including *A Narrative of the Life of David Crockett, of the State of Tennessee, Written by Himself,* 1834.)

———. *A Narrative of the Life of David Crockett by Himself.* Lincoln, NE: Bison, 1987.

Cummins, Light Townsend, and Mary L. Scheer. *Texan Identities: Moving beyond Myth, Memory, and Fallacy in Texas History.* Denton: University of North Texas Press, 2016.

Davenport, Harbert. "The Men of Goliad: Dedicatory Address and the Unveiling of the Monument Erected by the Texas Centennial Commission at the Grave of Fannin's Men." *Southwestern Historical Quarterly.* Vol. 43, no. 1 (July 1939), pp. 1–41.

Davis, William C. *Lone Star Rising: The Revolutionary Birth of the Texas Republic.* New York: Free Press, 2004.

———. *Three Roads to the Alamo: The Lives and Fortunes of David Crockett, James Bowie, and William Barret Travis.* New York: HarperCollins, 1998.

Day, James M. *The Texas Almanac, 1857–1873.* Waco, TX: Texian Press, 1967.

De Bruhl, Marshall. *Sword of San Jacinto: A Life of Sam Houston.* New York: Random House, 1993.

Delgado, Pedro. "Delgado's Account of the Battle." Reprinted in Barker, "The San Jacinto Campaign." *Quarterly of the Texas State Historical Association.* Vol. 4 (April 1901), pp. 287–91.

Dixon, Sam Houston, and Louis Wiltz Kemp. *Heroes of San Jacinto.* Houston: Anson Jones Press, 1932.

Dobie, J. Frank. "James Bowie, Big Dealer." *Southwestern Historical Quarterly.* Vol. 60, no. 1 (January 1957), pp. 337–57.

Ehrenberg, Herman. "A Campaign in Texas." *Blackwood's Magazine.* Vol. 59, no. 363 (January 1846), pp. 37–53.

———. *With Milam and Fannin: Adventures of a German Boy in Texas' Revolution.* Translated by Charlotte Churchill. Dallas: Tardy, 1935.

Featherstonehaugh, George William. *Excursion Through the Slave States, from Washington on the Potomac to the Frontier of Mexico; with Sketches of Popular Manners and Geological Notices.* New York: Harper & Brothers, 1844.

Field, Joseph E. *Three Years in Texas.* Greenfield, MA: Justin Jones, 1836.

Filisola, Vicente. *Memoirs for the History of the War in Texas.* Translated by Wallace Woolsey. 2 vols. Austin: Eakin Press, 1985. Originally published in 1848.

Flores, Richard R. *Remembering the Alamo: Memory, Modernity, and the Master Symbol.* Austin: University of Texas Press, 2002.

Folsom, Bradley. *Arrendondo: Last Spanish Ruler of Texas and Northeastern New Spain.* Norman: University of Oklahoma Press, 2017.

Foote, Henry Stuart. *Texas and the Texians.* Vol. 2. Philadelphia: Thomas, Cowperthwait, 1841.

Forbes, John. "Memorandum for Col. E. Yoakum," December 25, 1858. Personal Papers of Sam Houston, box 29, folder 36. Albert and Ethel Herzstein Library, San Jacinto Museum of History.

Fowler, Will. *Santa Anna of Mexico.* Lincoln: University of Nebraska Press, 2007.

Friend, Llerena. *Sam Houston: The Great Designer.* Austin: University of Texas Press, 1954.

Garrison, George Pierce, ed. Diplomatic Correspondence of the Republic of Texas. Washington, DC: Government Printing Office, 1908.

Garver, Lois. "Benjamin Rush Milam, Chapter III (continued)." *Southwestern Historical Quarterly.* Vol. 38, no. 3 (January 1935), pp. 177–222.

Gray, William Fairfax. *From Virginia to Texas, 1835. Diary of Col. Wm. F. Gray.* Houston: Gray, Dillaye, 1909.

Green, Rena Maverick, ed. *Samuel Maverick, Texan: 1803–1870.* San Antonio: privately printed, 1952.

Gregory, Jack, and Rennard Strickland. *Sam Houston with the Cherokees, 1829–1833.* Norman: University of Oklahoma Press, 1996.

Haley, James L. *Sam Houston.* Norman: University of Oklahoma Press, 2002.

Hardin, Stephen L. "The Félix Nuñez Account and the Siege of the Alamo: A Critical Appraisal." *Southwestern Historical Quarterly.* Vol. 4, no. 1 (July 1990), pp. 65–84.

———. "Line in the Sand; Lines on the Soul." In Cummins and Scheer, *Texan Identities* (2016).

———. *Texian Iliad—A Military History of the Texas Revolution, 1835–1836.* Austin: University of Texas Press, 1994.

Harris, Dilue. "The Reminiscences of Mrs. Dilue Harris." *Quarterly of the Texas State Historical Association.* Vol. 4, no. 3 (January 1901), pp. 155–89.

Hatch, Thom. *Encyclopedia of the Alamo and the Texas Revolution.* Jefferson, NC: McFarland, 1999.

Hatcher, Mattie Austin, trans. "Joaquin de Arrendondo's Report of the Battle of the Medina, August 18, 1813." *Quarterly of the Texas State Historical Association.* Vol. 11, no. 3 (January 1908), pp. 220–36.

Hatcher, Mattie Austin, ed. *Letters of an American Traveller: Mary Austin Holley, Her Life and Works, 1784–1846.* Dallas: Southwest Press, 1933.

Haythornthwaite, Philip. *The Alamo and the War of Texan Independence, 1835–1836.* London, UK: Osprey, 1986.

Hollen, W. Eugene, and Ruth Lapham, eds. *William Bolleart's Texas.* Norman: University of Oklahoma Press, 1956.

Holley, Mary Austin. *Texas.* Lexington, KY: J. Clarke, 1836.

Houston, Andrew Jackson. *Texas Independence.* Houston: Anson Jones Press, 1938.

Houston, Sam. *The Autobiography of Sam Houston.* Donald Day and Harry Herbert Ullom, eds. Norman: University of Oklahoma Press, 1954.

_____. *The Writings of Sam Houston, 1813–1863*. Amelia W. Williams and Eugene C. Barker, eds. 8 vols. Austin: University of Texas Press, 1938–43.

Hunter, Robert Hancock. *The Narrative of Robert Hancock Hunter*. Austin: Encino Press, 1966.

Huson, Hobart. *Refugio: A Comprehensive History of Refugio County from Aboriginal Times*. Woodsboro, TX: Rooke Foundation, 1953–55. Excerpted online at www.sonsofdewittcolony.org/goliadmorgan.htm.

Huston, Cleburne. *Deaf Smith, Incredible Texas Spy*. Waco, TX: Texian Press, 1973.

Jackson, Andrew. *Correspondence of Andrew Jackson*. John Spencer Bassett, ed. Vol. 1. Washington, DC: Carnegie Institution of Washington, 1931.

Jackson, Ron, Jr., and Lee Spencer White. *Joe, the Slave Who Became an Alamo Legend*. Norman: University of Oklahoma Press, 2015.

James, Marquis. *The Raven: A Biography of Sam Houston*. Indianapolis: Bobbs-Merrill, 1929.

Jenkins, John H., ed. *The Papers of the Texas Revolution, 1835–1836*. 10 vols. Austin: Presidial Press, 1973.

Johnson, Frank W. *A History of Texas and Texans*. Vol. 1. Chicago and New York: American Historical Society, 1916.

Jones, Oakah L. *Santa Anna*. New York: Twayne, 1968.

King, C. Richard. *Susanna Dickinson: Messenger of the Alamo*. Austin: Shoal Creek, 1976.

Kuykendall, Jonathan Hampton. "Reminiscences of Early Texans: A Collection from the Austin Papers." *Quarterly of the Texas State Historical Association*. Vol. 6, no. 3 (January 1903), pp. 236–53.

Labadie, Nicholas Descomps. "San Jacinto Campaign." *The Texas Almanac, 1857–1873*. Waco, TX: Texian Press, 1967, pp. 142–77.

Lack, Paul D. *The Texas Revolutionary Experience: A Political and Social History, 1835–1836*. College Station: Texas A&M University Press, 1992.

Lane, Walter P. *The Adventures and Recollections of General Walter P. Lane, A San Jacinto Veteran, Containing Sketches of the Texan, Mexican and Later Wars*. Dallas: DeGolyer Library, 2000.

Lester, Charles Edwards, ed. *The Life of Sam Houston, the Only Authentic Memoir of Him Ever Published*. New York: J. C. Derby, 1855.

Linn, John J. *Reminiscences of Fifty Years in Texas*. New York: D. & J. Sadlier, 1883.

Lord, Walter. *A Time to Stand.* New York: Harper & Brothers, 1961.

Maverick, Samuel Augustus. *Notes on the Storming of Bexar in the Close of 1835.* San Antonio: Frederick C. Chabot, 1942.

McDonald, Archie P. *William Barret Travis: A Biography.* Woodway, TX: Eakin Press, 1989.

Meacham, Jon. *American Lion: Andrew Jackson in the White House.* New York: Random House, 2008.

Moore, Stephen L. *Eighteen Minutes: The Battle of San Jacinto and the Texas Campaign.* Dallas: Republic of Texas Press, 2004.

Morgan, Abel. "Massacre at Goliad: Abel Morgan's Account." Available online at https://sonsofdewittcolony.org.

Morphis, J. M. *History of Texas, from Its Discovery and Settlement.* New York: United States Publishing Company, 1875.

Nackman, Mark E. "The Making of the Texas Citizen Soldier." *Southwestern Historical Quarterly.* Vol. 78 (January 1975), pp. 231–53.

"Notes on the Life of Benjamin Rush Milam, 1788–1835." *Register of the Kentucky Historical Society.* Vol. 71, no. 1 (January 1973), pp. 87–105.

Peña, José Enrique de la. *With Santa Anna in Texas: A Personal Narrative of the Revolution.* College Station: Texas A&M University Press, 1975.

Pierson, William H., Jr. *American Buildings and Their Architects: The Colonial and Neoclassical Styles.* New York: Oxford University Press, 1970.

Pohl, James W., and Stephen L. Hardin. "The Military History of the Texas Revolution: An Overview." *Southwestern Historical Quarterly.* Vol. 89, no. 3 (January 1986), pp. 269–308.

Potter, Reuben Marmaduke. "The Fall of the Alamo." *Magazine of American History.* Vol. 2, no. 1 (January 1878). Available online at https://sonsofdewittcolony.org.

Pruett, Jakie L., and Everett B. Cole. *Goliad Massacre: A Tragedy of the Texas Revolution.* Austin: Eakin Press, 1985.

Ramsdell, Charles. *San Antonio: A Historical and Pictorial Guide.* Austin: University of Texas Press, 1959.

Rather, Ethel Zivley. "De Witt's Colony." *Quarterly of the Texas State Historical Association.* Vol. 8, no. 2 (1904), pp. 95–192.

———. "Recognition of the Republic of Texas by the United States." *Quarterly of the Texas State Historical Association.* Vol. 13, no. 3 (January 1910), pp. 155–256.

Reid, Stuart. *The Secret War for Texas.* College Station: Texas A&M University Press, 2007.

Remini, Robert V. *Andrew Jackson and the Course of American Democracy, 1833–1845.* New York: Harper & Row, 1984.

Rives, George Lockhart. *The United States and Mexico, 1821–1848.* Vol. 1. New York: Charles Scribner's Sons, 1913.

Santa Anna, Antonio López de. *The Eagle: The Autobiography of Santa Anna.* Ann Fears Crawford, ed. Austin: Pemberton Press, 1967.

Santos, Richard G. *Santa Anna's Campaign Against Texas, 1835–1836.* Waco, TX: Texian Press, 1996.

Scheina, Robert L. *Santa Anna: A Curse Upon Mexico.* Washington, DC: Brassey's, 2002.

Schwarz, Ted. *Forgotten Battlefield of the First Texas Revolution: The Battle of Medina, August 18, 1813.* Austin: Eakin Press, 1985.

Sellers, Charles. *James K. Polk, Jacksonian, 1795–1843.* Princeton, NJ: Princeton University Press, 1957.

Shackford, James Atkins. *David Crockett: The Man and the Legend.* Chapel Hill: University of North Carolina Press, 1956.

Smith, Ruby Cumby. "James W. Fannin, Jr., in the Texas Revolution." *Southwestern Historical Quarterly.* Vol. 23, no. 2 (January 1919), pp. 79–90.

———. "James W. Fannin, Jr., in the Texas Revolution." *Southwestern Historical Quarterly.* Vol. 23, no. 3 (January 1920), pp. 171–203.

Smithwick, Noah. *The Evolution of a State; or Recollections of Old Texas Days.* Austin: Gammel, 1900.

Sparks, S. F. "Recollections of S. F. Sparks." *Quarterly of the Texas State Historical Association.* Vol. 12, no. 1 (July 1908), pp. 61–67.

Stenberg, Richard R. "The Texas Schemes of Jackson and Houston, 1929–1936." *Southwestern Social Science Quarterly.* Originally published in vol. 15 (December 1934); reprinted in fiftieth anniversary issue, vol. 50, no. 4 (March 1970), pp. 944–65.

Stephens, Rachel. *Selling Andrew Jackson: Ralph E. W. Earl and the Politics of Portraiture.* Columbia: University of South Carolina Press, 2018.

Sutherland, John. *The Fall of the Alamo.* San Antonio: Naylor, 1936. Available online at https://sonsofdewittcolony.org.

Swisher, John M[ilton]. *The Swisher Memoirs.* Rena Maverick Green, ed. San Antonio: Sigmund Press, 1932.

Taylor, Creed. "The Battle of San Jacinto," 1935. Available online at https://sons ofdewittcolony.org.

———. "The March, the Siege and the Battle for Bexar," 1900. Available online at https://sonsofdewittcolony.org.

Thompson, Frank. *The Alamo: A Cultural History*. Dallas: Taylor Trade, 2001.

Tolbert, Frank X. *The Day of San Jacinto*. New York: McGraw Hill, 1959.

Tucker, Phillip Thomas. *Exodus from the Alamo: The Anatomy of the Last Stand Myth*. Philadelphia: Casemate, 2010.

Wharton, Clarence R. *San Jacinto: The Sixteenth Decisive Battle*. Houston: Lamar Book Store, 1930.

White, Amelia. "Who Was the Yellow Rose of Texas?" *Alamo Messenger*. April 2015. Available online at https://medium.com/@OfficialAlamo/who-was-the -yellow-rose-of-texas-750c95617241.

Williams, Amelia Worthington. *Following General Sam Houston, from 1793 to 1863*. Austin: Steck, 1935.

Williams, Charlean Moss. *The Old Town Speaks: Reflections of Washington, Hempstead County Arkansas, Gateway to Texas, 1835, Confederate Capital, 1863*. Houston: Anson Jones Press, 1951.

Williams, John Hoyt. *Sam Houston: A Biography of the Father of Texas*. New York: Simon & Schuster, 1993.

Winders, Richard Bruce. *Crisis in the Southwest: The United States, Mexico, and the Struggle over Texas*. Wilmington, DE: Scholarly Resources, 2002.

———. *Sacrificed at the Alamo: Tragedy and Triumph in the Texas Revolution*. Abilene, TX: State House Press, 2004.

Winters, James Washington. "An Account of the Battle of San Jacinto." *Quarterly of the Texas State Historical Association*. Vol. 6, no. 2 (October 1902), pp. 139–44.

Wisehart, Marion Karl. *Sam Houston, American Giant*. Washington, DC: Robert B. Luce, 1962.

Wooten, Dudley Goodall. *A Complete History of Texas*. Dallas: Texas History Company, 1899.

Yoakum, Henderson King. *History of Texas from Its First Settlement in 1685 to Its Annexation to the United States in 1846*. 2 vols. Austin: Steck, 1935.

NOTES

PROLOGUE: THE LESSONS OF BATTLE

1. Thomas Hart Benton, Eulogy to Houston, reprinted in Lester, *The Life of Sam Houston (The Only Authentic Memoir of Him Ever Published)* (1855), p. 303.
2. Houston, *The Autobiography of Sam Houston* (1954), p. 12.
3. Lester, *The Life of Sam Houston* (1855), p. 35.
4. Houston, *The Autobiography of Sam Houston* (1954), p. 15.

CHAPTER 1: GENERAL JACKSON'S PROTÉGÉ

1. Lester, *The Life of Sam Houston* (1855), p. 22.
2. William Carroll, quoted in Williams, *Sam Houston* (1993), p. 71.
3. William Carroll, quoted in Williams, *Sam Houston* (1993), p. 260.
4. James, *The Raven* (1929), p. 157.
5. Thomas Jefferson to James Monroe, May 14, 1820.
6. Sam Houston to John H. Houston, January 11, 1830.
7. Gregory and Strickland, *Sam Houston with the Cherokees* (1967), p. 44.
8. De Bruhl, *Sword of San Jacinto* (1993), p. 130. As with many Houston anecdotes, details vary from biography to biography; other sources differ as to the origin of Houston's cane.
9. William Stanbery, quoted in *Niles Weekly Register*, April 14, 1832.

10. James, *The Raven* (1929), p. 162ff.
11. Ibid., p. 172.
12. Sam Houston to James Prentiss, August 18, 1832.
13. As he told Jefferson Davis; see Williams, *Sam Houston* (1993), p. 113.
14. See Stenberg, "The Texas Schemes of Jackson and Houston" (1970), p. 945.
15. Andrew Jackson to Sam Houston, June 21, 1829.
16. Andrew Jackson to Anthony Butler, February 25, 1832.
17. Sam Houston to John H. Houston, December 2, 1832.

CHAPTER 2: GONE TO TEXAS

1. Mary Brown Austin to Stephen Austin, August 25, 1821.
2. Bowie, "Early Life in the Southwest—The Bowies" (1852), p. 380.
3. Ibid.
4. Dobie, "James Bowie, Big Dealer" (1957), p. 343.
5. The town known circa 1835 as San Antonio de Béxar was, in the documents of its time, variously referred to as San Antonio de Béxar, San Antonio, Béxar, and Bejar. For the sake of clarity, this book will reference the place as simply San Antonio, except within quotations where the original authors' words will be retained.
6. Santa Anna, quoted in Brands, *Lone Star Nation* (2004), p. 227.
7. Sam Houston to Andrew Jackson, February 13, 1833.

CHAPTER 3: "COME AND TAKE IT"

1. Stephen F. Austin to the Illustrious Ayuntamiento of Béjar, October 2, 1833.
2. Stephen Austin to Mary Austin Holley, August 31, 1835.
3. Ibid.
4. Anthony Butler to Andrew Jackson, December 19, 1835.
5. *Texas Republican*, September 26, 1835.
6. Andrew Ponton to Political Chief, September 29, 1835.
7. Smithwick, *The Evolution of a State* (1900), pp. 102, 104–5. Accounts of the story vary, and some students of the battle believe the flag was made after the battle.
8. Joseph D. Clements to Lieutenant Castañeda, September 30, 1835.
9. Bennet, "Battle of Gonzales" (1899), p. 316.

10. David B. Macomb, "Letter from Gonzales," in Foote, *Texas and the Texians* (1841), p. 99.

11. Charles Mason, "Account," in Johnson, *A History of Texas and Texans* (1916), p. 270.

12. Macomb, in Foote, *Texas and the Texians* (1841), p. 101.

13. Smithwick, *The Evolution of a State* (1900), p. 101.

14. Hardin, *Texian Iliad—A Military History of the Texas Revolution, 1835–1836* (1994), p. 12.

15. Garver, "Benjamin Rush Milam" (1935), p. 186.

16. Ben Milam to Henry Smith, March 28, 1835.

17. S——— to ———, October 22, 1835. See Jenkins, *The Papers of the Texas Revolution, 1835–1836*, vol. 2 (1973), pp. 193–94.

18. Ira Ingram to S. F. Austin, *Austin Papers*, vol. 3 (1924), p. 181.

19. George Collinsworth to Mrs. Margard C. Linn, October 10, 1835.

20. *New York Star*, quoted in Nackman, "The Making of the Texas Citizen Soldier" (1975), p. 241.

21. Smithwick, *The Evolution of a State* (1900), p. 106.

22. Moses Austin Bryan, quoted in Barr, *Texans in Revolt* (1990), p. 6.

23. Stephen Austin to David G. Burnet, October 5, 1835.

24. General Martín Perfecto de Cos to Henry Rueg, quoted in Hardin, *Texian Iliad* (1994), p. 14.

25. Order No. 1, October 11, 1835.

26. Sam Houston to Isaac Parker, October 5, 1835.

CHAPTER 4: CONCEPCIÓN

1. Houston, *The Writings of Sam Houston*, vol. 1 (1838), p. 304.

2. Smithwick, *The Evolution of a State* (1900), p. 112.

3. Ibid., p. 138.

4. Stephen Austin to San Felipe Committee of Safety, October 11, 1835.

5. Stephen Austin to Captain Philip Dimmit, October 22, 1835.

6. James Bowie and James Fannin to Stephen Austin, October 22, 1835.

7. Ibid.

8. Smithwick, *The Evolution of a State* (1900), p. 111.

9. "San Felipe Circular," October 18, 1835.

10. Moses Austin Bryan to James F. Perry, October 26, 1835.

11. Stephen F. Austin to Council of Texas, October 26, 1836.

12. "The Most Eligible Situation" quote taken from James Bowie and J. W. Fannin, "Official Account of the Action of the 28thl ult., at the Mission of Conception, near Bejar," in Foote, *Texas and the Texians* (1841), p. 122.

13. Stephen Austin to James Bowie, October 27, 1835.

14. Ibid.

15. James Bowie and J. W. Fannin, "Official Account of the Action of the 28thl ult., at the Mission of Conception, near Bejar," in Foote, *Texas and the Texians* (1841), p. 122.

16. E. L. McIlhenny, quoted in Dobie, "James Bowie, Big Dealer" (1957), p. 399n4.

17. Davis, *Three Roads to the Alamo* (1998), pp. 440–41.

18. Bowie and Fannin, "Official Account" (1836), p. 123.

19. Smithwick, *The Evolution of a State* (1900), p. 114.

20. Ibid.

21. Bowie and Fannin, "Official Account" (1836), p. 123.

22. Smithwick, *The Evolution of a State* (1900), p. 115.

23. Austin, "Siege and Battle of Bexar" (1844).

24. Crimmins, "American Powder's Part in Winning Texas Independence" (1948), p. 109.

25. Stephen Austin to President of the Consultation of Texas, October 28, 1835.

CHAPTER 5: A SLOW SIEGE AT THE ALAMO

1. List of stores in Jenkins, *The Papers of the Texas Revolution, 1835–1836*, vol. 2 (1973), p. 251.

2. Stephen Austin to James Bowie and James Fannin, November 1, 1835.

3. William Travis to Stephen Austin, November 16, 1835.

4. Stephen Austin to William Travis, November 11, 1835.

5. Stephen Austin to President of Consultation of Texas, November 5, 1835.

6. Huston, *Deaf Smith, Incredible Texas Spy* (1973), pp. 1–5; Barr, *Texans in Revolt* (1990), p. 17.

7. Stephen Austin to President of the Consultation, November 3, 1835.

8. Anson Jones, quoted in Cantrell, *Stephen F. Austin* (1999), p. 326.

9. Austin, "Siege and Battle of Bexar" (1844).

10. Moses Austin Bryan, quoted in Cantrell, *Stephen F. Austin* (1999), p. 328.

11. Ehrenberg, "A Campaign in Texas" (1846), p. 39.

12. Moses Austin Bryan, quoted in Cantrell, *Stephen F. Austin* (1999), p. 328.

13. Two reports written the day after recount the events of the "Grass Fight." See Edward Burleson to the Provisional Government, November 27, 1835; and William H. Jack to Burlison [Burleson], same date. The latter contains the imaginative spelling of *mesquite*.

14. Barr, *Texans in Revolt* (1990), p. 40.

15. Bowie was probably closer to the mark. In his memoirs, Mexican general Vicente Filisola reported "fifty brave men . . . lying on the ground either dead or wounded." Filisola, *Memoirs for the History of the War in Texas*, vol. 2 (1848; 1985), p. 68.

16. Creed Taylor, quoted in Reid, *The Secret War for Texas* (2007), p. 52.

17. Sam Houston to James Fannin, November 13, 1835.

18. William Carey to Brother & Sister, January 12, 1836.

19. Samuel Maverick, December 4, 1835, in Green, *Samuel Maverick, Texan* (1952), p. 44.

20. Huston, *Deaf Smith, Incredible Texas Spy* (1973), p. 34. See also Foote, *Texas and the Texians* (1841), p. 165.

21. Taylor, "The March, the Siege and the Battle for Bexar" (1900).

22. Herman Ehrenberg, quoted in Huston, *Deaf Smith, Incredible Texas Spy* (1973), p. 36.

23. Ibid.

24. Taylor, "The March, the Siege and the Battle for Bexar" (1900).

25. Frank Sparks, quoted in Hardin, *Texian Iliad* (1994), p. 81.

26. Taylor, "The March, the Siege and the Battle for Bexar" (1900).

27. F. W. Johnson to General Burleson, December 11, 1835.

28. Edward Burleson and B. R. Milam to Provisional Government, December 6, 1835.

29. Field, *Three Years in Texas* (1836), p. 20.

30. Edward Burleson and B. R. Milam to Provisional Government, December 6, 1835.

31. Taylor, "The March, the Siege and the Battle for Bexar" (1900); Yoakum, *History of Texas*, vol. 1 (1935), p. 28.

32. Of the several retellings, Creed Taylor's is the most vivid. See "The March, the Siege and the Battle for Bexar" (1900).

33. William Carey to Brother & Sister, January 12, 1836.

34. Moseley Baker to Council at San Felipe, December 10, 1835.

35. Sherwood Y. Reams, quoted in Williams, *Sam Houston* (1993), p. 127.

36. Sion R. Bostick, quoted in Rives, *The United States and Mexico* (1913), pp. 300–301.

37. Barr, *Texans in Revolt* (1990), p. 52.

38. Filisola, *Memoirs for the History of the War in Texas*, vol. 2 (1848; 1985), p. 94.

39. Articles of Capitulation, Clause the First.

40. William Carey to Brother & Sister, January 12, 1836.

41. Texas General Council to Citizen Volunteers, December 15, 1835.

CHAPTER 6: THE DEFENDERS

1. *Telegraph and Texas Register*, January 2, 1836.

2. Sam Houston to Don Carlos Barrett, January 2, 1836.

3. Goliad Declaration, December 22, 1835.

4. Henry Smith to the President and Members of the Council, January 9, 1836; General Council to the People of Texas, January 11, 1836.

5. Sam Houston to Henry Smith, January 30, 1836.

6. J. C. Neill to Governor and Council, January 6, 1836.

7. Sam Houston to Henry Smith, January 6, 1836.

8. Lester, *The Life of Sam Houston*, p. 83.

9. Sam Houston to Henry Smith, January 30, 1836.

10. Ehrenberg, *With Milam and Fannin* (1935), pp. 124–25.

11. The principal source for Houston's speech was a volunteer named Herman Ehrenberg; in Leipzig in the 1840s he published the text as he remembered it, but in his native German. A number of scholars have expressed serious doubts as to its accuracy. See especially Crisp, *Sleuthing the Alamo* (2005), p. 27ff.

12. Sam Houston to Henry Smith, January 30, 1836.

13. Lester, *The Life of Sam Houston*, p. 85.

14. Ibid.

15. Dobie, "James Bowie, Big Dealer" (1957), p. 350.

16. J. C. Neill to Sam Houston, January 14, 1836.

17. James Bowie to Henry Smith, February 2, 1836.

18. Ibid.

19. William B. Travis, Last Will and Testament, May 25, 1835.

20. Green Jameson to Sam Houston, January 18, 1836.

21. Ibid.

22. Ibid.

23. For the most part these biographical details are drawn from the most reliable Crockett biography, James Atkins Shackford's *David Crockett: The Man and the Legend* (1956), supplemented by Crockett's own (and rather less factual) *Autobiography* (1834).

24. Shackford, *David Crockett* (1956), p. 296n11.

25. Crockett, *Autobiography* (1834), p. 40.

26. Williams, *The Old Town Speaks* (1951), p. 164.

27. Crockett, *Autobiography* (1834), p. 80.

28. *National Banner and Nashville Whig*, September 29, 1823.

29. Crockett, *Autobiography* (1834), p. 59.

30. *Niles Weekly Register*, April 9, 1836.

31. David Crockett to George Patton, November 1, 1835.

32. David Crockett to Margaret and Wiley Flowers, January [9], 1836.

33. Swisher, *The Swisher Memoirs* (1932), p. 18.

34. Ibid.

35. William B. Travis to Henry Smith, February 13, 1836.

36. Sutherland, *The Fall of the Alamo* (1936), https://sonsofdewittcolony.org. The story is also recounted in Davis, *Three Roads to the Alamo* (1998), pp. 533–35.

37. William B. Travis to Andrew Ponton, February 24, 1836.

CHAPTER 7: TWELVE DAYS OF UNCERTAINTY

1. Santa Anna, "Manifesto Relative to His Operations during the Texas Campaign and His Capture 10 of May 1837," reprinted in Castañeda, *Mexican Side of the Texan Revolution* (1928), p. 13. The most essential source for Santa Anna's biographical facts is Will Fowler's *Santa Anna of Mexico* (2007).

2. Minister of War José María Tornel, quoted in Lord, *A Time to Stand* (1961), p. 61.

3. Fanny Calderone de la Barca, quoted in Brands, *Lone Star Nation* (2004), p. 41.

4. William W. Travis to Fellow Citizens and Compatriots, February 24, 1836.

5. Enrique Esparza, quoted in Ramsdell, *San Antonio* (1959), p. 76.

6. José Batres to James Bowie, February 23, 1836.

7. William Travis and James Bowie to James Fannin, February 23, 1836.

8. William Travis to Sam Houston, February 25, 1836; Potter, "The Fall of the Alamo" (1878), p. 6.

9. William Travis to the People of Texas & all Americans, February 24, 1836.

10. William Travis to Sam Houston, February 25, 1836.

11. James Fannin to James Robinson, February 25, 1836.

12. John Sowers Brooks to A. H. Brooks, February 25, 1836.

13. James Fannin to James Robinson, February 26, 1836.

14. Crockett, *A Narrative of the Life of David Crockett by Himself* (1987), p. xxxii.

15. Santa Anna to the Minister of War and Marine, February 27, 1836.

16. Potter, "The Fall of the Alamo" (1878), p. 8.

17. Lord, *A Time to Stand* (1961). In keeping with the long tradition of historical disagreements regarding the Alamo history, historian (and former New York firefighter) William Groneman has expressed doubt regarding Crockett's fiddle playing.

18. "The Unanimous Declaration of Independence made by the Delegates of the People of Texas," March 2, 1836.

19. William Travis to the President of the Convention, March 3, 1836.

20. William Travis to David Ayres, March 3, 1836.

21. "Army of Operations, General Orders of the 5th of March, 1836. 2 o'clock P.M.—Secret."

22. Quoted in the *San Antonio Daily Express*, April 28, 1881. The historic record is hazy concerning Travis's March 5 actions and words. By some accounts he spoke long and movingly; by others, his words were few and pointed. Direct testimony concerning the events of the afternoon of March 5, 1836, is limited (and variable), but include a firsthand account in a late-in-life interview with Mrs. Almeron Dickinson, conducted in 1876, and a version that appeared in *The Texas Almanac*, in 1873, purportedly based on the recollections of the soldier who chose not to step across the line.

23. See McDonald, *William Barret Travis* (1976; 1995), pp. 172–73, 194n14.

CHAPTER 8: THE MASSACRE

1. Gray, *From Virginia to Texas* (1909), p. 137.

2. Peña, *With Santa Anna in Texas* (1975), p. 47.

3. Ibid.

4. Ibid., p. 46.

5. Ibid., p. 47.

6. Mexican soldier, in Chariton, *100 Days in Texas* (1990), p. 318.

7. Report of Francisco Ruiz, in Chariton, *100 Days in Texas* (1990), p. 325.

8. Wooten, *A Complete History of Texas* (1899), p. 215.

9. Peña, *With Santa Anna in Texas* (1975), pp. 42, 43.

10. Ibid., pp. 48–49.

11. Tucker, *Exodus from the Alamo* (2010), p. 235.

12. King, *Susanna Dickinson: Messenger of the Alamo* (1976), pp. 41–42. Almeron's words vary from one account to another, as do many of the details in the ensuing events of Mrs. Dickinson's life.

13. Peña, *With Santa Anna in Texas* (1975), p. 51.

14. Quoted in Houston, *Texas Independence* (1938), p. 143.

15. Letter of April 5, 1836, printed in *El Mosquito Mexicano*. Cited in Davis, *Three Roads to the Alamo* (1998), p. 734n104.

16. *Philadelphia Pennsylvanian*, July 19, 1838.

17. Letter of April 5, 1836, printed in *El Mosquito Mexicano*. Cited in Davis, *Three Roads to the Alamo* (1998), p. 734n104.

18. "Army of Operations, General Orders of the 5th of March, 1836. 2 o'clock P.M.—Secret."

19. Peña, *With Santa Anna in Texas* (1975), p. 52.

CHAPTER 9: BRING OUT THE DEAD

1. Quoted in Hardin, *Texian Iliad* (1974), p. 155. Accounts vary concerning whether Santa Anna referenced the dead as "chickens" on the night before or the day of the Alamo battle. Or both.

2. Crisp and Kilgore, *How Did Davy Die? And Why Do We Care So Much?* (2010), p. 15.

3. N. D. Labadie, "San Jacinto Campaign," in Day, *Texas Almanac* (1967), p. 174. Once again, there is an ongoing argument concerning Crockett's end.

4. Peña, *With Santa Anna in Texas* (1975), p. 53.

5. Santa Anna to José María Tornel, March 6, 1836.

6. Lieutenant Colonel José Juan Sanchez Navarro, "Memoirs of a Veteran of the Two Battles of the Alamo." Online at https://sonsofdewittcolony.org.

7. King, *Susanna Dickinson: Messenger of the Alamo* (1976), p. 70.

8. Morphis, *History of Texas* (1875), pp. 176–77.

9. Enrique Esparza, cited in King, *Susanna Dickinson: Messenger of the Alamo* (1976), p. 141n36. Other reports claim the sum gifted was two pesos rather than two dollars.

10. Santa Anna to the Citizens of Texas, March 7, 1836.

11. Report of Francisco Ruiz, in Chariton, *100 Days in Texas* (1990), p. 326.

CHAPTER 10: HOUSTON HEARS THE NEWS

1. Wisehart, *Sam Houston, American Giant* (1962), p. 167.

2. William Travis to the President of the Convention, March 3, 1836.

3. James, *The Raven* (1929), p. 227.

4. Lester, *The Life of Sam Houston*, pp. 90–91.

5. Ibid., p. 91.

6. Sam Houston to James Fannin, March 11, 1836.

7. Sam Houston to James Collinsworth, March 13, 1836.

8. Lester, *The Life of Sam Houston*, p. 95; Huston, *Deaf Smith, Incredible Texas Spy* (1973), p. 53.

9. Jackson and White, *Joe, the Slave Who Became an Alamo Legend* (2015), p. 207.

10. R. E. Handy, quoted in *Deaf Smith, Incredible Texas Spy* (1973), p. 53.

11. Robert Morris to James Fannin, February 6, 1836.

CHAPTER 11: FORT DEFIANCE

1. James Fannin to Sam Houston, November 18, 1835.

2. William Travis to James Fannin, February 23, 1836.

3. James Fannin to Joseph Mims, February 29, 1836.

4. James Fannin to James Robinson, February 22, 1836.

5. Sam Houston to James Fannin, March 11, 1836. Accounts disagree as to whether the letter was delivered late on March 13 or on the morning of March 14, 1836. See Huson, "Evacuation of Goliad," in *Refugio* (1953–55).

6. Ehrenberg, *With Milam and Fannin* (1935), pp. 169–70.

7. Ehrenberg, "A Campaign in Texas" (1846), p. 43.

8. Morgan, "Massacre at Goliad."

9. Shackelford, Jack. "Some Few Notes Upon a Part of the Texian War," in Foote, *Texas and the Texians* (1841), p. 231.

10. Ehrenberg, "A Campaign in Texas" (1846), p. 44.

11. Barnard, "Dr. J. H. Barnard's Journal" (1912), p. 16.

12. Shackelford, Jack. "Some Few Notes Upon a Part of the Texian War," in Foote, *Texas and the Texians* (1841), p. 233.

13. Ibid., p. 234.

14. Morgan, "Massacre at Goliad."

15. Barnard, "Dr. J. H. Barnard's Journal" (1912), p. 17.

16. Ehrenberg, "A Campaign in Texas" (1846), p. 45.

17. Barnard, "Dr. J. H. Barnard's Journal" (1912), p. 19. Accounts differ regarding the terms of the surrender and, very likely, Fannin got no explicit promises beyond Urrea's offer to use his influence with Santa Anna (see Urrea, "Diary of the Military Operations," in Castañeda, *Mexican Side of the Texan Revolution*, 1928, pp. 228–29). That said, Fannin, seeing no alternative, likely took Urrea's word and permitted his men to think their fate would differ from that of the defenders at the Alamo.

18. Urrea, "Diary of the Military Operations" (1838), in Castañeda, *Mexican Side of the Texan Revolution* (1928), p. 235.

19. Barnard, "Dr. J. H. Barnard's Journal" (1912), p. 22.

20. Account of Joseph Spohn, published in the *New York Evening Star*, as quoted in Brown, *Hesitant Martyr in the Texas Revolution* (2000), pp. 220–23.

21. The tale of the "Angel of Goliad," based on various references in the accounts of survivors, is a mix of confused names and details, many of which are summarized in "Angel of Goliad" at sonsofdewittcolony.org.

22. Dr. J. H. Barnard, quoted in De Bruhl, *Sword of San Jacinto* (1993), p. 195.

CHAPTER 12: THE TEXIAN EXODUS

1. Sam Houston to James Collinsworth, March 15, 1836.

2. "Kuykendall's Recollections of the Campaign," in Barker, "The San Jacinto Campaign" (1901), p. 295.

3. Lester, *The Life of Sam Houston*, p. 99.

4. Sam Houston to James Collinsworth, March 15, 1836.

5. Swisher, *The Swisher Memoirs* (1932), p. 33.

6. Sam Houston to Thomas Rusk, March 23, 1836.
7. Labadie, "San Jacinto Campaign" (1967), pp. 144–45.

CHAPTER 13: AN ARMY ASSEMBLES

1. Sam Houston to Thomas Rusk, March 23, 1836.
2. Sam Houston to Thomas Rusk, March 23, 1836.
3. With only minor differences, two Texian soldiers later told the story. See "Kuykendall's Recollections of the Campaign," in Barker, "The San Jacinto Campaign" (1901), p. 297; and Sparks, "Recollections of S. F. Sparks" (1908), p. 67.
4. Santa Anna, "Manifesto" (1928), p. 20.
5. Smithwick, *The Evolution of a State* (1900), p. 128.
6. Harris, "The Reminiscences of Mrs. Dilue Harris" (1901), pp. 155–89.
7. Moseley Baker, February 19, 1836, quoted in Moore, *Eighteen Minutes* (2004), p. 18.
8. Barker, "The San Jacinto Campaign" (1901), pp. 273–74.
9. Sam Houston to Thomas Rusk, March 29, 1836.
10. "Kuykendall's Recollections of the Campaign," in Barker, "The San Jacinto Campaign" (1901), p. 301.
11. Peña, *With Santa Anna in Texas* (1975), p. 102.
12. Tolbert, *The Day of San Jacinto* (1959), pp. 66–67; Santa Anna, "Report of the San Jacinto Campaign to the Minister of War and Marine," March 11, 1837, reprinted in Barker, "The San Jacinto Campaign" (1901), pp. 265–66.
13. Sam Houston to the Citizens of Texas, April 13, 1836.
14. Sam Houston to Thomas Rusk, March 31, 1836.
15. Labadie, "San Jacinto Campaign" (1967), p. 148.
16. David G. Burnet to Sam Houston, April 1, 1836.
17. Labadie, "San Jacinto Campaign" (1967), pp. 150–51; James, *The Raven* (1929), p. 241.
18. Sparks, "Recollections of S. F. Sparks" (1908), pp. 66–67; James, *The Raven* (1929), p. 242.
19. Santa Anna, "Manifesto" (1928), pp. 20–21.
20. Ibid., p. 22.

21. Sam Houston to John E. Ross, April 2, 1836.

22. Houston himself would acknowledge such thinking years later. See Davis, *Lone Star Rising* (2004), p. 252.

23. "Kuykendall's Recollections of the Campaign," in Barker, "The San Jacinto Campaign" (1901), p. 302.

24. King, *Susanna Dickinson: Messenger of the Alamo* (1976), p. 60.

25. Numerous versions of this story exist, the first written a month later; see W. B. Dewees to Clare Cardello, May 15, 1836. Subsequent accounts appear in Labadie, "San Jacinto Campaign" (1967), pp. 150–51; and in Hunter, *The Narrative of Robert Hancock Hunter* (1966), p. 13. The wagon master's name is variously spelled Rover and Rohrer.

CHAPTER 14: THE BATTLE AT SAN JACINTO

1. Delgado, "Delgado's Account of the Battle," in Barker, "The San Jacinto Campaign" (1901), p. 288; see also Tolbert, *The Day of San Jacinto* (1959), pp. 69–70.

2. Santa Anna to Vicente Filisola, April 14 [?], 1836.

3. "Kuykendall's Recollections of the Campaign," in Barker, "The San Jacinto Campaign" (1901), p. 303.

4. Coleman, *Houston Displayed* (1836; 1974), p. 18.

5. Bryan, "Reminiscences of M. A. Bryan," p. 20.

6. Sam Houston to David Burnet, April 25, 1836.

7. Lester, *The Life of Sam Houston*, p. 111.

8. Santa Anna, "Manifesto" (1928), p. 75.

9. "Kuykendall's Recollections of the Campaign," in Barker, "The San Jacinto Campaign" (1901), pp. 303–4.

10. Labadie, "San Jacinto Campaign" (1967), p. 155.

11. Lester, *The Life of Sam Houston*, p. 114.

12. Colonel Alexander Somervell, quoted in Labadie, "San Jacinto Campaign" (1967), p. 155.

13. Patrick Usher, quoted in James, *The Raven*, p. 203.

14. Sam Houston to Henry Raguet, April 19, 1836.

15. Lester, *The Life of Sam Houston*, p. 113.

16. Sam Houston to David Burnet, April 25, 1836.

17. Delgado, "Delgado's Account of the Battle," in Barker, "The San Jacinto Campaign" (1901), p. 290.

18. Labadie, "San Jacinto Campaign" (1967), p. 158.

CHAPTER 15: "REMEMBER THE ALAMO!"

1. Lester, *The Life of Sam Houston*, pp. 122, 124.

2. Calder, "Recollections of the Campaign of 1836" (1861), p. 449.

3. Labadie, "San Jacinto Campaign" (1967), p. 161.

4. Later scholarship suggests that the actual number in Houston's command was more likely in the range of 925 men.

5. Labadie, "San Jacinto Campaign" (1967), p. 162. See also Lester, *The Life of Sam Houston*, pp. 125–26.

6. Winters, "An Account of the Battle of San Jacinto" (1902), pp. 141–42.

7. Fowler, *Santa Anna of Mexico* (2007), p. 172.

8. Sam Houston to David Burnet, April 25, 1836.

9. Benjamin Franklin, quoted in Moore, *Eighteen Minutes* (2004), p. 269.

10. James, *The Raven* (1929), p. 251.

11. Foote, *Texas and the Texians* (1841), p. 311. See also Tolbert, *The Day of San Jacinto* (1959), pp. 111–12.

12. John Menifee, quoted in Tolbert, *The Day of San Jacinto* (1959), p. 141.

13. Labadie, "San Jacinto Campaign" (1967), p. 163.

14. Thomas Rusk, quoted in Foote, *Texas and the Texians* (1841), p. 309.

15. Taylor, "The Battle of San Jacinto" (1935).

16. Foote, *Texas and the Texians* (1841), pp. 310–11.

17. "A Bewildered and Panic Stricken Herd" from Delgado, "Delgado's Account of the Battle" in Barker, "The San Jacinto Campaign" (1901), p. 291.

18. Ibid.

19. Filisola, *Memoirs for the History of the War in Texas*, vol. 2 (1848; 1985), p. 225.

20. Thomas Rusk to David Burnet, April 22, 1836.

21. Houston, *Texas Independence* (1938), p. 228.

22. Hunter, *The Narrative of Robert Hancock Hunter* (1966), p. 16.

23. W. C. Swearingen to his brother, April 22, 1836.

24. Bryan, "Reminiscences of M. A. Bryan," p. 24.

25. Lester, *The Life of Sam Houston*, p. 133.
26. Pedro Delgado, quoted in Tolbert, *The Day of San Jacinto* (1959), p. 170.
27. Sam Houston to David Burnet, April 25, 1836.

CHAPTER 16: OLD SAN JACINTO

1. Among the various renderings of Santa Anna's capture—no two identical—are those of Dr. Labadie, Joel Robinson, and Sion Bostick, as well as James Sylvester's, of December 7, 1872, at https://sonsofdewittcolony.org.
2. As with Santa Anna's capture, numerous tellings of the tale survive. The primary sources here are Houston himself (Lester, *The Life of Sam Houston*, pp. 146–51) and Moses Austin Bryan ("Reminiscences of M. A. Bryan," p. 25ff), but other useful versions appear in James, *The Raven* (1929), p. 254ff; Labadie, "San Jacinto Campaign" (1967), p. 167ff; and Major John Forbes (see Haley, *Sam Houston* [2002], p. 153ff); and Santa Anna himself (*The Eagle: The Autobiography of Santa Anna* [1967]). Stephen Moore's *Eighteen Minutes* (2004) offers a quite complete compilation of the miscellaneous firsthand accounts. See also Brown, *History of Texas, 1685 to 1892* (1892), pp. 42–43.
3. Taylor, "The March, the Siege and the Battle for Bexar" (1900).
4. H. P. Brewster in Foote, *Texas and the Texians* (1841), pp. 314–15.
5. Santa Anna to Vicente Filisola, April 22, 1836.

CHAPTER 17: PRESIDENT SAM HOUSTON

1. "Address to the Army of the Republic of Texas," May 5, 1836.
2. Tolbert, *The Day of San Jacinto* (1959), p. 222.
3. *Telegraph and Texas Register*, August 30, 1836.
4. Thomas Green, quoted in Yoakum, *History of Texas*, vol. 2 (1935), p. 171.
5. "The Trial of Santa Anna," quoted in Yoakum, *History of Texas*, vol. 2 (1935), p. 179.
6. Santa Anna to Andrew Jackson, July 4, 1836.
7. Andrew Jackson to Sam Houston, September 4, 1836.
8. Foote, *Texas and the Texians* (1841), p. 318.
9. Santa Anna to Sam Houston, November 5, 1836.
10. Santa Anna, *The Eagle* (1967), p. 57.

11. Callcott, *Santa Anna* (1936), pp. 146–47.

12. Santa Anna, *The Eagle* (1967), p. 57.

13. William Wharton to J. Pinckney Henderson, March 15, 1837.

EPILOGUE: THE FOUNDING AND
THE FOUNDERS OF TEXAS

1. Houston, Directive of December 27, 1836.

2. That officer was José Enrique de la Peña; the book, *With Santa Anna in Texas* (1975).

3. E. H. Winfield, quoted in James, *The Raven* (1929), p. 331.

4. Bruce, *Life of General Houston* (1891), p. 217.

5. Coleman, *Houston Displayed* (1837).

6. Sam Houston quoted in Haley, *Sam Houston* (2002), p. 154.

AFTERWORD: OLD SAM AND HONEST ABE

1. Sam Houston, "Inaugural Address," December 21, 1859.

2. Sam Houston, "Address at Union Mass Meeting, Austin, Texas," September 22, 1860.

3. Jeff Hamilton, *My Master* (1940), pp. 72–73.

4. Temple Houston Morrow, quoted in Friend, *Sam Houston: The Great Designer* (1954), p. 338.

5. "General Sam Houston and Secession," *Scribner's Magazine*, vol. 29 (May 1906), p. 587.

6. Howard C. Westwood, "President Lincoln's Overture to Sam Houston," *The Southwestern Historical Quarterly*, vol. 88, no. 2 (October 1984), p. 140.

7. Smithwick, *The Evolution of a State; or Recollections of Old Texas Days* (1900), pp. 331–34.

8. Houston speech of April 19, 1861.

IMAGE CREDITS

1. Prints and Photographs Collection, Archives and Information Services Division, Texas State Library and Archives Commission, 102–280
2. FineArt / Alamy Stock Photo
3. GL Archive / Alamy Stock Photo
4. World History Archive / Alamy Stock Photo
5. Science History Images / Alamy Stock Photo
6. Bettemann / Contributor
7. By William Howard, James Perry Bryan Papers, di_04428, The Dolph Briscoe Center for American History, The University of Texas at Austin
8. Everett Collection Historical / Alamy Stock Photo
9. FLHC / Alamy Stock Photo
10. Public domain
11. Prints and Photographs Collection, di_11688, The Dolph Briscoe Center for American History, The University of Texas at Austin
12. The Picture Art Collection / Alamy Stock Photo
13. Public domain
14. Prints and Photographs Collection, di_02195, The Dolph Briscoe Center for American History, The University of Texas at Austin
15. The Picture Art Collection / Alamy Stock Photo
16. Chronicle / Alamy Stock Photo
17. World History Archive / Alamy Stock Photo
18. Public domain
19. Science History Images / Alamy Stock Photo
20. North Wind Picture Archives / Alamy Stock Photo
21. Public domain
22. Painting, *March to the Massacre* by Andrew Jackson Houston. Courtesy of the San Jacinto Museum of History
23. Niday Picture Library / Alamy Stock Photo
24. World History Archive / Alamy Stock Photo
25. Science History Images / Alamy Stock Photo
26. The Picture Art Collection / Alamy Stock Photo
27. The History Collection / Alamy Stock Photo
28. Bygone Collection / Alamy Stock Photo
29. Historical / Contributor
30. Public domain

INDEX

Note: Page numbers in *italics* refer to maps or illustrations.

AUTHOR BIO

Brian Kilmeade cohosts Fox News Channel's morning show *Fox & Friends* and hosts the national radio program *The Brian Kilmeade Show*. He is the author of six books, and he lives on Long Island.

Don't miss the other bestselling history books by Brian Kilmeade!

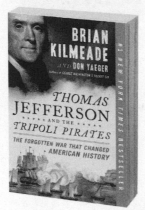

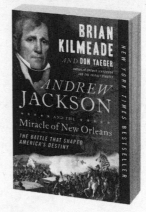

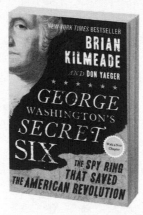

For more information, please visit
BrianKilmeade.com.